796.34
DAV   Davis, Pat   **8853**

Badminton

DATE DUE

BADMINTON

The Complete Practical Guide

BADMINTON

The Complete Practical Guide

Pat Davis

DAVID & CHARLES

Newton Abbot   London   North Pomfret (Vt)

To My Wife
P.A., critic and inspiration. Without
her constant encouragement this book
might never have seen light of day

Acknowledgements
My thanks go to all who supplied me with photographs,
in particular Mervyn Rees, FRPS, and to 'Den' Palmer,
who provided the sequence line drawings. I am much
indebted and most grateful.

British Library Cataloguing in Publication Data

Davis, Pat
  Badminton.
  1. Badminton (Game)
  I. Title
  796.34′ 5   GV1007

  ISBN 0 7153 8163 6

© Pat Davis 1982

Printed in Great Britain
by Butler and Tanner Ltd., Frome
for David & Charles (Publishers) Limited
Brunel House Newton Abbot Devon

Published in the United States of America
by David & Charles Inc
North Pomfret Vermont 05053 USA

Contents

Foreword

It is a rare experience to read a book of this nature and not be able to point at aspects that have been missed; but I believe that Pat Davis has called upon his wide experience and knowledge of the game, not only as a player but as a coach, official and journalist, to produce what can be truly described as 'The Complete Practical Guide'.

At whatever level a player may have reached, or has ambitions to reach, I feel this book cannot fail to guide them successfully on to better things. With his individual style of thoroughness, total dedication, and humour,

Pat has produced the combination of an instruction book for the complete beginner, an aid to the experienced player and future champion, and a life long maintenance manual for anyone whose game is in distress.

I consider it an honour to be included in his 'Top Thirty' and a great privilege and pleasure to have this opportunity to contribute in a small way to what must in time become a major addition to badminton literature – and an essential part of any sports enthusiast's library.

Thank you, Pat, for sharing the thoughts, experiences and vast knowledge that you have gained during your long and varied association with this wonderful game of ours.

Nora Perry, MBE

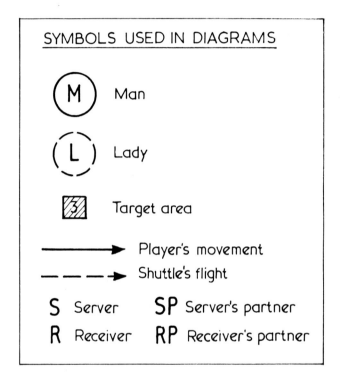

SYMBOLS USED IN DIAGRAMS

(M)   Man

(L)   Lady

▨   Target area

⟶   Player's movement
⤍   Shuttle's flight

S Server   SP Server's partner
R Receiver   RP Receiver's partner

Introduction

I have played badminton at every level from junior to club, and from county to international. I have coached all over Britain and overseas. My hope now is that by reading this book you too will share the tremendous pleasure that has been mine.

In the 1930s, a leading international, R.C.F. Nichols wrote 'coaching is definitely detrimental to playing . . .'. How wrong can you be! Today, every sport has a legion of coaches and a small library of instructional books. Not surprisingly overall standards have improved immensely.

Coaching is a short-cut. It is the distilled essence of years of experience. Use this book wisely and your play will improve rapidly. Wisely, in simple terms, means read and re-read one small section at a time and then practise until it is grooved into you. Then, and here Ralph Nichols was right, 'tournament and match play is essential'. You will best sharpen your ability on the steel of better players. Watch too and learn. Play three or four times a week if you can. Improvement will be rapid; enjoyment, doubled.

Let the written word become the spoken; the author, the coach. If some of the ideas late in this book seem to have a familiar ring, you are under no delusion. They have — and for a purpose. It is done — as a coach recaps — to make sure that early points are not forgotten, that their full impact is hammered in.

You will notice too that in the chapters on stroke production, simple tactics are also included. You cannot play a stroke intelligently in a vacuum; its point is lessened if you know only 'how', not 'why' and 'where' as well. Revise this detail when you come to basic tactics where it would have been wearisome for the eager reader had I particularised yet again.

Remember too that Den Palmer's charming illustrations and the brilliant photos of Louis Ross and Mervyn Rees are not just pleasant optional extras. Study them thoughtfully. They speak volumes.

The better you play, the greater the enjoyment. So go to it! There are years of pleasure, fitness and fun ahead of you.

PART I

BASIC PLAY

1 The Joys of Badminton

What is badminton's charm? Most important, it is easy to pick up initially; you can have a game (of sorts) within an hour of starting. Secondly, it is especially challenging to climb the competitive ladder and well worth it, for the view from the top is a truly international one.

It is played in every town (and most villages) of this country, so popular, it is now the fastest growing participant sport in England. And badminton ripples have spread round the globe. With over sixty countries now members of the International Badminton Federation its growth has been phenomenal.

Its very equipment is a joy to handle and easy to do so almost from the cradle to the grave. A racket is a streamlined masterpiece of modern engineering. Though the apparently fragile shuttle, made of cork, kid and goose feathers, weighs a mere 80 grains, it can withstand a barrage of power strokes that start it speeding on its way at up to an estimated, incredible 180 kph!

Basically a winter game, though a growing number of enthusiasts play the year round, badminton provides exercise and fun whatever the weather. Its devotees I rate 'gold star', well above average both for sociability and sportsmanship. For them and for you, the well organised Badminton Association of England provides a wide range of leagues, county competitions and tournaments of varying standards that cater for the novice and the tiger alike.

The game itself? A fascinating mixture of varied strokes and tactics. One moment you are hitting a smash with every ounce of power you can muster, the next you are caressing the shuttle a mere two inches with micrometer accuracy so that you couldn't slip even a visiting card between it and the net-tape. And with so light a racket there is the Paul Daniels magic of deception to enjoy. Movement is fast and graceful – with fitness a very worthwhile by-product. Tactics are satisfyingly chess-like and varied.

And still more! It offers three types of game: each with its own character, its own particular genius. Singles are as demanding of stamina as of patience in man-to-man (and, of course, woman-to-woman) combat. Men's and ladies' doubles are power games of long, fluctuating rallies in which attack rapidly follows defence and defence, attack; whilst mixed doubles, a subtler, more delicate cat-and-mouse game, brings into play yet different skills.

You will get tremendous pleasure from badminton. Persevere and practise, for the better you play, the more you will enjoy the game. Then, your pleasure is doubled.

(*Overleaf*) Plate 1. The joy of badminton! Hadinata Christian and big Ade Chandra (both Indonesia): winners of the 1980 Friends' Provident Masters Tournament in the Royal Albert Hall, London (*S. Perry*)

2 Equipment

RACKETS

Buying one's first racket is nearly as important as going to one's first date. The same trepidation and delight are there. And a bad choice in either is disastrous.

It is an important but difficult preliminary. Department stores seem to bristle with legionnaire squads of rackets. All are differently labelled, yet, to the novice, all appear much the same. The small specialist shop with an assistant who really knows his stuff and with a smaller range may be a better bet.

A racket with a pedigree will seldom let you down. Dunlop, Slazenger, Grays, Carlton, Yonex, Jaguar, Kawasaki, are all names to conjure with. But you are still left with a wide choice. Narrow it first by deciding if you will buy a racket with a wooden frame or a metal one.

Pick them up; swing them judiciously. How do they feel? This is the criterion. Remember that a racket should be neither heavy in the head nor in the handle. It should balance on your finger roughly halfway along its length. If it does this, then the racket will almost seem to lift itself.

The wooden-framed racket, even if it is an 'Under 5' (ounces) will be heavier than the metal, weighing-in at an amazing 3½oz. The wooden one will put a little more weight into your shots; the metal will be more easily and quickly manoeuvrable, less tiring to use, and probably more durable. 90 per cent of players now choose metal.

Grip

Feel includes the grip. The bevelled wooden handle covered with a spiralled leather grip comes in sizes ranging from 3¼in to 4in. Get it right. Too small: you grip too tightly and use of the wrist is inhibited; you will develop a palm

Plate 2. A wooden-framed racket – the famous Dunlop Maxply 'Under 5' (ounces) *(Dunlop)*

15

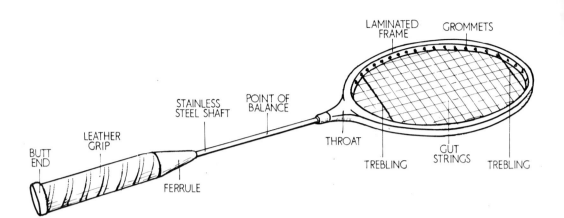

LAMINATED FRAME · GROMMETS · POINT OF BALANCE · STAINLESS STEEL SHAFT · LEATHER GRIP · BUTT END · FERRULE · THROAT · TREBLING · GUT STRINGS · TREBLING

Fig. 1 Wooden-framed racket

rather than a finger grip. Too big: you may lose not only touch but even the racket itself!

If you are of the hot and sweaty-handed type, a towelling grip helps but it may become hard and matted. It can be replaced or alternatively you can try an easily replaceable gauze that sticks only on itself. At least make sure the leather grip has tiny perforations in it that make for better 'drainage' and grip. Whatever you choose, be certain it helps you to grip the racket firmly, to avoid unwanted slip or twist at impact.

Shaft

Now for the shaft. Strength and whip are the key factors. Stainless steel quite adequately supplies both; carbon graphite goes just one better. The difference perhaps is for the expert.

Hold the racket by head and frame; press upwards with the thumbs judiciously and you will see how much whip there is in the shaft. Too much may mean too little control. Manufacturers of twin-shafted rackets claim this feature gives them 'directional stability'. In other words the head does not turn and send the shuttle off course.

Shaft shape is another consideration. You will be overwhelmed by 'slim', 'tapered', 'flat-waisted' and 'squeezed' types. Don't be too worried – the effective difference again is slight.

Stringing

What is of much more importance is the stringing. And here it is worth buying the best. Pure gut undoubtedly has greater resilience

than synthetic. It will string tighter and maintain that tension longer. Top quality No 1 gut (preferably Weddell's) should be fine, unmarked, clear and a pale gold in colour.

Synthetic strings come in a multiplicity of forms. If you can't afford gut, choose that known as the 'multi-miniscule thread pack centre'. This means that within the outer core float myriad, hair-like, loosely packed, nylon threads. (Oxide-T is probably the best.) Synthetic strings haven't quite the same 'oomph' as gut but they are less allergic to damp and generally more durable.

To check all-important tension, there are two common tests: First, place your fingers under the strings on each side of the frame. Press down with your thumbs. There should only be minimal give. Secondly, flick a fingernail across the strings; this should give a high pitched 'ping' and not a rather puddingy 'ploof'.

Look for aids to longevity in strings. Plastic guards ('grommets') in the stringing holes should protect the string from fraying on the metal. Rather similarly, the top of the head should be channelled so that strings do not protrude and become frayed when shuttles are scraped up from the floor with the racket head.

Price

The range is wide: £5–£40. Generally speaking go for the middle to upper figure. Your racket can do a lot for your game so pay a little more than you can afford – it's worth it.

Racket Care

After purchase, thoughtful care and respect for craftsmanship will prolong life. Store your

racket in cool, dry surroundings. Never throw it about. If it is wood-framed, keep it in a press. Never continue to play with it if a string breaks; you may well double or treble the damage.

Your racket is sleek and featherweight. It withstands tremendous stresses in play. Choose it well and it becomes almost a living part of you and your play.

SHUTTLES
Choice here is of vital importance too. A wise one should give you a shuttle of durability, correct speed, flight and touch at a reasonable cost.

Your initial choice must be between feathered shuttles and synthetic shuttles. The former, the perfect shuttle, is more expensive and less durable than the synthetic. Despite this it is the choice of top players who, accustomed to it, cannot adapt to the synthetic's differences of touch and flight.

Shuttle manufacturers (RSL – Reinforced Shuttlecocks Ltd – for feathers; Carlton and RSL for synthetic are the big names) and their

Plate 3. Metal-framed rackets are lighter and therefore easier to manoeuvre than those with wood-frames *(Carlton)*

scientists have been working on the problem for thirty years. Yet the synthetic, though vastly improved, is still not quite the same as the feather shuttle. It is nevertheless perfectly suitable until you reach top league status.

Feathered Shuttles
Feathered shuttles consist of sixteen perfectly matched goose feathers secured in a cork base. (For top quality shuttles, it takes two geese to provide the necessary number.) These are strengthened and their spread (2⅛in–2½in) which affects the speed of the shuttle, is kept uniform by a double circle of glued thread round the quills. Left and right wing feathers must not be mixed in the same shuttle.

Inside the precision dome-shaped cork is a tiny lead pellet to give it the requisite weight for its particular speed. If it is dislodged, the shuttle becomes so light that it has difficulty in

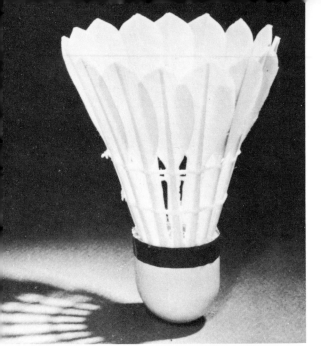

(*Left*) Plate 4.   A feathered shuttle in all its delicate beauty *(RSL)*

Plate 5.   A synthetic RSL Competition Tourney shuttle; cheaper and more durable than feathered *(RSL)*

(*Below*) Fig. 2   Feathered shuttle. Always treat it with respect

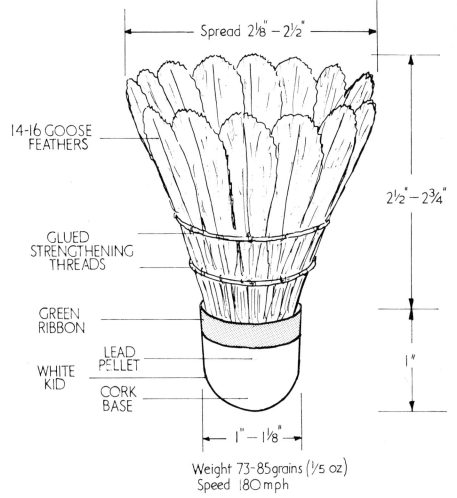

Spread 2⅛" – 2½"

14-16 GOOSE FEATHERS

2½" – 2¾"

GLUED STRENGTHENING THREADS

GREEN RIBBON

LEAD PELLET

WHITE KID

CORK BASE

1"

1" – 1⅛"

Weight 73-85 grains (⅕ oz)
Speed 180 mph

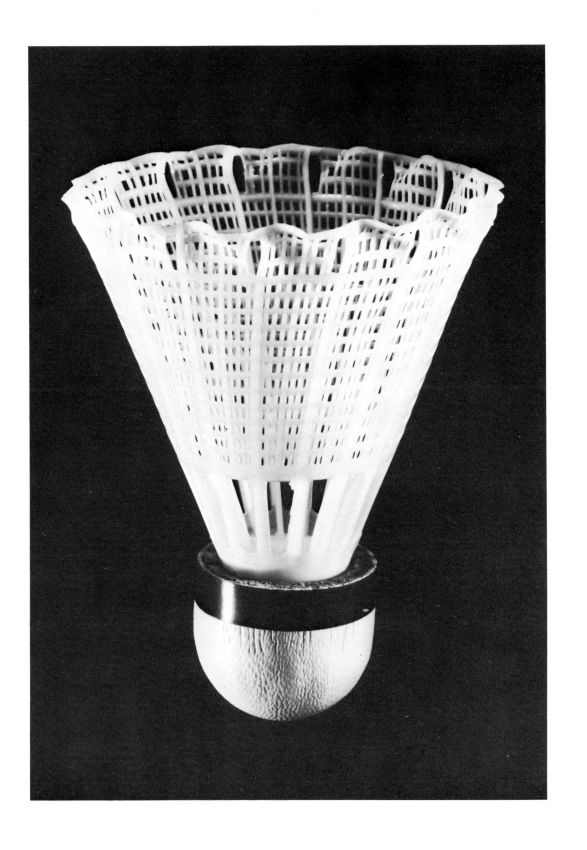

overcoming air resistance and scarcely flies. Covering the domed base of the cork is kid leather, glued and further secured by a coloured ribbon. The kid must have the correct co-efficient of friction so that it 'grips', not slides, on the strings. Shuttle weight? A bare one-fifth of an ounce.

It is quite on the cards that by the time this book is published feathered shuttles made in this country will be available only for major championships. The high cost of feathers and labour have rendered them no longer a viable commercial proposition.

Synthetic Shuttles

Basically, synthetic shuttles are very similar to feathered. In cheap brands, the base may be rubber or plastic; in more expensive ones it will, as in a feathered shuttle, be of kid-covered cork. It is possible that the IBF, the ruling body, will decree that rubber-based shuttles are non-regulation.

The difference lies in the lack of feathers. As these are fragile, in short supply because of ever-growing demand, and highly expensive, they are replaced by a synthetic 'skirt'. This may be all in one piece, though (like teabags) highly perforated, or it may be shaped like real feathers.

RSL Competition-Tourney shuttles are also available in 'Cold' and 'Gold'. The former last better in cold halls; the latter are more easily visible against light-coloured walls.

The Difference

This is mainly in cost. Both feathered and synthetic shuttles are available in different qualities at different prices. Top quality feathered shuttles cost some £16 per dozen; synthetic, £7. A big difference indeed. So too in durability: a feathered shuttle, unless a feather is broken by a single mishit, should last two or three games; a synthetic, five or six. Penurious or economically minded players will find that it is possible to give a shuttle new, if temporary life. Carefully take out the damaged feather and replace it with one taken from another stricken bird.

Touch, flight and speed are the other issues. Even now a synthetic shuttle does not feel quite the same on the racket as does a feather, nor does it have quite the same consistent flight, or turnover in net-shots. There, it is a little more difficult to control. But what you've never had, you won't miss.

Finding the Right Speed

Correct speed is vital. Synthetic shuttles were once uniformly slow. Now, like feathers, they are available in a wide range of colour-coded (slow-medium-fast) or numbered speeds (73–85). The latter gives the greater accuracy in assessing speed.

What speed is correct? This depends entirely on air resistance. And this in turn depends on altitude, size of hall and temperature. Forget altitude, unless you play in Johannesburg (7,000ft) or with Paddington's Aunt in Highest Peru (12,000ft). In a warm, one-court gym or church hall the air resistance is much less than in a cold, four- or eight-court sports centre. In the former probably use a 76–78; in the latter, an 81–83. To be exact you must test for yourself.

What do the figures indicate? The weight of the shuttle in grains. For if the spread of the feathers or skirt is uniform, the speed will vary with the weight: the heavier the shuttle, the faster and further it will fly.

How do you find out if the chosen speed is correct? Law 4 of the badminton rule book lays down explicit instructions but all too seldom are they followed. Stand a foot behind the base-line so that the shuttle is actually held directly above it. Hit the shuttle upwards at 45° and parallel to the side-line with an underhand stroke. The striker should be of average strength.

The shuttle is of correct speed if it drops on or up to 18in behind the back doubles service line. Short of that area it is slow; beyond it, fast. Too many players flout this law by using a shuttle that drops anything from 12in–18in short of the line. Greater control and skill are needed to keep the standard speed shuttle in court.

Long Life for Shuttles

1. Smooth ruffled feathers regularly between thumb and forefingers.
2. Use shuttles of correct speed; slow shuttles have to be hit harder.
3. Never hit a shuttle on the half volley.
4. Don't scrape shuttles back to your

opponents; it is hard on racket, shuttle and your reputation.

5. Knock-up gently for a minute or two; initial mishits break feathers.

6. Never bang a tube of shuttles on the floor to open it.

7. If shuttles are stuck together, part them gently.

8. Always store feathered shuttles where it is cool and not dry.

9. Use 'Cold' and 'Gold' synthetic shuttles where appropriate.

10. Repair feathered shuttles.

SHOES

Willing to face any charges of immodesty, I would suggest that of all your 'clothing', shoes are by far the most vital. Ill-fitting, heavy shoes are worse than near nudity. Upon a wise choice depends not only your comfort and freedom from foot injury, but also your speed about court. Shoes are the foundation of your game.

To achieve speed look for these points: A light shoe is the first essential. Nylon mesh uppers help in this respect and also provide ventilation. Suede tends to discolour. Secondly, see that the sole, although flexible, has a well-defined tread to give you grip for quick starting, stopping and turning on a slippery floor. It should be of a soft rubber, rather than a hard synthetic. Though light, it must be thick enough, or have a sorbo inner-sole, to prevent jarring – and weary feet at the end of a match. It should also be wide enough to protect the whole sole of the foot. Black soles are often vetoed by sports centres.

As for the heel, additional cushioning prevents tiring heel-jar. If it is rounded, it allows a more natural rolling of the landing foot into normal stride without jolting.

A slightly raised heel helps prevent injury to the Achilles tendon. Whether or not such injury is further prevented by a raised heel-tab or protector is a matter of debate. Some manufacturers maintain it offers useful support; others that it merely causes pressure and so possible injury.

Plate 6. A typical modern shoe. Note the strong toe cap and well padded heel *(Dunlop)*

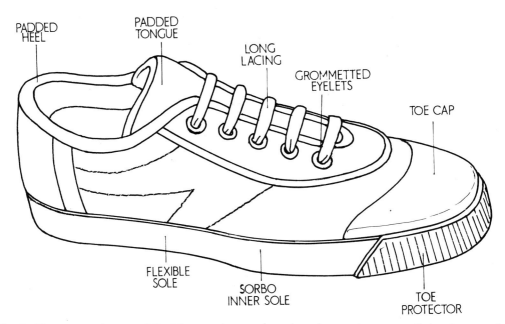

PADDED HEEL · PADDED TONGUE · LONG LACING · GROMMETTED EYELETS · TOE CAP · FLEXIBLE SOLE · SORBO INNER SOLE · TOE PROTECTOR

Fig. 3 Choose your shoes carefully. They are the most important item of clothing

Padding on the collar and tongue makes for comfort but may add to the weight. Long lace-up from toe to instep helps make foot and shoe feel as one.

For long life, make sure that your shoe has a strong toe cap. This prevents wear when you drag your foot as in a lunge. Protection too on the front of the toe helps to prevent sole and upper parting company if drag is accentuated.

Do not be overwhelmed by this wealth of necessary qualities. Look for them — for shoes are the wings of your feet.

CLOTHING

This is obviously more a matter of personal taste and preference — certainly in regard to style. Neither I nor the Laws dare pontificate on this subject. But the rule for many tournaments is: 'Clothing shall be predominantly white'. An all-red shirt, for example, would not be acceptable but a white one with red placket, yoke or side-panels would be. Do resist the current trend for a hotch-potch of colours. Whites, with a touch of colour, look neatest.

Men wear socks, shorts, shirt and sweater. Ladies too sometimes, but more usually a skirt rather than shorts, or a dress. And extremely attractive ones are available. A little morale-boosting glamour is not out of place here, or for that matter in the underwear department.

So stick to whites, take your choice and use commonsense. The latter dictates that your clothing shall be as light as practicable. If shirts are too tight they will certainly hamper deep breathing; if shorts are too tight they may split in moments of stress and strain. They should be short enough not to hamper movement but not so short as to embarrass you — or your partner. Choose an absorbent material — you can get very hot at badminton — and one that is easily washed out and drip-dried.

For ladies, the Warner All-Gold bra can be recommended as it is specially designed for comfortable firmness that reduces breast movement and consequent abrasion.

Woollen socks, ankle or shin length, help to keep well-talced feet fresh and blister free.

A tracksuit is a most useful optional extra for either sex. And here you can go to town on colour. It keeps you warm, especially if hooded, during the inevitable waits between games and so obviates the dangers of initial stiffness and of pulled muscles. Make sure that the trouser legs are either flared or have zips at the bottom. This enables you to slip out of them easily without having to take off your shoes or do incredible and precarious one-legged balancing acts.

Wear your tracksuit during the knock-up but

please take it off once the game starts. To wear it then must hamper movement. It is also a condescension to your opponent, breaches the 'predominantly white' rule and spoils the look of otherwise 'all-white' courts. Nothing looks sloppier! This is a simple commonsense courtesy to be observed, not broken. If, after an active knock-up, you are cold on court, it is only because you are not moving.

COURTSIDE BAG
Another wise provision is a courtside bag. In it, carry those seemingly unimportant accessories, but ones which in a crisis, can make all the difference between winning and losing.

A towel for a quick mop-up. Sweat bands too. If you wear spectacles, a demisting agent. Elastoplasts for blisters in their prime or synthetic skin for those which have burst. A salted glucose drink to ward off cramp and restore flagging energies. Safety pins for bra

Plate 7. Badminton clothing can be most attractive *(Rucanor)*

straps or shorts fastenings that crack under the strain.

New shuttles of varied speeds for the knock-up. (The customary broken-feathered wreck will merely deaden your touch.) A spare racket or three, of course. Strings do break and even a hastily borrowed 'twin' is never quite the same.

Spare laces — and better still, a spare pair of shoes with smooth soles in case the court is tacky, as on a Hova court where lack of give can lead to injury. Powdered resin if you have a perspiring and slippery hand. A bandeau for unruly, sight-impeding, long hair. Even a copy of the laws for amicable settlement of an unfriendly dispute.

Some shopping list! But play once started must be continuous — no chance to nip back to the changing room.

3　How the Game is Played

THE LAWS

All players should know the Laws of Badminton fully; 99 per cent, however, have never read them, and never will read them. Assuming you are one of the 99 per cent, I intend to fill these pages with a brief summary that you will read, rather than the full twenty-two lengthy laws that you won't.

That said though, you must have at least a basic knowledge of them. So please read on. Those very important ones relating to serve and return of serve I deal with relevantly under those headings. Study them.

If you are one of the one per cent, I apologise and suggest you invest in a 20p rule-book obtainable at most sports shops.

Summary:

The posts, 5ft 1in in height, should be placed on the side-lines.

The net should be stretched taut 5ft in height at the centre.

Shuttles should be of correct speed. (See page 20).

The shuttle shall be volleyed by a player of each side alternately until a fault is made. (Players of the same side do not have to take it in turn to hit the shuttle.)

It is a fault if:

A serve does not fall within the boundaries of the diagonally opposite service court.

A shuttle is hit into the net or out of court or fails to cross the net or goes under it.

A player touches the net whilst the shuttle is in play, or invades the opponents' court with person or racket.

A shuttle be caught or held on the racket and then slung during a stroke.

The shuttle is hit twice in immediate succession by the same player.

The shuttle hits the racket, person or clothing of one player (in or out of court) before being returned by his partner.

A player, although not ready, attempts but fails to return a serve.

The receiver's partner touches or returns the opponent's serve.

It is not a fault if:

The shuttle strikes the net-cord tape and then falls over into play.

The server completely misses the shuttle.

Any part of the shuttle lands on any part of the boundary line.

For service faults see page 39.

For return of service faults see page 62.

SCORING

It is essential that you learn to score from the very outset. If you don't, the game will lose its competitive edge. At best you will be prey to the occasional muddle-head or cheat; at worst, you will be regarded (quite rightly) as a ninny. More, when you reach match and tournament standard, you will not be able to take your fair share of the chores of umpiring.

So, learn now. It is part and parcel of the game and much simpler than it may appear. It's not a question of 'I've no head for figures' — unless, of course, you can't add up by ones.

The easiest way is to plough through the following until you've roughly got the hang of it. Then ask an experienced player if you can just 'stand in' as he scores. Follow the score for a while. Then try calling the score mentally to yourself, checking against the actual scorer's call. When they generally tally, ask if the scorer will stand by whilst you score. And in two or three games you will have cracked it.

Fig. 4　Court nomenclature and dimensions

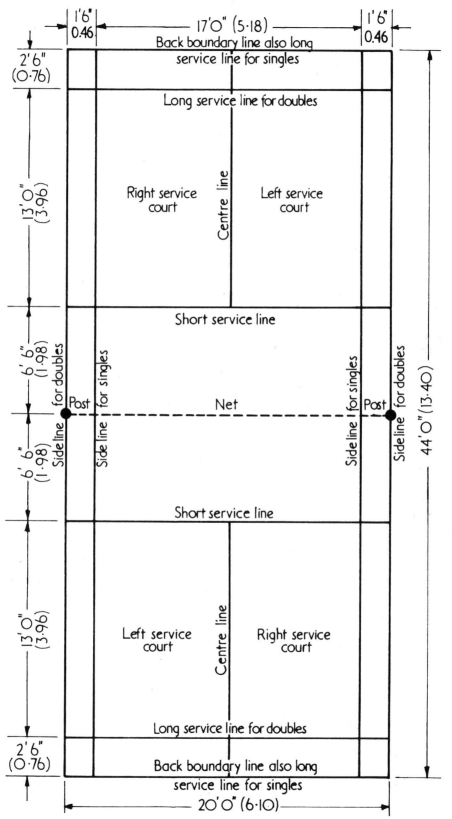

It really is quite simple and can be summarised as follows:

Basic Points for Doubles

1. When you or your partner are serving and you win a rally you:
   (i) add one point to your score, and
   (ii) change sides (so that the serve is now to the other opponent).
   Your opponents do nothing – merely grin and bear it.
2. When you are serving and you lose a rally:
   (i) obviously, no points are scored (you don't deserve one!). Nor are sides changed, and
   (ii) the server loses his serve. This then passes to his partner who continues to serve until another rally is lost. Both partners having served, the serve now passes to the opponent in the right hand court.

Additional Points

3. The opponents each serve in turn until a rally is lost. When two rallies have been lost the serve will revert to you.
4. The pair who open the serving at the very start of the game are allowed only one serve, that of the player in the right hand court where service always starts. Thereafter both players in a pair have a serve.
5. A game is 15 points up except in ladies' singles when it is 11.
6. If the score becomes 13 all, the pair who first reached 13 may decide either (i) to play through, or (ii) to set. If (i), scoring continues as normal to 15. If (ii), the score reverts to 'love all' and the first to score 5 additional points wins the game. (Although the final score may be called 5–2, say, it is recorded as 18–15).
7. The same applies at 14 all, though setting is now 3 up, not 5.
8. In ladies' singles, setting is at 9 (3 up) and 10 (2 up).
9. Failure to set at the first opportunity does not prohibit setting, if desired, at the second.

Calling the Score

10. Always call the server's score first (3); follow it with the receiver's score (6), thus

3–6 (not 6–3). Add, after the score, the phrase 'second server' when the first server has lost his serve. Most important – or there will be unhappy wrangles as to whether or not a player has served.

11. For example the score is '3–1, second server'. The 'in' or serving side lose the rally. Service passes over to the other pair so the score is now 1–3. They lose the next rally: '1–3, second server'. They also lose the following rally so the first pair are serving again, '3–1'.
    Note: 'First server' is not called; it is implicit in '1–3' or '3–1'.
12. In matches, the best of three games are played. Sides are changed at the end of each game and also when the score reaches 8 in the third. The winning pair (either of them) open the serving.

Always call the score aloud after every point. There should be no doubt in anyone's mind. If anyone wishes to challenge the correctness of the score they must do so then. To call the score only spasmodically invites argument. '4–8? I'm quite sure we're 6 and I don't see how you could possibly have scored 8 points!' It can happen just occasionally – and leave a nasty taste in the mouth. And even an amicable haggle is a waste of good playing time.

As a check, remember in which court you started – right or left. When the score is even, you should be in that same court; when odd, you will be in the other court.

ETIQUETTE

Every worthwhile game has its conventions, its code of conduct. Badminton is no exception. To break the code, even unwittingly, puts the beginner at a red-faced disadvantage.

1. To decide choice of ends or who serves first, one player will spin his racket in his hand. The answer to 'Call!' is 'Rough' or 'Smooth'. This is found by rubbing the forefinger along the coloured string(s), the trebbing, at the bottom of the racket. Modern rackets often do not have this so you may have to improvise with 'Maker's

Plate 8. Good manners are essential on court. Left to right: Nora Perry, Barbara Sutton, Karen Chapman and Karen Bridge shake hands – and then acknowledge the umpire (*Louis C. H. Ross*)

name side'. If correct, choose 'This end' or 'We'll serve'.

2. At the end of a game, say 'Thank you!' to your partner and opponents.
3. If it is a match, shake hands all round. In a tournament you will also shake hands with the umpire and the service judge.
4. If you hit a shuttle into the net or if it lands on the floor near you, pick it up. Pass it to your partner or your opponent not by scraping it along the floor like a frantic hockey player but by accurately passing, throwing, or hitting it. Never kick a shuttle when it's down!
5. Give line decisions for your half of the court only. Your opponents will do the same for theirs; never query their decision unless they appear to be deliberately dishonest. Then you can ask for an umpire or linesmen.
6. If certain about decisions on your side, call clearly 'in' or 'out' and brook no argument. If in slight doubt, give your opponent the benefit.

If really unsure, or unsighted, ask for a 'let'. This should be rare.

7. Immediately call any 'fault' of yours such as (i) a sling; (ii) touching the net; (iii) the shuttle grazing your hair or clothing.
8. Encourage, never blame, your partner.
9. Congratulate your opponents if they win; commiserate, if they lose.
10. Never walk across or behind another court when the shuttle is in play.
11. Don't ask players much better than yourself to play. You will spoil their game and not enjoy yours.
12. Never dispute an umpire's decision — by word or look.
13. Pay your subscription early and unasked.
14. Do your share of the club chores.
15. Never lean on or pull down the net when discussing a point with your opponents.
16. When watching, applaud good strokes impartially but never bad ones even though they give your side a point.

Stick to these rules and you'll be a popular club member.

4　Foundations

KNOW YOUR BADMINTON BODY

To play badminton well you will certainly have to make a full-blooded and a full-bodied effort. But some parts of your body are obviously more important than others so it's just as well to appreciate their vital role. Let's take a quick inventory.

Eyes

Everything starts with the eyes.

Reflex They must, by trained and acute observation, pick up the shuttle's speed and line of flight at the first possible split second. Then they can instantly relay 'All systems go' signals to send your arms and legs into early action.

Consistency In addition to giving you speed they will give you consistency (another of the Seven Virtues). Watch the shuttle all the way from your opponent's racket to your own (not always easy). Then you will avoid red-faced misses and mishits. And even for a fraction of a second after impact, it is a matter, as in bingo and golf, of 'Eyes down'.

If you give few points away, if you don't make careless unforced errors, you will be hard to beat. At the same time that you thus improve your own efficiency, you are undermining your opponent's. If he can't rely on your generosity to bring play to a swift end, he will start worrying about his own physical fitness to sustain long rallies. And in addition he will have to play to finer margins of accuracy if he is to penetrate your defences. It is then that his errors begin to multiply.

Peripheral Vision Your eyes must not be entirely single-minded, concentrating solely on the shuttle. They must also keep track of your opponent's whereabouts so that they can direct racket-fire to the weaker player, to the awkward parts of the body, and to wide open spaces.

This they do by peripheral vision. At first you will be concentrating so hard on the shuttle itself that you will be virtually blinkered. But as strokes become more automatic, more grooved, so you will learn to observe the wider scene.

Self-criticism Employ too the 'inward eye'; the eye that is constantly reviewing your own strokes and tactics; enabling you to assess their strengths and weaknesses, their effectiveness. It is incredible how much pleasurable success the average club player loses because he is purblind. Month after month the same shots, weak tactically or technically, lead to summary execution. But the lesson is never learnt. Post-mortems are not necessarily the prerogative of bridge-players. Nor need they be dismal affairs. Use your brain, use your critical faculty: see the error of your ways. Give yourself 'the eye' sometimes!

Read your Opponent like a Book Learn your badminton alphabet – how to 'read' your opponent's strokes. Not anticipation this, but close observation of your opponent's action before impact and the racket-head's speed, trajectory and direction at impact. The first, slow or fast, will give you an idea of whether a delicate or a power shot will be played. The second, downwards or upwards, shows whether you must prepare for an underhand or an overhead reply. The third, to right or left, will show whether it is aimed at your forehand or backhand. Remember it is *impact* you observe, for a skilled player can mesmerise you with a deceptive change of speed, flight or direction almost up to impact.

Practise this 'reading' as surely as you practise a stroke. It will pay even higher dividends.

1. Initially get your partner to shadow strokes on court. Reading them, run to the target area, shadow an appropriate shot, return to base, bounce, and read the next stroke.

2. Sit behind a court and try to 'read' each stroke. Two or three such five-minute (that's as long as you will concentrate) reading lessons each evening will bring much richer rewards than you will find in the cafeteria!

Feet and Legs

If eyes are the alarm signal, feet and legs are the motive power. They are the foundation of your game. Train them by sprinting, jumping, and skipping; trigger them into action with an observant eye and you will take the shuttle early. This is the hallmark of the good player. It is a double-edged sword. Be aware that in as little as a tenth-of-a-second a shuttle will drop to comparative safety below tape level. So never wait for it to come to you. Go and meet it! Then, very often, you can attack.

On the other hand, it means you have given your opponent a tenth-of-a-second less in which to play his return. A mere tenth on its own may not be enough to hurry your opponent into error. But, add two- or three-tenths together in a rally. Then a third-of-a-second lost by your opponent can mean a snatched shot, one played off balance or a shuttle never even reached.

Dancing Feet Once the serve has been struck your feet should never be still. Bounce lightly on the balls of your feet so that body inertia does not have to be overcome. You become lighter; move more easily.

After each stroke, drive your feet into instant recovery. Sometimes back to your base to await developments, a base that places you equidistant from all possible returns, that leaves no obvious gaps. Sometimes, adventurously, direct to the point of arrival of the anticipated return. Don't make a wild, crystal-ball guess but a computer-rapid assessment of the returns that could possibly be made from your shot; of those your opponent can play; and of those, shrewdly observed, that he is in the habit of making. After each stroke — except the rally-ender (and even then never assume the rally is over until

the shuttle is actually dead on the floor), there is no time to stand and stare, no time for self-admiration. Be on your toes and you'll feel like moving.

Keep your Balance Such movement will be the speedier — and recovery the easier — if you are on balance. If you are lazy, slow or awkward in moving backwards you will be off-balance as you hit the shuttle, a sad fact that will probably rob your stroke of power and accuracy if not of life itself. Even if you manage a passable return you will totter one (or more) unnecessary steps backwards — and a further one or more are then needed merely to regain lost ground. Two or four unnecessary, fatal perhaps, steps!

So too in running forwards. Never run onto or over-run the shuttle. Your return will be cramped and you will again take an unnecessary step forward. Rather reach forward, lunge comfortably on balance, to take the shuttle at full stretch. Make sure your brake linings and reverse gear are in good order.

Knees Here lies drive. Never be stiff-legged. There is as much push in them as in a piece of wet string. Before you can push off fast, you will first have to bend your knee before you straighten it. Two actions instead of one. For drive — keep your knees bent.

Arm and Wrist

Arm It is the pronation (turning inwards) of the forearm and the snapping straight of the fully bent arm that supplies power. It is the strong uncocking of your wrist that adds the vital extra snap. Use your left arm always as a counter balance. Raised thus in overhead shots it can also be a useful sighter that keeps your eye on the shuttle.

Wrist Consider your wrist. It is a veritable universal joint, able to move in all directions. First, in conjunction with your forearm, it can turn your hand from left to right, or vice versa. This enables you to make a deceptive last-second turn of the wrist to wrong-foot your opponent by deflecting the shuttle to the other

Plate 9. Thomas Kihlstrom (Sweden) uses *all* his body: feet, legs, torso, shoulders, arms, wrists, hands and eyes *(Mervyn Rees)*

side of the court. Also, it enables you to turn the racket, which you generally hold side-on to the net, square to the shuttle at impact.

Secondly, still more important, it can bend backwards and forwards, or cock and uncock. And, as in a gun, it is this cocking and uncocking of the wrist that can give lethal sting to your strokes. As you swing your racket back in all strokes, cock back the wrist to have hidden power at your command. In all power strokes uncock it crisply just before impact to add wrist speed to arm speed.

With a light but firm grip use your wrist to the full in badminton. Wielding a mere 3½oz racket it is your staunchest ally. But until you have the action fully controlled, don't over-use it. A racket-head that is twisting and turning at impact like a dancing dervish brings only error.

Body

As wrist is used in nearly every stroke, your body should be used in all. Even in the gentlest of strokes, such as low serves or net-shots, sway your body into the shot.

In power strokes you use it more purposefully. Always have your weight on the back foot at the end of the backswing. Turn your shoulders, then with body both turned and arched backwards, you can spiral it upwards into overhead strokes; swing it into sidearm and underarm ones.

Never, in your hurry to recover, sway back or sway away from the shuttle at impact. Your body will draw your racket away from the shuttle either to lose power, mishit or even miss altogether.

Fourteen stone of bone and muscle (or even 8½) swung into your stroke makes a difference – a big one.

Brain

This is as vital as brawn. It is dealt with more fully in chapter 7. Let it suffice now to say tactics are simple logic; that there should be a reason for every position you take up, for each shot you play. Never do anything thoughtlessly. Ask yourself if your shots are successes or failures – and if not the former, why the latter. Think about your opponent's strengths and weaknesses. Things happen fast in a game so do develop a 'badminton brain'.

STROKE PRODUCTION

No one is going to pretend that badminton is easy. Nothing worthwhile ever is. But one of the game's many virtues is that it is fairly simple to pick up right from the start. This is so because all strokes are based on an action most of us have done all our lives – that of throwing. Admittedly this is a skill more familiar, even today, to robust lads than to delicately nurtured young ladies. Even so there are analogies that may help.

Types of Stroke

For the men? Strokes may roughly be classified into three groups. Overhead strokes are played with the same action as throwing a cricket ball from the boundary or a stone far out to sea. Side-arm strokes have their equivalent in cricket throws from cover point or skimming flat pebbles across a pond. Underarm strokes are duplicated in the boundary throws of the arthritic-shouldered aged or the joyous 'how high can you chuck it?' of the young.

And for the rather less sportingly inclined ladies? Overheads correspond to the vigorous flicking down by duster of cobwebs in high places; side-arms to the stinging slap to the face inflicted on some small, odious and over-venturesome male. Carpet-beating has the same action as does the whipping of a giant top. Underarms? These correspond to tossing washing into varied piles in the kitchen or (low serve only), lobbing a ball very gently to a three-year-old.

Stroke Phases

Each stroke within these categories consists of five phases that can be more conveniently telescoped into three because of the very speed of their flow: (i) backswing (or preparation); (ii) forward swing and impact (or hitting action); (iii) follow through and recovery; the latter is too often forgotten but should be an integral part of every stroke. Strokes can be shadowed (played without a shuttle) and built up phase by phase or learnt as a whole. The details will be described more fully in each stroke. Let it suffice here to make these brief points.

Backswing (preparation) This, of course, includes movement to the shuttle, so that, perfectly balanced, the body is correctly

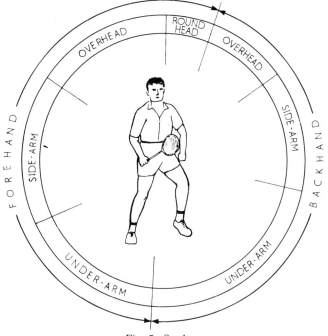

Fig. 5 Stroke areas

positioned for arm and racket to make the correct point of impact. The backswing must be made as you move, not belatedly when you arrive.

For power strokes, it must be full – with both arm fully bent and wrist cocked back. Just as important, it must be completed early, ie for a clear, when the shuttle is just starting its downward flight, for a lob or a drive just before the shuttle crosses the net. Only then will the stroke be straight-armed and unhurried. Late preparation is the downfall of many beginners, so start it far earlier than you feel you need to.

Forward Swing The smooth, no pause, transition is accomplished generally, with the heel of the hand leading, by snapping the bent arm straight (another word to print indelibly on your mind). Extra power is added by strongly uncocking the wrist. This is done just before impact. Thus the racket head is moving at its fastest, where it is most effective; that is, in the 'zip' area extending some 2ft to either side of the point of impact. This is the secret of timing.

Point of Impact Feet must position the body in just the right place so that impact is made at precisely the right spot. If it is not, error or an incorrect stroke will result. Generally impact is just in front of the body. The racket-head should be as square to the shuttle as possible. Generally hit into and through it, but for some strokes your racket-head will slice (cut smash), stop at impact (drop-shot), or even give slightly (return of smash).

Follow Through For control, always try to keep shuttle and strings in contact as long as possible. Keep the racket-head aimed at the target throughout. Avoid any sudden turning or snatching of the wrist.

Recovery As soon as, but never before the shuttle has been cleanly struck away from the racket, instantly regain your base, immediately bringing yourself and your racket back to the position of readiness.

Underarm and side-arm strokes are produced in virtually the same way as overhead ones except in a different plane. In each case the racket-head is somewhere near the small of the back, and the arm and wrist are bent. Power is obtained by snapping these straight as the weight is transferred from back to front foot.

33

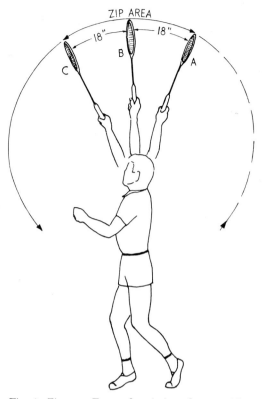

ZIP AREA

Fig. 6 Zip area. For perfect timing of an attacking clear your racket must be moving at its fastest in this area

Power strokes are like the coiling and uncoiling of a spring or − if you are more romantically inclined − a snake. Each part of the body smoothly adds its quota of power (and maintains it) to build up acceleration to its maximum precisely at impact. The secret is technique and timing rather than brainless bashing.

MOVEMENT

I make no apology for adding a little more detail on running, for movement is badminton's life blood. Move not at all and obviously you won't even hit the shuttle. Move very late and you will play a weak or a defensive stroke upwards from well below the tape. Worse still you will be off-balance and so slower still to your next shot. And if even fractionally late in the forecourt, you've missed your chance of hitting down for a winner.

Expect every shuttle to come to you. Move early! Move fast! Recover quickly! Then you're attacking: in on a winner, snapping up half-

chances, putting your opponent under pressure, and having fun.

Position of Readiness

Your movement springboard is your position of readiness. This is the alert stance you try to take up in between each stroke as you wait to move again to the shuttle. But in a hectic rally things happen fast, so it is not always feasible, as you may have to run through this position.

But whenever possible, this is your stance. Be perfectly balanced on the balls of your feet with the latter about shoulder width apart. You are never still. To overcome initial body inertia either do a quiet Mohammed Ali shuffle or a Virginia Wade bounce. Your knees are slightly bent to give you quick and vital drive. Your racket is held slightly to one side or directly in front of the body, pointing slightly upwards or nearly flat, according to whether you anticipate attacking or defending. Your eye is on your opponents and the shuttle. Your concentration is 100 per cent − nothing else exists outside the court.

This is your racing start: a stance that gives you a glorious feeling of movement and aggression. Never, never stand racket down, as limp as a wet umbrella, and flat-footed like an old age pensioner queuing for bingo. It must be a dynamic all-systems-go stance.

Running

How actually to move? In general, use short, floor-caressing, driving steps to get you off the mark. These will keep you compact, on balance. They will enable you to change direction more easily. Position yourself finally with a longer stride, which will also act as an instant disc-brake, if you are hurried.

At all costs you must get *behind* the shuttle and be on balance. Such landing is not three-point. For straight overhead and underarm strokes it is a sideways position with the left foot and hence the left shoulder at 90° to the net. For sidearm strokes you will be lined up almost parallel to the net, not at right angles to it.

You will always run forwards but going

Plate 10. Champion Liem Swie King (Indonesia) does a perfect backswing: elbow up, arm bent, wrist cocked back, racket-head down *(Mervyn Rees)*

FRIENDS' PROVIDENT B

backwards you may skip, glide, or run. The latter is preferable. Sideways movement is generally two or three skips followed by a longer stride across with the inside leg. This enables you to change direction quickly up to the last moment if deception is employed by the enemy camp.

Recovery from a shot must be as full of zip as the movement put into it. There's no time to hang about.

Movement is everything. Always go to meet the shuttle at the earliest possible moment. Never wait and let it come to you. 'On your toes' is the watchword. Throw inhibitions to the wind and RUN. Your difficulty will be not knowing where your opponent's return is likely to go. Note from this book what returns are likely. Use your commonsense and think what return you would make in such circumstances.

Remember too that the eye plays as important a role in speed as the legs and feet. If by acute observation you can pick up the shuttle's line of flight almost as it is hit, and not as it is crossing the net, you should both start and arrive early. The best movers are the early starters and recoverers, rather than the fastest sprinters. After all you can't make up much time in a three metre dash now, can you?

As perfect examples watch the feather-light dancing feet of Lene Koppen, the bounce and dash of Liem Swie King, the easy unhurried glide of Prakash Padukone. Such is movement!

PRACTICE DOESN'T MAKE PERFECT

Not a shuttle hit on court yet! But ignore this section at your peril.

Of course you want to enjoy games but wise practice will improve your game faster than just another routine, thoughtless club game from which nothing was learnt. I am going to prescribe a shrewd mixture of the two.

Forget that hoary old fallacy that 'practice makes perfect'. Only *perfect* practice achieves that end. So let's give it a little thought and save ourselves a lot of heartache.

Obviously the more you practise intelligently the faster you will improve. Try to play two or three times a week at least.

'Where and when' is the next cry. Although the club seems to be geared solely to games you can still practise if you adopt these methods: Arrive early or stay late when the courts are often free. Use, where possible, the space to the side of the court. String another net across. Explain to the committee member on duty that instead of a game you wish to practise for 10–15 minutes. That's fair, isn't it? Join the Local Education Authority evening class where practice should be the rule not the exception. Best of all, book a court at one of the now very numerous sports centres.

Equipment? Use good shuttles of the correct speed, not tatty throw-outs and a partner of the same enthusiasm and mind.

Be methodical. Plan just what you will practise each session. Let's say (i) High serve and clear, (ii) smash and push return, (iii) a game of singles. Always bear in mind your aim. Advance towards it by progressions which stretch you but which can be achieved. Success is a great fillip! Keep a record of these steps towards your target, noting both consistency and accuracy, eg 20 drop-shots: 2 in net, 12 good length, 4 too deep, 2 hit upwards.

Take it in turn to feed or to practise for a set time (5 minutes) or a set number of hits (30). Don't constantly switch. Play to and from correct court positions. Remember that accurate feeding is half the battle; if you can't hit the shuttle accurately (good practice in itself) throw it with a badminton action (more practice). Discuss reasons for failure. Never continue once your concentration or enthusiasm is burnt out: that breeds disillusion. End on a note of success if you can – and with an enjoyable game.

Don't try to run before you can walk! If timing is a problem, *start* with the racket swung back. Master the stroke from there, then gradually build up the backswing. In the same way, if running to the shuttle is the problem, start where you intend to hit the shuttle. Cut out the running. Then slowly add a pace or two of movement until you are naturally running to the shuttle.

Start too by playing one shot at a time. When you can play it reasonably well then try a rally. Start rallying too early and both feeding and stroke production become erratic. When you can rally two or three different strokes reasonably well then build up a game-routine, eg:

A Singles high serve   –   B Drop-shot
A Lob (not too deep)   –   B Smash

A Push return   –   B Lob
A Drop-shot   –   B Lob
A Smash   –   B Push return etc.

Move on to play conditioned games, ie a normal game except for an additional rule imposed to ensure repetition of the desired stroke. 'All high serves' will ensure smashing and push return; 'no lobbing' ensures net-shots; 'drops landing beyond front service line penalised' ensures tighter drop-shots.

Next, as your standard really improves, try pressure-training with two players versus one. The aim of the two is to make few mistakes and so keep long rallies going. They are there to stretch to the limit, not to beat. They too will learn accuracy and consistency.

Competitive games, especially against better players, are an essential part of practice. Work hard to be selected for a club team; enter as many tournaments as you can.

Practise regularly and intelligently; improve fast.

5 The Strokes

THE GRIPS

As you sow, so shall you reap. Less biblically, as you hold your racket, so will you play.

If you are to do yourself full justice you must get the grip right from the very start. It controls the racket-head which in turn controls the all-important flight of the shuttle.

Do not be deterred by the fact that there are five possible grips. In the comfort of your own home, you can practise the easy change from one to the other of the three with which I am going to start you. Or, you can play all the strokes there are with just one of them – the basic.

Whichever you use remember just two things. For control and touch, hold the racket in the fingers rather than in the palm. Your grip should be firm but relaxed so that the wrist remains flexible. Don't clutch it as a drowning man clutches a straw.

Basic

Every shot in the book can be played with this one grip. Hold the racket by its throat in your left hand so the handle points towards you. Now simply shake hands with it. After all, you're going to be partners. Or place it on the floor and then pick it up as if it were a chopper; edge on to the floor.

Check three points:
1. The V between thumb and forefinger lies roughly along the top bevel in line with the shaft.
2. The fingers, especially the forefinger, are spread out, not bunched like carrots.
3. The butt end of the racket, for power and reach, nestles in and does not protrude from the hand.

Hold the racket well out in front of you. Now you should see that it is a continuation of your arm, with the racket-head as a second hand; the sides of the thumb and forefinger do most of the gripping with the other fingers curled round the bottom of the handle to help.

Backhand

As for all changes of grip, relax your hold and roll the racket in your fingers. Roll it about 30° to your right. This will bring the flat of your thumb onto what is now the back bevel to give you greater leverage and so power, as well as control. This action you will notice has 'closed' the racket face. To 'open' it, or you'll be hitting downwards into the net, turn your wrist up slightly to the left.

Frying-pan

To achieve this aptly named grip, first take the basic or chopper grip. Roll the racket a full 90°. Now the racket-head is not sideways on to the net but square to it.

Use this grip only when hitting downwards near the net. Never use it at the back of the court because it inhibits full use of the wrist. At the back it is all too easy to cheat in bringing the racket face square to the shuttle. Don't take the easy way by just turning the racket in the hand. Do turn the wrist – and so the racket. It comes quite naturally.

Obviously you can – and must – practise these at home until the change becomes as automatic as breathing. Start with the basic; then 'backhand': roll the racket in your fingers; 'frying-pan': roll it again; 'forehand', and so on.

Later, move the racket as you practise the above to the appropriate position in relation to your body: left (backhand); centre (dab); right (forehand). A little later still, actually shadow backhand, dab or forehand strokes, changing grip as you do so.

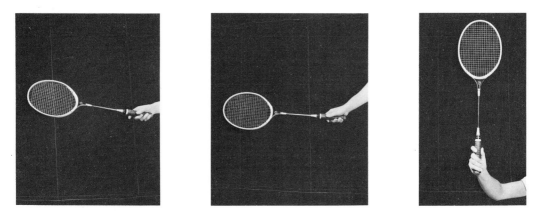

So much depends on the hand (and wrist) that control the racket face at impact. If the latter is wrongly turned, or turning, so that the racket face is not square to the shuttle at impact the shuttle will be missed, mishit or sliced, in order of venality. Many beginners' errors start – and stop – here.

So, when you actually hit the shuttle (except in deliberately cut shots) ensure that the racket is square to the shuttle at impact. Don't overuse the wrist so that the racket-head is turning erratically as you hit the shuttle. Good racket-head control cuts down error.

HIGH SERVE AND CLEAR
As a stimulating starter to your badminton banquet let's try the high service and clear. Complementary one to the other, each shot has its own distinct flavour. The high serve is the epitome of leisurely grace and ease; the clear, the acme of robust defence. Neither is a particularly difficult shot basically, though you will have to work hard to obtain the essential length.

High Serve
First you must know the Laws relating to service so that you do not unwittingly gain an unfair advantage – and probably an unflattering reputation.

Laws Relating to Service
At impact:
1. No part of the shuttle to be above the waist.
2. Whole of the racket-head, pointing downwards, to be clearly below the whole of the racket-hand.
3. Feet to be in court, not touching a line.

Plate 11. Grips. (i) Backhand; (ii) Forehand; (iii) Frying-pan

4. Both feet, or part of them, to be in contact with the floor.
5. There must be no feinting: ie the racket speed may be slowed down or speeded up but the movement must be continuous, without pause.
6. There must be no undue delay in serving. This is difficult to assess in seconds. It is rather a matter of whether it upsets the receiver or is used as a means of regaining breath after a hard rally.

Aim: The aim of a high serve is threefold:
1. To drive your opponent as far back in court as possible to blunt his power of attack.
2. To move him from his base and to open up the forecourt.
3. To give him problems in timing a high-hit, steeply falling shuttle. Throughout your practice therefore check and re-check that you are achieving the necessary length (within 12in of the back service line) and height (as high as ceiling and rafters, etc permit).

Despite this, such a serve, in a single stroke, does give your opponent the attack. Use it a lot in singles when its length can be increased by that safeguarding extra 2½ft to the base-line. Use it more sparingly in level doubles: when your opponents are weak smashers – or, as a gambling variant, when nothing else goes. Don't use it in mixed where defence is at a discount; unless, of course, the opposing lady's answer is a weak clear.

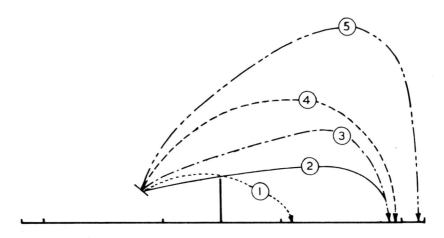

Fig. 7 Serve trajectories. (1) Low. (2) Drive.
(3) Flick. (4) High – doubles. (5) Very high – singles

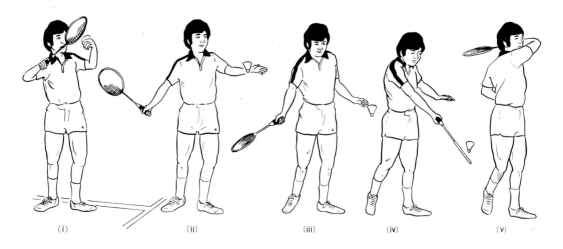

(i) (ii) (iii) (iv) (v)

Fig. 8 High serve. (i) Starting position; relaxed, unhurried. (ii) Slow start of downswing. (iii) Racket speed accelerating; wrist still cocked; eye on shuttle. (iv) Impact forward of right foot; wrist uncocked; eyes down. (v) Follow-through on line

Why start with it then? Simply because badminton is a game of overhead shots (with a 5ft high net, it needs to be!). And to practise overhead shots you must have an underhand stroke to hit the shuttle up. Have no fear, I'll explain the better alternatives, the low and flick serves, a little later.

Since you are going to 'practise as you will play', take up a position 2–3ft behind the front service line: Front foot (the left) at an angle of 45° to the net, back foot almost parallel to the net. Left shoulder pointing at your opponent (real or imaginary) in the diagonally opposite court. Weight evenly balanced. Knees very slightly bent; body erect and relaxed. (Yes, the latter is very important – nothing ever comes out of tension, except awkwardness and the twitch.) Shuttle feather or skirt held between thumb and forefinger (arm slightly bent) at shoulder height so that the shuttle will fall some 12in in front of your leading foot and just to the right of it. Racket-head up alongside the shuttle. Look at definite target area.

40

Backswing Sweep the racket down as far as it will go. Then, by bending the elbow outwards, allow it to swing up without pause. It should be almost vertical, just to the right of and about 1ft from your right shoulder. The wrist is cocked back; the elbow still bent, and the weight now on the back foot. Simpler still, you can just start in this position from the outset.

Forward Swing Now you are ready for the forward swing. Push the heel of the hand down and forward so that the arm straightens. Your body pivots at the hips, squarer to the net, and your weight sways forward onto the front foot. Just before the arm straightens, slightly bend the knees, uncock the wrist, and hit upwards for height. But to get the even more vital length, you must at the same time sweep the racket forward as well as upwards.

Don't desperately swish your racket down as though your life depended on it. The shuttle is a feather; it floats down – not plummets. Hit too fast and racket-head, like some impatient lover, arrives at its tryst too early only to find that the leisurely bird hasn't even arrived. 'Slow and steady with gently increasing acceleration' is the order of the day. You're not hitting the full length of the court so don't give it all you've got. Rhythm and timing are the answers.

Impact Actual impact is desperately important. The racket-head must squarely meet the shuttle without any exaggerated last-second wrist twitch. It must be aimed at the target and kept on course. Avoid the natural tendency to hit cross-court. Then (and for a split second after) it's head down to *see* the shuttle actually hit the strings and away.

Follow-through and Recovery Follow through easily on target line as long as you can. The racket-head finishes high in front of your left shoulder. Stroke over, draw it down and dance into a position of defensive readiness at the appropriate base.

Likely Pitfalls
1. Too tight a grip: prevents full use of wrist for height.
2. Too fast down-swing: shuttle missed.
3. Head up just before impact: shuttle missed.

4. Racket-head not aimed squarely at targets: hit out.
5. Wrist turned sideways at impact: mishits.
6. Shovelling or pushing action with no sweep through: lack of length.
7. Not enough hitting firmly upwards results in loss of height; too much, in loss of length.
8. Short backswing, and failure to use wrist or push through: lack of length.

Practices
Use a shuttle of the same speed each time you practise.
1. From the front service line see how far you can hit the shuttle. (Don't rush it!) Note your best distance.
2. Repeat in your next practices until you can (i) reach the back doubles service line; (ii) the singles back service line.
3. When (2) is achieved, check that by using wrist strongly you are hitting the shuttle roof-high.
4. Move back a foot at a time to a base 3ft from the front service line still maintaining length and height.
5. As above but serve cross-court not straight.
6. Using an outspread newspaper as target, count your successes out of ten attempts.

Defensive (or High) Clear
The clear, lacking the bravura of the smash, is nevertheless a solid, satisfying, down-to-earth, workaday stroke without frills. It is easier to play, full-blooded, and provided it has all essential length, gives you temporary respite.

Although I am a firm believer in attack I offer this defensive stroke first because of its comparative simplicity. It offers a solid foundation on which to build the other overheads: the smash and the drop. It is an excellent practice stroke too because clear can be answered with clear.

Aim: to hit the shuttle overhead, high, from base-line to base-line.

You will find that a defensive clear is almost never used in mixed doubles because its player formation is weak defensively and a clear is always open to attack. It is used more in men's

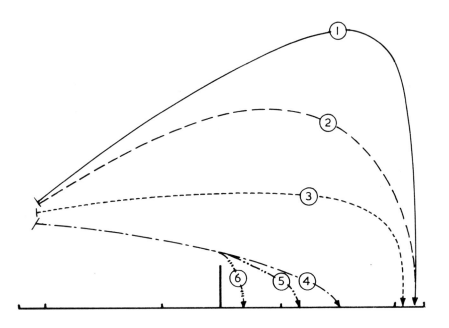

Fig. 9 Overhead trajectories. (1) Defensive clear. (2) Clear. (3) Attacking clear. (4) Smash. (5) Fast drop-shot. (6) Slow drop-shot

and ladies' doubles where strong defensive positions can be mounted, although an attacking shot is obviously a preferable alternative.

In singles where it may well be dangerous to attack from the base-line it is used much more. In conjunction with the complementary drop-shot it is the means of running your single opponent up and down the court.

Remember, a clear hit short of the back doubles service line is wide open to attack. Every foot short of that is added danger. Length therefore is a prime virtue.

A secondary one is height. As with the high serve, a high, steeply falling clear is difficult to time and hit cleanly. It has the added merit that it gives you (the striker) ample time to recover in good order to your base before your opponent can have a crack at it.

In practice, take up your position of readiness (on your toes) on the back doubles service line. Initially, to make sure your stroke is unhurried and will be completed with a straight arm, start your backswing slowly *as the server starts his.* This may seem much too early but, believe me, it isn't, at this stage.

Preparation and Backswing As the shuttle is hit you must judge whether to move forwards, backwards or sideways, so that, if allowed to fall, the shuttle would hit you on the head! As you do so complete your backswing. It is absolutely vital that you learn to synchronise the two. As your back foot goes down, feel the racket-head hit the small of your back.

The racket-head, to achieve power, must be brought fully back. This can be achieved in any of three ways. Do whichever comes naturally – and effectively.

1. Simply raise the racket then, by cocking back the wrist, drop it, head first, over your right shoulder. This, both for speed and power, is used by most top players in over-heads. As you improve, your backswing will be made later and your follow-through curtailed in the cause of instant racket-head recovery. Your overhead strokes will have the swift menace of a striking cobra or a karate chop.
2. Sweep the racket sideways, upwards, round the shoulder, to the small of your back.
3. As in a tennis serve, sweep the racket-head down behind you as far as you can; by

Plate 12. Liem Swie King again. High serve: arm straight but wrist still cocked back; knees bending, body turning, eyes on shuttle *(Louis C. H. Ross)*

turning the arm outwards, bending the elbow inwards and then sweeping it upwards, the racket-head is dropped down the back. If you sweep the racket-head firmly downwards it will automatically sweep up behind you to the correct position.

Whichever way you adopt, and (1) is the quickest and simplest, the racket-head should be in a 'back-scratching position' in the small of the back. To achieve this your elbow is bent and your wrist fully cocked back. (I defy you, unless double-jointed, to achieve this without the latter.)

At the same time, you have turned sideways, knees bent, left shoulder to the net, and with body turned, weight on the back foot. Your left arm is upraised as a counter-balance and pointed at the shuttle as a 'sighter'.

Forward Swing Non-stop, in one smoothly accelerating action, the upward and forward swing commences. And if the backswing was 100 per cent important, the forward swing is 200 per cent! With the heel of the hand leading, the bent arm is snapped straight in a throwing, not a straight-armed, bowling action. The racket-head must be thrust upwards as well as forwards. If you only push the racket forward, (and many ladies unversed in the art of throwing will do so), you will become that badminton anathema − a bent arm dabber, a darts player, a pusher! One who will never know the full glory of a lusty, good length clear. So, throw that hand upwards to the ceiling.

Meantime, as with the high serve, your body is turning square to the net and your weight moving across on to your front foot. Just before impact the wrist is firmly half uncocked.

Impact, Follow-through and Recovery Impact should be made with a *straight* arm high above the right shoulder. The racket-head should be at about 45° in order to achieve maximum length and height. Don't uncock the wrist too fully, and feel you are hitting upwards.

If you make impact when the shuttle is behind you, you will achieve height but little

Plate 13. Gillian Gilks plays an overhead stroke: straight arm, perfect balance and eyes on shuttle *(Mervyn Rees)*

length. If, when it is in front of you, it will lack both height and length. So position yourself carefully.

Keep shuttle and strings aimed at the target, and in contact as long as you can. Let the racket swing through and down to waist level.

If you have driven up with your bent knees and spiralled your body upwards and forwards into the shot strongly enough, your right leg should automatically swing forward. Thus you both put body weight into the shot and take a first quick step to your central base. Always try to reach it before your opponent plays his stroke.

Pitfalls
1. A slackly strung racket and an arm without muscle: no length.
2. Little or no backswing: no power.
3. Late backswing − bent arm: little power, no height. Start with racket in backswing position.
4. Letting shuttle drop: flat and no power.
5. Uncontrolled racket-head at impact: mishit or hit out.
6. Stiff wrist: lack of power.
7. Square to net; dabbing not throwing: lack of height and length. Check grip and stance.
8. Not getting behind the shuttle: no length.

Practices
Use shuttle of same speed each time.
1. In pairs, throw shuttle high across width of court to each other.
2. Using same upward throwing action (*not* a dab or push) shadow the stroke with your racket.
3. Stand on base-line. Feeder hits high serves. Mark length of best clear. Seek to better this in each practice.
4. As above, but count number of clears landing between the two back lines out of ten.
5. As in (3) but now running back from a base first one pace, then two, then three, in front of base line.
6. Each player stands mid-court. A serves high to B who clears back to A who in turn clears to B to maintain a rally. Keep a count.

45

(i)   (ii)   (iii)   (iv)   (v)

7. As in (6) but gradually move base further back to rally over longer distances, seeking to hit the shuttle from base-line to base-line.

SMASH AND PUSH RETURN

Now for two of the most important strokes in the game. The smash – the spearhead of attack; the push return – the bulwark of your defence.

Smash

This is a great stroke! Fascinating alike in its sheer power – and as a safe means of uncorking bottled up inhibitions and ill temper. It is a stroke that you've got to play meanly. It is the rally-ender, the point-winner, the ego-satisfier.

Aim: to hit downwards as hard and steeply as possible to end the rally or at least force a weak return that can be 'killed'.

All overhead strokes must be played with identical actions until the last possible second. In this way your opponent may be deceived as to whether you are going to clear, smash or drop. Play your smash therefore exactly like your clear until fractionally before impact.

Impact This must be made not over the head but as with the clear but earlier, some 18in in front of it. The wrist must be fully and crisply uncocked. In this way your racket-head will come over the shuttle to hit it *downwards*.

Fig. 10 Smash. (i) Start of backswing over shoulder. (ii) End of backswing – 'back scratch'. (iii) Just before impact; body swinging forward. (iv) Impact; racket-head over shuttle. (v) Follow-through and recovery to attack return

The follow through will be rather longer, generally down beside the left leg. Otherwise what we have said of the clear applies. (See Fig. 9.)

Many players, especially ladies, find this downward-hitting action difficult. Note the pitfalls carefully.

Pitfalls

1. As Pitfalls (1), (2), (5) and (6) for the clear stroke.
2. Not getting behind the shuttle: hit flat.
3. Belated forward push or dab instead of an *early upward throw*: hit flat.
4. Racket-head not brought crisply over shuttle by use of flexible wrist: lacks steepness.

Practices

1. Striker stands on *front* service line: racket-head down behind back. Feeder throws or hits shuttle fairly high to drop 18in in front of him. Striker, moving feet if necessary, has only to

46

throw racket gently up and bring wrist and racket-head over to return down to feeder. Steepness, not power, is the aim. Repeat ten times. When he is successful, striker moves back a yard and hits down from there. Repeat gradually moving back up to back doubles service line.

2. Repeat (1) but start with racket-head held in front of body at (i) shoulder level then (ii) at waist level.

3. With backswing (2) mastered, feeder must place shuttle so that striker has to run back first one yard, then two, then three, and so on.

4. For placement: spread an open newspaper as target about 15ft from the net. Striker smashes from back doubles service line.

5. For steepness: draw a line across the court some 13ft from the net. Shuttle must land within that line.

6. For consistency: feeder has six shuttles that he hits up at regulated intervals to different parts of the court. Striker smashes one after the other. None to be hit out or into the net.

Push Return

There is little learnt simply by picking up a shuttle smashed to the floor. So, pursuing our policy of complementary strokes and 'two for the price of one', let's play one of the five returns to the smash.

Aim: To return *flat* your opponent's main attacking shot, with least risk of error, and so prevent him playing another strong attacking shot.

So, let's play a defensive push return. It has two great advantages: (i) it is comparatively simple; (ii) it should early inculcate the old military truth 'Attack is the best method of defence'.

As soon as you lift a shuttle expect trouble! You'll rarely be disappointed. So keep your return flat whenever you can.

With high service, lob or clear completed, it's back to mid-court defensive position and position of readiness square to the striker. Be on your toes, that opponent of yours is quite capable of a drop-shot in front of you or a clear behind you – both deceptively played with a smash action. Have that racket held across your stomach (a likely target) and thus equidistant from flanking attacks to backhand or forehand. *Above all have your eyes on your opponent's racket-head so that you can instantly pick up the shuttle's line of flight.* Then, and only then, have you the time to play a calm, unhurried return. Spot the shuttle only as it hurtles into your forecourt and a panic-stricken snatch or missed shot results.

Watch that bird with the same close observation and keen interest, gentlemen, with which you observe the other even more beautiful and no less expensive variety.

If the smash is travelling fast you probably have no time for footwork and little for backswing. Therefore, still square to the striker, if needs must, play the shuttle without footwork. Your backswing will be limited to a foot or so. Not to worry. At this stage we aren't in the power-stroke business. This is 'the soft answer that turneth away wrath'!

With bent arm tucked into your side if possible and with your wrist firm, take early and simply push or block the shuttle back flat. Relaxed but not sloppy grip; racket-head angled slightly upwards; a little body sway; a very limited follow through; and head down, completes the stroke. The shuttle, travelling just fast enough to avoid interception by the opposing net player, skims the tape and falls just short of the smasher. (See Fig. 11.)

Pitfalls

1. Not picking up speed and line of flight early: snatching.

2. Not watching shuttle onto racket: miss or mishit.

3. Using too much wrist: mishit.

4. Using too much backswing: miss.

5. Angling racket upwards too much: shuttle lifted – and killed stone dead by your opponent.

Practices

1. Feeder using smash action throws shuttle from just beyond net onto forehand – striker plays push return.

2. As above but throws to backhand.

3. As above, alternating.

4. As above, but thrown at random backhand or forehand.

Plates 14(i) and (ii). Champions both. (i) Rudi Hartono (Indonesia), forehand, and (ii) Liem Swie King, backhand, show watchful agility in push return of smash *(Louis C. H. Ross and S. Perry)*

5. Striker hits high doubles serve; feeder smashes as above; striker plays flat return. Power of smash can be gradually increased.
6. As in (5) but place a net-player opposite the striker; he will try to intercept push return.

DROP-SHOT AND LOB

Two more new strokes to master.

Have no fear. Both are only slight variations of strokes you are already playing: the lob of the high serve; the drop-shot (sometimes called the 'drop') of the smash. Neither therefore presents unknown perils.

Fig. 11 Sidearm and underarm trajectories. (1) Defensive lob. (2) Attacking lob. (3) Drive. (4) Half-court push. (5) Net-shot

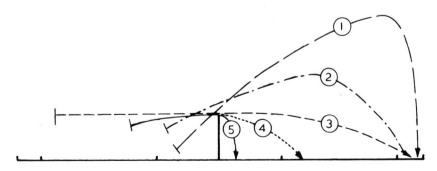

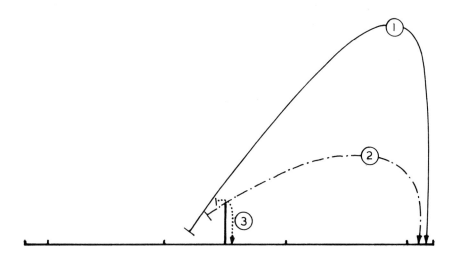

Fig. 12 Underarm trajectories. (1) Defensive lob. (2) Attacking lob. (3) Net-shot

Both are a delight. The drop exudes delicacy and deception. The lob is a saving, last-ditch stand, played with an athletic grace beloved of photographers.

In accord with our softly, softly approach let's take them one at a time. It's cart before the horse perhaps, but, the lob first; it's simpler.

The Lob (or Underarm Clear)

Aim: To return a drop-shot or net-shot falling well below tape-height in the fore-court, high and deep to the baseline. It is a defensive shot that relies on length and height for survival.

How then to play it? Exactly like the high serve except that you take the shuttle at full stretch and nearer the floor. You lunge to it — front knee well bent. This, partly because in a game it may be your only desperate means of preventing it hitting the floor; partly because at least your back foot is therefore still fairly near base. If you just run, you are likely to run right up alongside it. This will cramp your return. Worse still, you will have run a yard further forward than you needed to. And you will have a yard further to go back as well. Two yards wasted. So put on the brakes. Make sure you are on balance.

For full recovery all that is needed is a strong push back with your front foot. This initially will probably be your left. If it is your right, don't worry as we shall advocate that later.

So much for movement. Now for the hitting action. This is the same as for the high serve, though not quite so much backswing is necessary. You are hitting a shorter distance —

only just over half the length of the court. It is therefore all too easy to hit out. And because it is easy to hit out then we tend to be over-cautious and hit short. We are caught between Scylla and Charybdis. Length however is essential for nothing is more damaging to your ego and your person than to have a shuttle smashed sharply between your eyes as you retreat in some disorder 'to base'.

Make sure, therefore, that as your front foot goes forward your racket goes *back*. There is no power in a shovelling action from a racket held stiffly in front of you. And just as control is essential for length, so it is for direction. In 'plugging' your opponent's deep backhand it needs only a slight turn of the racket-head to hit the shuttle out over the side-line. It may be marginal but all the more infuriating, because a point lost. As service laws do not apply here the racket-head on occasions may be at impact more horizontal than vertical, well to the right of your leading foot, not just alongside it. And whilst you must do all you can to make that impact as high as possible (the early take) often it will be only inches off the floor.

At this stage you will not be as physically agile as a cat, nor as mentally agile as 'Mastermind', so, with a strong uncocking of

(*Overleaf*) Plate 15. The epitome of athletic grace, Lene Koppen (Denmark) sweeps in to play a lob at pressured full stretch (*Mervyn Rees*)

49

Fig. 13 Forehand lob. (i) Running to shuttle. (ii) Starting backswing en route. (iii) Halfway to impact; lunge; wrist cocked. (iv) Impact, beside right foot; balanced. (v) Follow-through on line

the wrist, hit *high* as well as deep. This will give you time to be back on base before your opponent can have another crack at it.

Pitfalls

1. Over-running the shuttle: this will cramp your return and delay your recovery. So, lunge!
2. Head lifted just before impact: shuttle missed.
3. No backswing as front foot goes forward: lack of length.
4. Too much wrist and not enough push through: height but poor length.
5. Uncontrolled turn of wrist at impact: mishit or hit out.

Practices

1. Stand side on, racket back in high serve position, a yard behind the front service line. Partner throws shuttle underhand, short, so that you have to lunge to make contact. Partner runs backwards to catch shuttle in front of him, runs in, and repeats. (Useful and necessary footwork practice: running backwards, never letting a shuttle get behind you.)
2. Progressions: striker (i) initially stands sideways, racket back; (ii) then stands square, 1, 2 and 3 yards behind service line so having to turn and run in to shot; (iii) after impact, runs backwards until shuttle is caught, then in again. (Footwork and pressure.) Always check *length* by noting if opponent's back foot is behind the base-line.

The Drop-Shot (Slow)

Now for the drop-shot – the third of the trinity of overhead strokes. It is to a beginner something of a paradox. A gentle shot – yet one classed as 'attacking'. But, played downwards, deceptively, and to a length, it is just that. It surprises your opponent who, belatedly lunging forward and taking it near the floor, has little option but to lift, perhaps short.

Aim: To drop the shuttle a minimum distance from the net so forcing your opponent to make a maximum run and to play a weak, lifted return. Target area: from net to front service line (See Fig. 9).

In singles, in thoughtful co-operation with the clear, it is used to run your opponent up and down the court into exhaustion and error. In doubles, to maintain the attack when a smash is not 'on'.

In singles, it will bring you outright winners, doubly delectable because they were achieved by subtlety and with minimal expenditure of energy. In doubles, it will force a short lob that you can then proceed to dispatch painlessly by smashing.

Remember, the drop-shot is played *downwards* from between the two back lines to lose speed quickly and fall as near the net as possible (2–4ft). Hit it beyond the front service line and your opponent has scarcely to move; caress it, stroke it perfectly within 2ft of the net and he has to lunge desperately. Hit it upwards and even the most leaden-footed opponent virtually has time enough to go for a quick 'cuppa', return, and still be able to dispatch it with considerable relish.

Delicate, slow stroke that it is, it survives solely by subtlety. You must play it exactly like a clear or a smash to hobble the marauding opponents who will otherwise be fast in for the kill. It must look like a power-stroke down even to the very last nuance, down to the face-contorting grimace of hate that goes with a smash.

Play it therefore with the full-blooded wind up and forward swing of a clear or smash. Obviously the speed of arm and wrist must be slowed down a foot or two before impact. The later, the more deceptive. Point of impact too differs. For the drop, it is between that for the smash and the clear; just inches forward of the head. But the arm should still be straight. The follow-through is shorter but even firmer. Almost push the shuttle over, keeping strings–shuttle contact as long as possible.

Target areas? Generally speaking, in singles, the corners to make your opponent travel; in doubles, down the middle to cause doubt as to who shall take it, or nearer the slower moving or more error-prone opponent. In mixed, of course, eschew it, as in that branch of the game there is a nippy young lady specially stationed at the net to give it full military honours!

Pitfalls
1. No backswing, just dabbing at the shot: no deception.
2. Hitting upwards: gives opponents time to run in and kill it.
3. Letting shuttle drop and playing bent arm push: no downward angle or deception.
4. Hitting too hard: opponent unmoved!

Practices
1. Feeder plays high singles serve: striker plays drop, downwards. Count number falling between net and service line.
2. As in (1) but feeder plays a return lob. Players rally and help each other by calling 'Good' or 'Short' or 'Too deep' as appropriate.
3. As in (2) but feeder and striker do not maintain static conditions; they run in and out between shots. Do not run so far as to preclude easily regaining base to play a series of well-balanced shots.
4. Drop-lob single: Play only drops and lobs. Any lob not falling between the back lines and any drop-shot not falling between net and front service line are regarded as faults. Use full width of court and keep a score.
5. As in (4) but instead of just letting short lobs fall to the floor, smash them.

DRIVE
Even if the shuttle has fallen to just above tape-height it can still be attacked – with a drive. Used mainly in mixed doubles by the man, it drives the shuttle down the side-lines, into the body, or cross-court. Hit with a whip-like action, it is a cracking shot that thrills by leaving an opponent stranded by sheer speed. (See Fig. 11.)

Aim: to hit a shuttle which has dropped to tape-height, hard, fast, and flat, or slightly downwards.

Your racket is prepared by swinging it back sideways at shoulder level so that the racket hand is by your right shoulder, and the racket-

head, parallel to the ground between your shoulder blades.

At the same time, pivot on your right foot and stretch across onto the left foot so you are parallel to the net. Then, with arm bent and wrist cocked back, *fling* the racket outwards in the widest possible arc at the shuttle. Use, but do not overuse the wrist, and pronate the forearm. Meet the shuttle just above tape-height and just in front of the leading foot. Your racket-head angle is vitally important and depends on the shuttle's height in relation to the net. If the shuttle is above, your racket face is slightly closed; if it is below, slightly open. And if it is level, almost vertical. Leaning well forward, hit into and through the shuttle keeping the racket face square to the shuttle as long as possible to drive it down the side-line. To hit it cross-court, simply make your point of impact some two feet further forward when

Plate 16. Indonesia's Ivana has drive! Right foot across, well balanced, bent arm and cocked wrist crisply straightening to fling racket-head at shuttle *(Mervyn Rees)*

Fig. 14 Forehand drive. (i) Running to shuttle. (ii) Right foot across; swinging racket back. (iii) Halfway through forward swing. (iv) Impact, in front of body; straight arm. (v) Follow-through and recovery

your racket is swinging across your body. The follow-through is across the body at chest height.

From the drive, stem two other useful strokes. Each is played with the drive action (deception again!) but with reduced power. The **push** is hit just hard enough to beat the net-player and fall 2–3ft behind the front service line, between net- and back-players. This is particularly effective in mixed doubles.

The **drop-shot** is played more gently still, (but with full and apparently powerful swing), to skim the tape and land just beyond the net. As the shuttle travels slowly, hit slightly upwards to nullify the downward pull of gravity. Both are excellent alternatives to the brainless wallop upwards that brings only destruction in its train. Gently played though they are, they maintain the attack.

55

Pitfalls

1. Racket *pushed* in short arc, not *flung* in wide arc: no power.
2. Shuttle taken late when past body: hit out.
3. Racket face too closed: hit into the net; too open: lifted, or so sliced that speed is lost.
4. Cross-courting too often: take shuttle later.

Practices

1. Feeder, 8–10ft from the striker, throws shuttle underhand. Already positioned with left foot across and racket back, merely sweep shuttle carefully back to feeder. Repeat, gradually moving further apart.
2. Stand some 14–15ft from the net and 3ft from the side-line. Feeder, from other side of net, hits shuttle 2–3ft above tape height, 2–3ft to *your* right. Stroke the shuttle smoothly back to him.
3. Gradually increase power, hitting full length of court straight and cross-court into hands of 'shuttle fags' stationed in the back 'box', and mid-court on the far tram-lines.
4. Players, each mid-court, play a rally of drives: (i) cross-court, forehand to forehand; (ii) straight, forehand to backhand.
5. Using same power-action, practise the push as in (1) and (2).

NET-SHOTS

These are strokes played in returning a shuttle from very near the net: strokes in miniature but nevertheless ones that are often winners. Played upwards, they should just trickle over the tape and immediately down the other side – a matter of mere inches. Played downwards, they hit the floor only a few feet behind the front service line. Their rewards are out of all proportion to the energy expended. The former call for rare delicacy of touch; the latter, quick reflexes and the snap of finality.

Downward Net-Shots

Aim: to hit any shuttle above net height steeply and crisply downward with a dabbing action.

Know the Law It is a fault (i) if, over-eager, you hit the shuttle before it crosses the net, or (ii) if in the course of your stroke you hit the net, no matter whether you merely graze it with your clothing or completely uproot it with your racket or (iii) put so much as a toe *under* the net.

You may however, hit the shuttle on your side of the net and then follow through over it.

Practise these downward strokes first because badminton's basic maxim is to hit *down* at every opportunity. With net-shots the opportunity is often fleeting; a shuttle has to drop only an inch or two to find sanctuary below tape-height. It is therefore imperative that you adopt the correct stance for split-second net attack.

Your base is on the T-junction. Stand square to the net, knees bent, bouncing lightly on the balls of your feet. If you are tall or worried about being hit in the face, crouch down below net-height. Not only is this safer but it also makes it easier for you to control the shuttle. Hold the racket just forward and to the right of your head in a basic or a frying-pan grip. The latter is simpler, (page 38), but do not use it except in 'rushing' low serves or in downward net play.

Watch your opponents observantly to see who is shaping to play the shot – and to which side of the net. When you are so near your opponents, it is as essential to have an early warning system as it is to be highly mobile. You are working in split seconds.

Dab If the shuttle is played to you just above tape-height then your stroke is a quick dab – no more. No more is needed to score a winner. And there is no time for a long backswing or the shuttle will drop below tape-height.

So, bring the racket back about a foot. Then smartly extend the forearm and slightly uncock the wrist to dab crisply down. Down is the key word; hit it flat, without wrist, and it will fly out, a golden opportunity wasted. Stop the racket on impact so that there is no follow-through. Aim straight at your opponent or into a gap. Instantly recover the racket to its original position, for if the shuttle is returned at all, it will come back quickly. You must be ready to maintain the attack.

A useful variant is the following. Instead of always dabbing down crisply, slow down the action just before impact, as in a drop. Then,

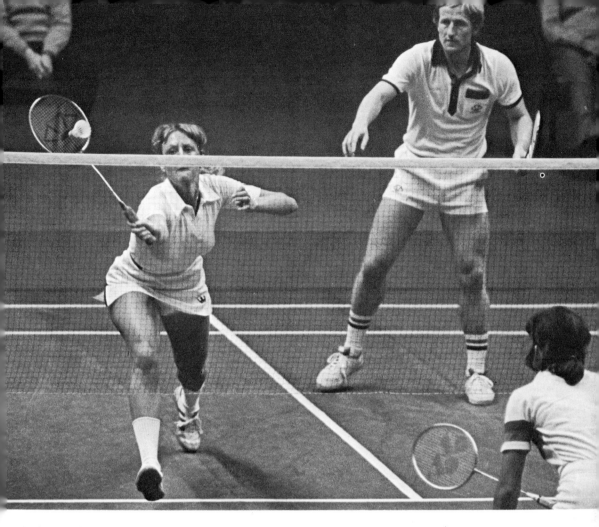

played with relaxed grip and almost a dead racket, the shuttle will fall much shorter (only a foot or two over the net) than your opponents anticipated.

Smash If the shuttle on rare occasions is cocked up several feet about head-height, then use the smash. It will however have to be quickly played and played therefore with a shortened 'straight up and over' backswing and a very much curtailed follow-through. Don't be tempted to move far back into your partner's area. If there is any doubt whose shot it is, a crisp 'Mine' (provided always that it is solo and not duet) should prevent decapitation.

Equally, beware greed. It is tempting indeed to have a go at everything that rises above the tape. Be selective. Go only for those you can take in front of your ears and therefore control. Leave the others to your partner who is moving

Plate 17. Peerless Nora Perry races in – just in time to dab down a low serve *(Mervyn Rees)*

forward and has more time than you to judge the shuttle's flight. It is easier for him!

Pitfalls
1. Sluggish feet.
2. Too long a backswing: shuttle drops and is hit into the net.
3. Shuttle hit flat, without wrist: out!
4. Slow racket recovery: opponent wriggles off the hook.
5. Taking too much: uncontrolled shots.
6. Standing *too* near the net: not enough time to intercept fast-moving shuttle.
7. Racket held downwards: chance missed.

57

Plate 18. Big Steen Skovgaard (Denmark) gets down to it to play a delicate net-shot at tape height (*S. Perry*)

Practices

Bounce on the T-junction – a feeder stands opposite about 11ft from the net. (Always on the balls of your feet, positioning yourself behind the shuttle – not just stretching for it.)

1. Dab down slowly to feeder who returns shuttle just above tape-height with side-arm push defence. To sustain the rally, aim for his racket.
2. As in (1) but slowly increase tempo.
3. As in (1) and (2) but playing on his backhand.
4. Dab down alternately to forehand, backhand, forehand, etc.

5. Dab down to either side without set pattern.
6. Feeder returns along full width of net to run you about.

Upward Net-Shots

These strokes are the epitome of delicacy and touch. If the shuttle cannot be hit down, take it as high as possible and stroke it just over the tape to trickle straight down close to the other side of the net. If the shot is played correctly your opponent cannot hit down and has difficulty even hitting up.

Aim: to return the shuttle so close to the net that your opponent is forced to lift.

When hitting down is risky, or impossible, then you should hit up. But do it with a surgeon's silken delicacy and millimetre accuracy.

You will have only a split second in which to decide whether to hit down or up. A difficult choice. Be neither rash in hitting down and into the net, when you should have hit up, nor timorous in hitting up when you could have hit down.

Always take the shuttle early – and therefore as high – as you can. At the tape if possible. Your stroke is a perfect miniature: with racket-head up, a 6in looped backswing; then a forward swing and impact in the same compass; and a miniscule follow-through.

With a relaxed grip, basic or variant, bent arm, a firm wrist, and a hint of body sway, scarcely breathe on the shuttle, just stroke it, coax it, will it – to tumble over the tape and vertically down the net on the other side. Don't desperately stab or jab like a berserk D'Artagnan. Equally, don't dilly-dally with it or it will die on you.

Play out to the corners away from your opponent. When you have drawn him out there you can play a cross-court net-shot. For this simply turn the wrist crisply inwards to send the shuttle tape-skimming, fast, falling near the far side-line.

Pitfalls

1. Not taking the shuttle early, tape high: opponent given time; shot more error-prone.
2. Jabbing wildly at it: mishit or in the net.

3. Hitting too hard with a tight grip: shuttle hit too high above tape and killed by opponent.

Practices

1. Start with yourself and feeder mid-court. The shuttle is hit underhand, low, wrist cocked, one to the other. Both slowly move into the net, hitting ever less hard by gradually shortening both backswing and follow through. Keep the racket up and eventually meet the shuttle near the net, tape-high. Be on your toes; watch that bird; relaxed finger grip; don't hurry it; take care. Success!
2. A serves low. B returns shuttle to the net. Then, still using upward net-shots only, a 'single' is played along the length of the net.
3. As above but uppish net-shots may be dabbed down provided shuttle lands within line marked 11ft from the net.

Hair-pin Its name clearly describes its flight. It is hit almost vertically upwards some 6–12in above the tape, makes the narrowest of loops, and then drops vertically down almost touching the other side of the net.

This renders an accurate return very difficult if not impossible. It should be played only when your opponent is sluggish or deep in court. Otherwise he will delightedly kill the high-rise shuttle!

LOW SERVE

If the smash is the king of strokes, the low serve is undoubtedly the crown prince. It is the simplest yet the most difficult; it yields the biggest returns for the least effort; it offers too, the joy of achievement against the odds. Can one say more of a single stroke?

Aim: To get the shuttle safely into play. To force your opponent to play a lifted reply – be it net-shot or lob – to you or your partner.

The first stroke of the rally is hit underhand. It rises slightly upwards but drops (to safety) to skim the tape and fall up to 12in beyond the front service line and near the T-junction, so narrowing the angle of return. (See Fig. 7.) Its aim, 'to get the shuttle into play' may sound pathetically negative. But consider again the

Laws (see page 39) that shackle you and prevent any kind of McEnroe or Tanner blistering aggression. These should be as immutable as the Laws of the Medes and Persians! Especially numbers (1) and (2). The latter particularly is far too often broken. That's cheating! Look too at the eager receiver waiting to pounce on the shuttle if it is a mere inch or two above the tape.

The odds are stacked against you in your prime aim of forcing your opponent to lift, of preventing him from hitting down. No glorious heart-warming aces here. But do not let me shake your infant confidence. (It is an essential in low serving.) The main threat is an aggressive, agile tiger of a receiver toeing the front line opposite. Fortunately they are few and far between at this stage. Later, though, you will meet them. So, even now strive for tape-skimming perfection.

Production

To some extent the low serve is a miniature, emasculated high serve. There is the same basic position and stance but as you're going to hit the shuttle a bare 16ft, bring shuttle and racket initially closer together. The shuttle, at chest height, should fall now just to the right of and level with your leading foot. Your racket generally (though service swings vary enormously) is pointing downwards to the right of and just behind or forward of (take your choice) the thigh. Grip is relaxed and wrist fully cocked back. Weight is on the back foot.

Thus, comfortably poised, linger a moment. Do not rush headlong and thoughtlessly to disaster. Take your time. It's the only occasion you can do so. Be relaxed. Be confident. (Think you'll fail – and fail you will.)

Doubtless William Tell took a long, long, look at that fateful apple. Do the same at your targets – the tape and a precise spot up to 12in beyond the front service line. Register them on the computer brain that must accurately activate the hand, wrist and arm. Then, with the targets still in your mind, look at the shuttle. No blithe cavalier 'hit and swipe' approach here. Look at badminton on TV and you see 100 per cent concentration. (See Plate 19.)

Take 100 per cent care, too. As you drop the shuttle, sway forward, arm close to the body.

Plate 19. Gillian Gilks, relaxed but 100 per cent
concentrating, illustrates the all-essential 'wrist
cocked back' *(Mervyn Rees)*

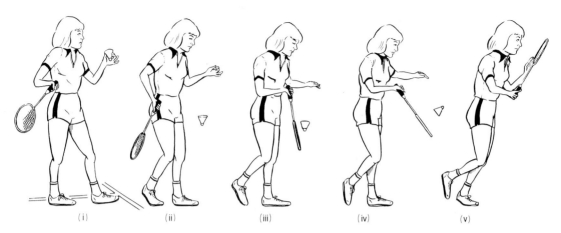

Avoid 'curtseying'! The heel of the hand pushes slightly down and forwards. The arm partly straightens; the weight shifts; the body turns — but the wrist stays immutably cocked back.

Impact is made at mid-thigh level with the racket face only minimally out of the vertical. But it is angled enough for the shuttle to skim the tape. Stroke the shuttle flat, on target. (No last-second panic wrist-twitch.) It's a matter of nerve — don't let a grim-faced receiver intimidate you. Even if he hits at you, you can always duck. You've a partner behind you. Maintain shuttle–strings contact as long as possible. Stroke, almost push the shuttle over — don't hit.

Eyes still down, follow through almost to waist level. Then as you move in to the net to threaten any net return, raise the racket tape-high, instantly ready for quick action.

If you watch a number of people serving you will I expect notice that there are nearly as many different methods as there are Heinz products. The above is a good middle-of-the-road style. Provided the wrist is back and impact is correct, it doesn't matter if your swing differs from it, provided a good serve results.

Pendulum Push

This is a variation you might find useful. Shorten your grip by holding the handle further down, ie nearer the head. Bend your elbow fully so that the racket-head is as high as possible. Some players (All-England Junior Champion Mary Leeves is one) sway up on to their toes at impact to gain a couple more inches of height. Such a serve, though you may initially find cramped, is so simplified that it

Fig. 15 Low serve. (i) Ready position, upright stance; shuttle high; confident, thoughtful, unhurried and relaxed grip. (ii) Halfway to impact; weight transfer. (iii) Impact; body turned, wrist and racket still angled back; eyes on shuttle. (iv) Follow-through; wrist still cocked and racket pushing through after shuttle. (v) Following in to threaten net-return; racket up

reduces the margin of error, and makes for a flatter trajectory.

A further variation, the backhand serve, is described on page 69.

Whichever style you adopt (do experiment) remember a relaxed grip does help.

Pitfalls
1. Shuttle held too low or a crouch stance.
2. Shuttle held too far ahead of foot.
3. Wrist uncocked even minimally.
All three will result in too steep an upward trajectory.
4. Lack of deliberate aim and care.
5. Weak follow-through: shuttle falls short. Surely you're not so undernourished you can't propel 80 grains of shuttle some 5 yards! Unforgivable! Two or three possible points lost in one careless stroke!
6. Racket face turned sharply at impact: 'out' or mishit.
7. Faulty timing of shuttle-drop and racket movement: neither too fast nor too slow.

Practices
1. Without a shuttle, simply sway and

push. Check each time at the end of your forward swing that the wrist is still cocked back, that the racket head even now is below the hand.

2. With the wrist now under control, practise serving, diagonally, to a target.
3. As in (2) but include a receiver, racket up, standing 5ft back, for the target. He threatens mutely but not so aggressively that he gives you the 'twitch'.
4. As your confidence increases the receiver moves in until he is some 3ft from the front service line. Now he actually returns serve – with an upward net-shot that does not shake your new-found confidence and does give you practice in watchfully following-in your serve.
5. All out server–receiver confrontation, but only when you have mastered the flick and can slip it in occasionally to hobble the receiver. Otherwise he would know you had played all your aces! It is important that the latter never shakes your essential confidence by over-aggressive attack, secure in the knowledge that every serve is to be low.

RETURN OF SERVE

'Serve and return' trip off the tongue as indissolubly as Fortnum and Mason, or Morecambe and Wise. They are part and parcel, one of the other. If good serving is vital, so too is receiving. The former enables you to score points; the latter prevents your opponents from doing so. A formidable combination, one on which very often the whole outcome of a game depends.

So having set you thinking about low and high serves, let's deal with their return. Then you will be able to practise one against the other, so learning doubly fast. You'll see both sides of the coin, I hope.

Aim: To meet rising serves early so that the attack can be seized or the rally won outright by a downward, attacking shot.

To do this you've got to move as short a distance as possible, as fast as possible. Only then will you meet the shuttle whilst it is still above tape level and so in danger. So, let's look intelligently at your position and your stance in

that position in relation to *doubles*. But first the Laws.

Laws Concerning the Receiver

You must not:
1. Move before the server strikes the shuttle.
2. Delay unduly before taking up your stance.
3. Balk (put off) your opponent.
4. Have a foot off the floor or on a line.

Position This is a personal matter depending entirely on your own speed and temperament, or lack of it. As in war, your base should cover, be equidistant from the likely points of attack – the front and back service lines. Just as important, don't leave your vulnerable flank (the backhand) exposed. So, in the right court, stand some 4–5ft back and within 18in of the centre line. In the left court, stand the same distance back. The only difference: move further to the left, about 5ft from the centre line. Then neither forehand nor backhand is exposed.

So far, so good. Now, let's face it. Your main difficulty will be in running – backwards! After all we don't do it often. Your main fear will be of looking silly with a high serve falling smack behind you, immobile. Unless you have a devil-may-care attitude you will probably cower 6–7ft behind the front service line, thus covering your rear but leaving your front exposed. So too, in the right hand court, you will tend to hug the centre line to coddle the sickly backhand and leave the forehand highly vulnerable.

Unless you really are hippo-ponderous moving backwards, alter this. Be cheeky. Stand a little further forward than you think you dare: say 5ft from the front service line, and each week now, faster forward and back, advance your base an inch or two. Then you will really be able to attack.

Stance This is all-important. Instant reaction is vital, for we are dealing in those split seconds in which even a slow-falling shuttle drops to safety. 'Move' is your watchword. The picture I want is one of eager, restless mobility: the racing start with engine ticking over.

Cast aside your inhibitions. To achieve the

(i)   (ii)   (iii)   (iv)

crouched athlete, we want left foot forward, knee half bent, only the ball of the foot on the floor; right leg outstretched, knee bent again, only the toes in contact with Mother Earth; body leaning slightly forward – for you will probably go forward more often than back. A wide but balanced stance. Bent knees offering instant drive – forward or in reverse.

Hold your racket just to the right of your head at tape-height. There it has the minimum distance to travel to return a low serve. Left hand – claws out – is in a roughly similar position to counter-balance you and complete the picture.

It must be a picture of aggression. This is a vital war of nerves. Look milk and water and you will deter no one. Look as meanly determined (difficult for some I know) as you can and you will rattle a server who needs steady nerves to survive. Then, the first trick is yours!

So much for the body. What of the mind? What will be your thoughts in those half-dozen seconds before the server strikes the shuttle? Neither panic-stricken nor irrelevant, I hope.

Observation Thoughtful positioning and aggressive stance should give you mobility. All that you need now is 'early intelligence'. And only your eyes can give that to you. So watch your opponent, his position, his eyes, his backswing. Above all, observe racket and shuttle speed and direction at impact. From this at first

Plate 20. Even charming young Wendy Poulton, claws out, must look menacing for psychological domination of server *(Louis C. H. Ross)*

Fig. 16 Return of serve (dab). (i) Stance: agression! (ii) Fast movement to shuttle; little backswing. (iii) Impact; lunge; dab *down.* (iv) Short follow-through

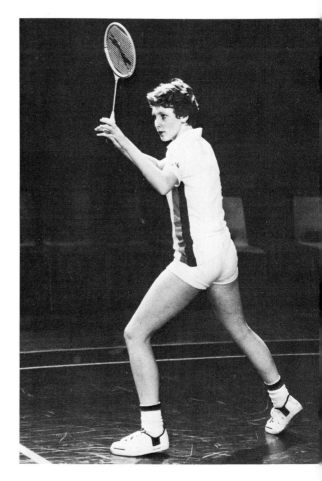

63

Plates 21 and 22. (*Above*) Flemming Delfs
(Denmark) uses reach to dab a low serve down off
the tape. Note his very alert partner, Steen
Skovgaard. (*Right*) Steen Skovgaard, fractionally
later, has to return serve with a tape-hugging net-
shot. Very unalert partner — flat footed and
straight legged (*Mervyn Rees*)

blurred impression, 'intelligence' will soon learn to spot the point of attack – where and how the enemy is going to hit the shuttle. Low or high? To forehand or backhand?

Movement The whole key to returning low serve is to move as soon after the server strikes the shuttle as is humanly possible. Ideally you are moving with short driving steps (or a step and a lunge) as the shuttle leaves the racket, not as it crosses the net. If only you can achieve the former, with racket extended, you will meet the low serve *chest high, in front of the front service line.* If the latter, the shuttle will have crossed that line, fallen, and be too low to attack. Never just stand and let the shuttle come to you. Go to meet it.

Returns of Low Serve
Having reached the shuttle, what shots to play? Much depends on the height of the shuttle – not as it crosses the net – but at actual impact. If it is above tape-height, dab it down crisply. No time for any backswing; simply extend the forearm and uncock the wrist.

If it has fallen anything up to 2ft below the tape, then play an accurate *upward net-shot* to the corner away from the server if he is following in.

And if it is lower than that (though Heaven knows this means you started appallingly late or moved snail-wise!), then there's nothing for it but to *lob* the shuttle to the base-line, preferably to the backhand corner. In each case, to save yet another split second, stretch out and play the shuttle as far in front of your body as possible.

A word of warning: remember the stakes are high. An error means a point lost with a single stroke; a winner, an opponent's serve and chance of points captured. Attack, but attack with care.

It is all too easy to see the shuttle above tape-height as it crosses the net and think that it is still at that height as you hit it. Result: the shuttle is 'rushed' into the net. Instead you must realise that, on occasions, it has dropped below tape-height, and quickly change from dab to upward net-shot. Remember also how easy it is to hit out at the back if you dab flat – and not down. Use your wrist. Steepness is more important than sheer speed.

Returns of High Serve
These also depend on your speed both of reaction and movement. They in turn will dictate the all-important factor of where the shuttle is going to be at impact in relation to your body.

If only you can drive back fast and get behind the shuttle, then you are able to smash, probably to score a winner. Be fractionally slower in movement or starting and only just keep pace with the shuttle just over you, and you will have to play a drop-shot. Be so slow back that you never get behind the shuttle at all then there's nothing for it except an ignominious clear that loses you the attack; unless of course you simply don't hit the shuttle at all.

Run and Swing All of this, perhaps rashly, presupposes a ready racket. But too often beginners are so occupied with running back and looking at the shuttle that they forget the racket. And so they arrive back, with racket trailing at their ankles and 'Oh, horror', a shuttle fast descending. All that can come of such an unhappy conjunction is a miss, a mishit or a bent arm push; none of them anything to proudly write home about!

Remember therefore as your feet move so must your racket. 'Run and swing' is the maxim. Make sure that as you make your last dancing step back with the right foot, your racket head is dropped down between your shoulders. Only then will you have time to play a powerful straight arm stroke.

Practise the movement off court until it is quite automatic. There's nothing to it.

Pitfalls
1. Ill-balanced court position: gaps left.
2. Undynamic stance: no racing start; no domination.
3. Failure to read your opponent's serve: late start.
4. Lack of killer-spirit: no aggression.
5. Rash shots played without due awareness of shuttle's height or position at impact: cheap points for your opponents.

Practices
1. With feeder serving low, move forward

from your normal receiving base to 'lob'. Shuttle must fall between two backlines in backhand corner.

2. As in (1) but play a net-shot: play it to the corner.
3. As in (1) but dab downwards *if* shuttle is above tape-height.
4. Play not just the one reply as above, but whatever return is appropriate to the serve and your position.
5. Feeder serves high: play smash, drop or clear as appropriate.
6. Feeder serves high or low: play fifteen serves and returns then reverse roles. Keep a tally of your returns which force your opponent to lift. Advance your receiving base as you become faster off the mark.

Remember few practices can yield such high dividends, in so vital a phase of the game.

BACKHAND STROKES

These are strokes played on the left-hand side of a right-handed player. They are therefore played at impact with the *back* of the hand, not the palm, to the net – hence backhanded.

Although they are often considered to be the bête noire of beginners this need not be so. The action does come a little less naturally than that for the forehand and, if you don't move your feet, is rather more cramped. But the main reason for weakness is simple, and ridiculous. You just don't practise them as much as forehand strokes, do you?

And yet they offer a double reward. Each time you practise them you are strengthening a possible Achilles Heel. And each time your backhand is unsuccessfully attacked be reminded that your opponent, not having practised as zealously as you have, may be vulnerable. So hammer your opponent's backhand. He will certainly test yours. And as a bonus: backhand strokes seem to have a certain cachet and a very definite grace.

When you are practising bear in mind these simple fundamentals:

1. Ordinary or backhand grip (page 38).
2. Right foot pointed at the shuttle's line of flight.
3. Right hand brought back to or near left shoulder in the backswing.
4. Elbow, pointing into the shuttle, leads as the arm is snapped straight and the racket head is *flung*, not pushed, in the widest possible arc at the shuttle.
5. Point of impact just in front of the forward foot.

Pitfalls and practices are much as for forehand strokes.

Lob

In the unlikely event that you are a left-handed golfer, you will appreciate the analogy that the badminton backhand lob is played in much the same way as you drive. If you are neither left-handed nor a golfer (and the odds are heavily on both) you will be more appreciative of an analogy that shows that the lob is very like a

Fig. 17 Backhand lob. (i) Moving eagerly to shuttle. (ii) End of backswing. (iii) Lunge; wrist just uncocking. (iv) Impact; eyes down; balanced. (v) Follow-through and recovery

(i)   (ii)   (iii)   (iv)   (v)

Plate 23. Nicola Aspell (Hampshire) shows good
footwork, bent-arm, wrist-cocked backswing, eyes
on shuttle – and enjoyment *(Louis C. H. Ross)*

stroke you have already learnt: the high serve (though played at stretch and in reverse).

Lunge, right foot forward. Swing racket back so it is almost vertical by left shoulder, arm bent, wrist cocked. Now sweep down, to point of impact beside leading foot. Straighten the arm, uncock the wrist and hit through the shuttle and up, high above the right shoulder. As in golf (sorry to mention it again), keep the head down as you hit and fractionally afterwards. Look up just before you hit to see where the shuttle is going − and often the shuttle won't go anywhere at all!

Drive

Here, a more helpful analogy, known well to both giver and receiver: the incensed female's backhander bestowed on the over-amorous male; or, more simply, throwing a frisbee.

Backhand grip. Draw your racket back so that the shaft is on your left shoulder, and the racket-head behind it. If the latter is parallel to the floor, this will ensure a strong pronation of the forearm for added power. Then, with right foot across, fling it in a wide arc to make impact tape-high or above, just in front of body. Lean into the stroke keeping racket square to the shuttle and on target as long as possible. Follow through well across body.

For the cross-court drive simply meet the shuttle earlier, 2ft in front of your body. The shuttle is then hit with the natural cross-court swing.

Danish Wipe or Swedish Swish

This delightfully named stroke, the first to be taught to Danish players, is a hybrid: a cross between a lob and a drive. And like most hybrids, it is hardy. It is too something of a paradox, an underhand 'lob' played from the *back* corner. And a joy to play − a definite 'oomph' shot that digs you out of backhand corner trouble, and confounds a hopeful opponent. But it is mainly for ladies.

With a shuttle fed deep into your backhand corner prepare as for a drive. Instead of hitting flat, sweep the racket *down* to knee height, then hit *up*, through the shuttle, and finish with racket above your right shoulder. It needs arm and body power ('wipe') as well as wrist ('swish') united in perfect timing. A most satisfying stroke! Master it early as an insurance policy before moving on to take the shuttle earlier and with more variation in the high overhead backhand (page 131).

Serve

Once regarded as the prerogative of top players the backhand serve is now often taught to beginners because of its almost foolproof sim-

Fig. 18 Backhand drive. (i) Movement; pivoting across on left foot. (ii) swinging racket back behind shoulder. (iii) Forward fling; arm nearly straight; wrist still cocked. (iv) Impact; eye on shuttle; leaning into stroke. (v) Follow-through and quick recovery

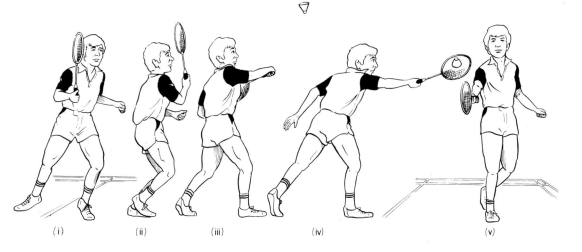

(i)   (ii)   (iii)   (iv)   (v)

Plate 24(i). Lancashire's Rita Heywood puts plenty of 'zing' into the Danish wipe. Plate 24(ii) (*inset*). Note balance, eye, straight-arm impact (*Louis C. H. Ross*)

Fig. 19 Danish wipe. (i) Movement. (ii) End of backswing; right foot across; racket well back. (iii) Forward swing; racket sweeping down. (iv) Impact; racket now flung *upwards*. (v) Strong follow-through and body turn

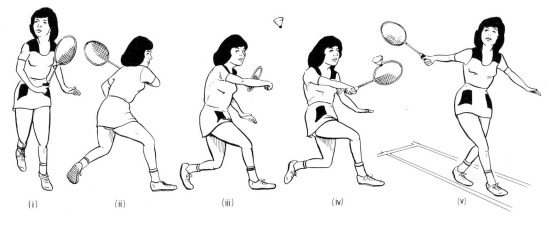

(i)   (ii)   (iii)   (iv)   (v)

Plate 25.   Ray Sharp (ex-England player), toe-to-line, elbow up, demonstrates longer backswing *(Louis C. H. Ross)*

plicity. It outpoints the forehand serve on three scores:

1. The flight of a white shuttle held in front of white shorts or skirt is not quickly picked up.
2. Played at waist height (just below) and from in front of the front service line, it travels flatter and gives your opponent less time to deal with it.
3. Even now, when it is no longer a stroke solely for the elite, it holds a certain eastern magic that spellbinds the unaccustomed receiver.

Its only disadvantage at this stage is that its essential complementary stroke, the flick, though highly effective, needs a stronger wrist than you may have yet achieved. Anyway have a go. It's novel (just). And it's piquant. Even if you are already in the groove with a forehand low serve it's a useful 'mixer'. Use it to spring a surprise – or if the forehand version isn't up to scratch.

As with the forehand serve, it can be played with widely different backswings and stances. The following is pretty standard; variations will be mentioned later.

After the preliminaries described for the forehand low serve (page 59) stand, facing diagonally with your right foot forward and right up to (but not on) the front service line (weight slightly forward); hold the shuttle with a straight arm pointing down at about 45°. This should place the shuttle, legally, below your waist line and just inside and ahead of your front foot.

With elbow bent, and up, and with wrist cocked back, place the racket head vertically downwards immediately behind the shuttle. This is the preparation.

Now, by bending the forearm inwards, bring the racket back slowly as far as the stomach allows. Then, without pause, smoothly, slowly advance the racket. Release the shuttle only fractionally before impact, virtually hitting the shuttle out of the hand. It is this, not having to time the fall of the shuttle, that makes it simpler than the forehand version. Keep the wrist cocked back, and *push* the shuttle forward. Only with the shuttle on its way should you then quickly raise the racket (and eyes) to deal with any return to the net.

Variations are these: Some players, the Indonesian, Chandra, is one, stand almost square to the line. Yorkshire's Paula Kilvington is certainly another. She also has a very distinctive almost 'do-it-by-numbers' action. Her racket is placed with deliberation plumb-line straight in front of her. Pause. Next, the shuttle is placed (the only word) within half-an-inch of the strings. Pause. The racket is moved back no more than 2in before an equally abbreviated forward push ('swing' is not the word!) and strong follow-through.

Another lady, another Indonesian, World Mixed Champion Imelda Wigoeno, also employs a limited swing, perhaps 6in, and cuts the shuttle slightly. On the other hand, many players, of whom former English international Ray Sharp is one, use a much longer backswing. The racket is drawn well back under the left armpit before smoothly moving into a long forward swing.

6 Tactics

THE KNOCK-UP

The pre-game knock-up (limited to three minutes) is generally desultory to say the least. Too often it is merely a sluggish hotchpotch of strokes played with too little care and even less thought. On occasions it becomes a negative, under-cover sparring match with both players concerned only with concealing their own weaknesses but revealing their opponent's.

Intelligently practised and played, the knock-up is valuable. Preliminary warm-up and stretching exercises should be done in the changing-room. These will not only supple you and get your adrenalin flowing but also help prevent pulled muscles. (See page 97.)

Then, on court, you can devote all your time, care and concentration (the words are carefully chosen) to actually hitting the shuttle. In that way you start your game, match-tight. With touch and length established and with careless errors drained from your system, the first vital points should be yours. Vital because they give a boost to your morale, and a corresponding depression to your opponent's.

In singles you must obviously knock with your opponent. In doubles it is preferable to knock with your partner who knows your method. Admittedly this deprives you of the chance of weighing up your opponent: his strengths and weaknesses.

This is much better done by thoughtful analysis of his play observed in a game situation before you actually play against him. Many an opponent looks depressingly strong in a knock-up but in a game proves to have feet of clay tactically, or under pressure. If you can spot only a single weakness or predictable return, your effort has paid far better dividends than a while-away-the-time chat in the tearoom or bar. This ability to analyse from both on and off

court, can prove decisive in a game between evenly matched opponents.

In the doubles knock-up you are interested in your own strokes, not those of your opponents. In just three minutes you must practise a number of strokes. But only those needed in the particular branch of the game you are about to play. At the same time you must get movement, eye, concentration, length and touch, up to concert pitch. No mean order?

Plan and work out the routine with your partner. It will differ as between men's doubles and mixed doubles. For the sake of example, let's take the men's doubles: A few, very few, clears. Then your partner serves a high doubles serve; you smash. He plays a push return. You recover quickly to play a net-shot which he lobs to restart the cycle. Similarly you can play drops which your partner lobs. During both of these, concentrate on real match movement and keep a keen eye on length, or lack of it. Call 'Short', 'Long', 'Right' so that you are aware of that all-important virtue.

Above all, do not forget (though many do) those most vital strokes: the low serve and net-return. Don't use the 'kill' or you could break your partner's essential nerve and confidence before the game even starts. The net-return you can use as the springboard to a rally of tight upward net-shots. If time allows throw in a few backhands to take the stiffness out of them.

A game of mixed doubles uses rather different strokes or places a greater emphasis on some. And the strokes needed by you the man, are not those used by the lady. Your knock-up must therefore be adapted to this.

Take the lady first. She (like you) needs low serve and return practice. In particular she will need net-shots, which will be the greater part of her game. These will be not only upward ones, played as part of your service practice, but downward ones and interceptions. If you drive at her and she returns to you with downward dabs, two birds are killed with one stone. Lastly as these can be fatal flaws she must practise (i) returning drive serves to her backhand with dabs, and/or (ii) running backwards to hit high serves down and then quickly regaining the net.

All of which seems to leave far too little time for the equally fallible man. Low serve, return, drives and defence have however been jointly practised. What is left? A few steep smashes – and, most certainly, backhand strokes, especially the drop. Your opponent is sure to test your backhand early on in the proceedings.

In all strokes strive for easy timing rather than crude power. Now, moving, concentrating, playing to a length, and rid of early error, you should be off to a flying start.

SINGLES
Even if you are fat, forty and unfit, don't hurriedly skip this chapter. Admittedly it can't change your age but it can do something for your other attributes.

Fig. 20 Singles. Court positions and areas to attack. R = Receiving S = Serving B = General base (1) Clears. (2) High serves. (3) Smashes. (4) Drop-shots. (5) Net-shots

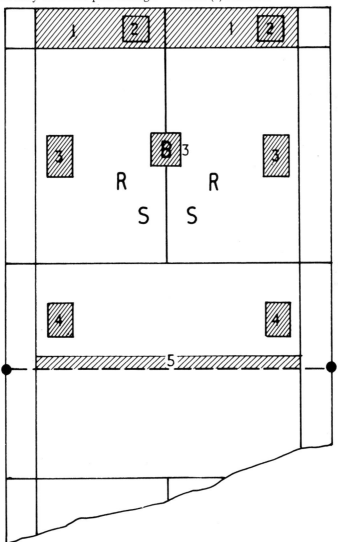

Singles are not merely a testing game in themselves, they are also excellent practice. To avoid massacre you must learn to hit to a *length* and to develop an all-round armoury of basic strokes (especially the backhand). With no partner to rely on you will learn to move fast. You're out on your own – and that's no bad thing.

Another bonus is that with only two players on court, tactics are fairly simple as well as commonsense and there's a little more time to think.

With a court 22ft long and only 17ft wide it is obviously better to run your opponent up and down the court rather than to and fro across it. Your main strokes therefore will be high serves and clears to run him to the back of the court, and drop-shots and net-shots to bring him hurrying in to the front. Finally, a smash to finish off the rally when you've outmanoeuvred him so that he has left a gap in his defences or only scrambled a short and vulnerable clear or lob to you.

So, to a rather more detailed plan of campaign. At this stage it will be kept simple in order to avoid confusion. In Part II it will be elaborated. But remember that what you learn here is the solid foundation of all later play.

If court-time for singles is a problem, try 'half-court singles'. Divide the court longitudinally by the centre-line with a pair playing in each half. You can add, if you like, any spare space outside the side-lines but initially you may well find half a court is enough to cover.

Play it safe. Shots dangerously down the middle should be left and a let claimed. Next time at the club, why not try two half-court singles instead of one doubles? You'll get more play.

Serving
Stand close to the centre line and about 5ft behind the front service line. For the moment stick to the high serve. If hit really deep you have already got your opponent on the run and created a fore-court opening. If hit very high, the shuttle will be harder to time and hit cleanly. If hit just high enough to avoid interception, it will hurry him. Length is everything so move in a foot or three if necessary to achieve it.

From the right court, aim 18in to the left of the centre-line. This 18in gives you a margin for error; the 'centre-line' cuts down your opponent's possible angles. From the left court, aim 18in from the side-line. This has a twofold effect. It may force him to play a weak backhand; it will almost certainly prevent him attacking yours.

Position of Readiness
Having opened the attack you must now prepare yourself for immediate movement to his return. By stepping back a pace astride the centre-line you will be roughly equidistant in time, if not distance, from a return to any of the four corners. A return to your rear-court has a longer 'travel time' than one to the fore-court; on the other hand, running backwards is slower than running forwards.

Be on this base and in the alert position of readiness already described *before* your opponent hits the shuttle. Never be caught moving *as* he hits it or he may woefully wrong foot you. On occasion, if you anticipate well or are hard-pressed, you will by-pass or move straight through this position. But it is an ideal to be achieved when possible after every stroke.

In this connection too, use height wisely. When you need time to recover, clear or lob high; when you wish to pressurise your opponent, hit only just high enough to avoid spring-heeled interception.

Return of Serve
Your choice here lies between the three overhead strokes – and is full, as tactics inevitably tend to be, of 'ifs' and 'buts'.

If the serve is short of the back *doubles* service line and if you think you can score an outright winner or at least put your opponent in real trouble, then go for it and smash. If the length is too good for this then it must be clear or drop.

Which you use depends, again as do all tactics, on your skills and those, or the lack of them, of your opponent. If you can clear to a length or he has a weak smash, then play a clear. You may not have gained the attack but at least you've returned the compliment and put him in the same rather negative rear court position you were in.

If your clear is weak and his smash strong then a deceptive, good length drop is the answer. After all it is a downward, attacking

shot. If he is slow of foot or anticipation he may not reach it at all or only play a mediocre lob. You have forced a lift. Now three options are open to you: (i) a smash if he is out of position or still tottering back to base; (ii) a clear to the open space your drop created at the back of the court; (iii) yet another drop, if, fearful of (ii), he has hurriedly retreated too far. Much depends on your opponent's position, on 'the gap'.

General Play
The remainder of the rally will be based on the same principles. Play a series of good length clears and drops to the corners to make him run a maximum distance and to force a weak return. Do not play to a set pattern that he can anticipate. Sometimes attack the same corner two or three times in succession when he is obviously expecting you to switch it.

Singles is a war of attrition, so plug away carefully. Play more drops than clears. For the former, maintain the attack, for the latter, give it away. Play to the backhand more often than the forehand, it is generally weaker. Smash, only when fairly sure of a winner, into the body or away to the side-lines − not onto the racket.

Plate 26. Hartono's early return of Liem Swie King's drop-shot has the latter unusually slow following in, caught off guard (G. Habbin)

What of defence? An observant eye and eager feet, eager in advance and recovery alike, are your foundation stones. Return smashes with flat 'blocks' to the front corners. Return drop-shots with good length lobs or, if you take them early and high, even with net-shots. Answer net-shots with better net-shots or lob safely to the base-line.

Counter his attacks on your backhand in three ways: (i) make your base a foot nearer that side; (ii) try, by quick movement, to take everything you can forehanded; (iii) play on *his* backhand.

MEN'S AND LADIES' DOUBLES
Men's doubles, popularly regarded as the most spectacular branch of badminton, is a game that see-saws excitingly from rampaging attack to last ditch defence and back. Spot-on serving and aggressive return are part and parcel of a swash-buckling battle. Ladies' doubles, though not so cut-throat, has basically the same tactics.

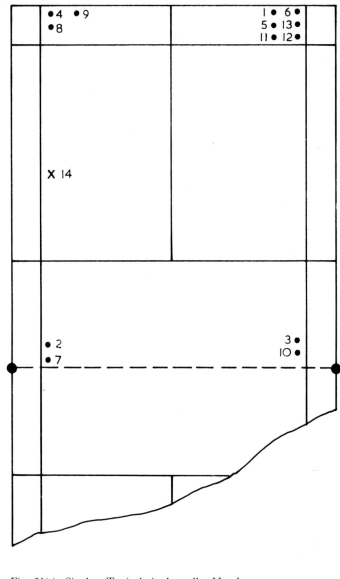

Fig. 21(a) Singles. Typical singles rally. Numbers
represent sequence of strokes played

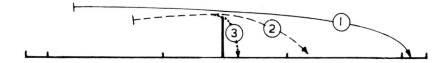

Fig. 21(b) Sidearm strokes. (1) Drive. (2) Half-court
push. (3) Drop-shot

At this stage, tactics can be kept simple because much has already been explained under the relevant stroke. They will be elaborated in Part II by which time you will be able to think more of where to hit the shuttle and less of merely how to hit it. Meantime, your basic aim is to hit *down*, not up.

Court Positions

Initially, for simplicity, you may play 'sides'. This means that each player is responsible for his half of the court from net to base-line. The forehanded player will best deal with high shots down the middle; the backhanded with the low.

This rule of thumb method has disadvantages so the next step is to 'modified sides'. If one player A is obviously stranded at the back or at the net and unlikely to reach a distant return shot, his partner B, calling 'Mine', (or A calling 'Yours') moves to his partner's side to play the return. Simultaneously A then quickly moves across to cover B's now empty half-court.

From this it is but a short step to the best formation of 'In and Out'. This is an amalgam of two formations so that you get the best of both worlds. When a pair having lifted, are on the defence they play 'side by side' with each player covering his half of the court as described above. When the shuttle is lifted to one of them and they are attacking (hitting down or in a way which will force another lift) they adopt a back and front formation.

When the shuttle is lifted to one, he goes back to smash and the other immediately (no waiting!) moves into the T-junction to attack net-shots. They remain in this formation until one of them lifts, then, with their opponents now attacking, they drop back to 'sides' for defence. In doing this, the last player to hit the shuttle moves into the nearest half-court. His partner drops back into the other.

In the opening phase of the game both pairs, optimistically, adopt a back and front formation, the server near the front service line, his partner, alertly poised to defend, a couple of paces immediately behind him, mid-court. The receiver is as near the front service line as he dare; his partner safely positioned to his rear. After one or two sparring shots one player or another will lift. That pair then drops back to 'sides', the other, attacking, remains back and front.

Serving This is all-important. Serve, unhurriedly low to the centre, hoping to force a lift. If your serve is attacked you will have to revert to the high serve. To blunt your opponents' attack it must be of good length. Experiment sometimes by hitting to the corners to see if your opponents have a weakness there. In the former case, the server goes in to the net; in the latter, drops back to sides to defend. In both cases be alert to attack the weak return.

Receiving Equally important. So please revise chapter 5, where positioning and stance as well as the possible returns of both low and high serves were dealt with. Little more need be added at this stage. But do remember you must move quickly and early. Only then will you be able to wrest back the serve by dabbing low serves *down* or into the body, or returning them with accurate net-shots; and by hitting high ones down with smash or drop to the centre or to the weaker player. Don't lift needlessly or aimlessly.

Attack

This need not necessarily be a powerful smash. It can just as well be a drop-shot or a net-shot provided it forces a lift by your opponents.

At the Back If you have been forced back to the base-line a smash will have little power. It is better therefore to play a drop to the centre in the hope that it will create confusion or force a short lob. This you can then attack with a *steep* smash to the body or into a gap. Maintain the attack with smashes or drops. Don't sacrifice the attack with a clear unless you need time to recover balance.

At the Net Again most of what you must put into practice is in chapter 5. Remember: racket up and on your toes. Hit down whenever you can with a virtually no-backswing dab. If you're too late to do that, play an upward net-shot to maintain the attack rather than a lob that loses it.

Defence

Your main strokes will be the push return to counter the smash and the lob to return the drop-shot (see page 47 and page 49). In both cases try and take them early. If you can do that

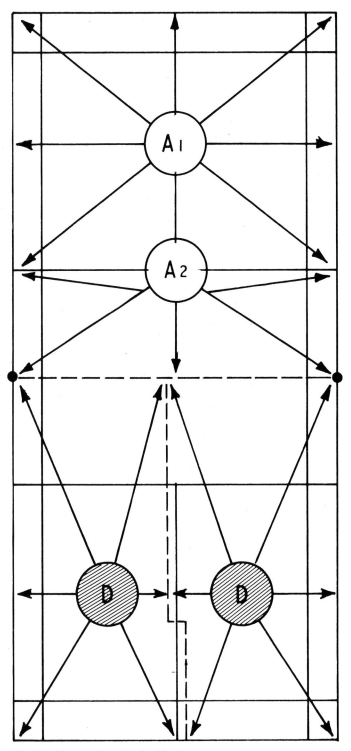

Fig. 22 Men's and ladies' doubles basic positions.
A1 = Attack at back. A2 = Attack at net. D = Defence
(side by side)

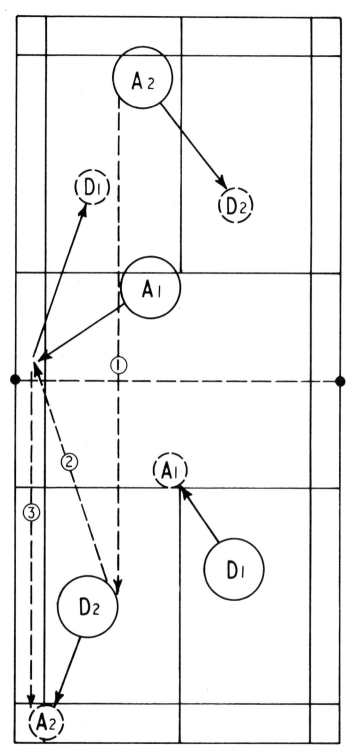

Fig. 23 Men's and ladies' doubles change of
positions. D1 and D2 move from defence to attack
(A1 and A2) when A1 lobs D2's net-shot and D2
intercepts; A1 and A2 move from attack to defence
(D1 and D2)

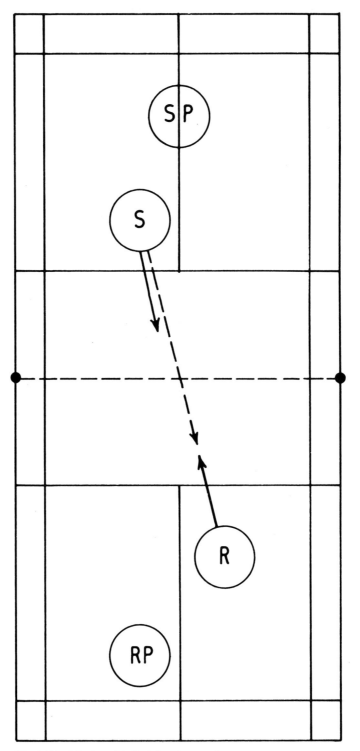

Fig. 24(a)   Men's and ladies' doubles opening
positions − from right court

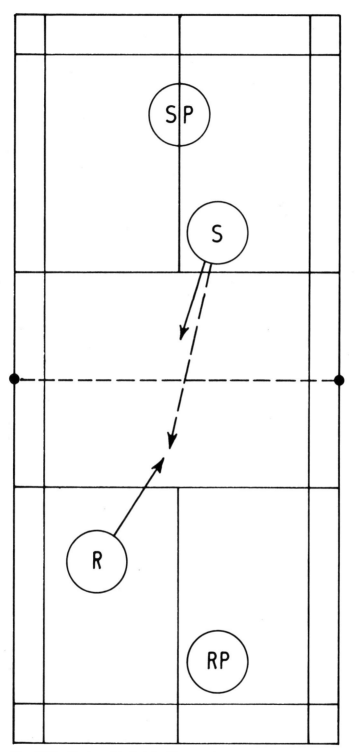

Fig. 24(b)   Men's and ladies' doubles opening
positions – from left court

there is a chance of dabbing down or pushing the return of smash back flat, or of playing a net-shot off the drop. And again you've got the lift.

Always seek to turn defence into attack. And throughout, take care; concentrate 100 per cent. Then there will be few unforced errors and you'll be hard to beat.

Ladies' Doubles
Basically use the tactics outlined above. But remember two differences. Ladies neither smash as hard nor run as fast as men though their defences may be equally good. On the one hand therefore, it is safer to lob. And on the other hand, the game becomes more a war of attrition using drops and low clears to evoke a short return that can be dispatched. Backhands

Plate 27. All-out attack: Amazon Verawaty (Indonesia) smashes from back; Wigoeno (Indonesia) is alert at the net to kill a weak return *(Mervyn Rees)*

Plate 28. Active defence: Wahjudi and Tjun Tjun (both Indonesia) show agile eagerness to turn defence into attack *(J. Potter)*

too will be weaker so concentrate on that corner.

Comparative lack of speed means that fewer low serves will be rushed and high serves will be more effective *if* the receiver stands in. Confidently, therefore, seek to obtain an early lift, then maintain a steady attack.

MIXED DOUBLES
Mixed doubles is a fascinating and delightful branch of the game; not solely because it brings the sexes together, but rather because though power and speed are needed, mixed is more a matter of delicacy of touch and placement; of deception, and varied tactics. Craftsmanship rather than crude power is the deciding factor.

In mixed, the faster, stronger man covers two-thirds of the court from front service line to base-line; the lady utilises her talents of touch,

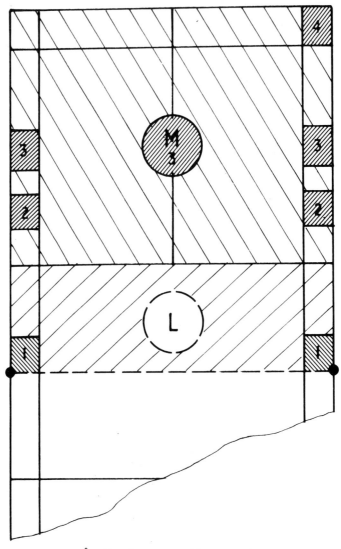

Fig. 25 Mixed doubles. Areas covered by man and by lady. Points to attack with (1) Net-shots. (2) Half-court pushes ('divorce area'). (3) Smashes. (4) Drives, attacking lobs or attacking clears

eye and agility in the remaining one-third at the net. In case the lady feels this is male chauvinism or sex discrimination let me assure her she would not enjoy playing back. The opposing man could invariably outrun and out-hit her. As it is, hers is a key role which sets up many a delightful crisp winner.

Hers is also a more difficult role than the man's. At the net, cramped, she has less time to see a faster moving shuttle; she has to serve from nearer an aggressive receiver than her partner – and stay there under heavy attack. It's high time the mere male appreciated this. Only then will his barely suppressed groan accompanied by a grimace of despair when the lady errs, become a murmur of genuine commiseration. Then too the lady can relax – and play the better for it.

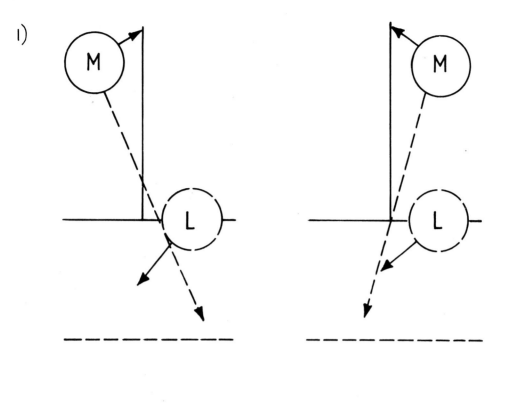

1)

2)

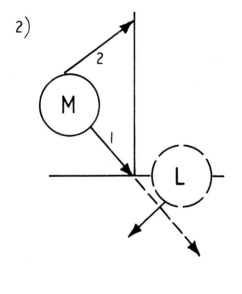

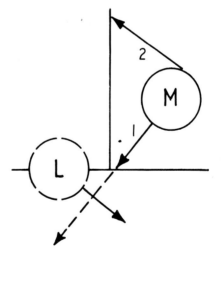

Fig. 26 Mixed doubles. Opening positions:
(1) Man serving. (2) Man receiving

85

Seven Roads to Success
DO:
1. Play strokes that help your partner score winners, not ones that put him/her deep in trouble. You are a pair!
2. Attack the weaker opponent – often, but not always, the lady.
3. Play to the gaps down the side-lines.
4. Use the full width of the court to stretch your opponent.
5. Attack the man's deep backhand corner.

DON'T
6. Lift – instead, hit down flat, or tightly upwards.
7. Overuse the cross-court shot. Wait until you have opened up the centre by drawing both opponents to one side-line before hitting to the other.

The Lady's Role
Positional Play Her base is a central one on the T-junction. She adopts the same positions from which to serve and receive as she does in ladies' doubles.

Changes however are necessary when her partner is the striker. When he is serving, she always stands in the left-hand court as near the centre-line as possible without obstructing him or their opponents. When he is receiving, she positions herself in the other court again as near the centre-line as is safely possible. It is imperative that she takes up this central position as soon as the shuttle is in play to ensure no inviting gaps are left open.

Serve and Return The lady will serve low, really low, to the centre to force a lift, either to the net which she, following in, will deal with, or high to her eager partner behind. The only variation will be high to the opposition lady, to see if she is too slow moving backwards or hits weakly upwards. If the latter smashes effectively, the lady should revert to the low serve.

It is equally important that she doesn't just lift her own return of serve to the man. She must move quickly to high and low serves alike. Then she will be in a position to hit down the high serve and dab down the low ones, or at least play an accurate net-shot.

Having hit down from the back she must quickly follow in to deal with a net return. If she can't do this the man will have to help out but this does break up their basic formation.

It is all too easy for her to snatch belatedly at shots she will miss, or, just as bad, hit but can't control. Far better if she is in doubt to leave it to her partner who has so much more time.

Man's Role
Serving The man's general base is alertly astride the centre-line, mid-court. With the lady in front of him he serves from about 6–7ft behind the service line. His serving will be much the same as the lady's: low to the man; low and/or high to the lady.

Receiving All that has been written before applies. Two points however should be borne in mind. He should take a chance in attacking the lady's serve. If successful, this will rattle her not only in serving but also perhaps in general play. On the other hand, he has no partner *behind* him, so he must score a winner or play a deceptively slower push or tight net-shot to enable him to regain his base.

General Play He must move quickly to take the shuttle early and high. He will then be able to jockey for position with a series of accurate side-line net-shots or deceptive half-court pushes that eventually gain him the lift. Softly, softly . . .

If the lift is only a foot or so he can attack wholeheartedly with straight or cross-court drives to the lines. If it is really high he has two alternatives: from the base-line, a half-smash down the side-lines; from forward of the back doubles service line, a steep smash to the side-lines or the man's body.

When he is on the receiving end, *defending*, he is on his own. The lady stays in at the net. Agile and reading the stroke, he must answer where possible with flat pushes to the 'divorce area' to regain the attack. If in trouble, he must play net-shots if the opposing lady is not sharp, lobs to the deep backhand corner, if she is. He should try where possible to safeguard his own backhand (overhead) by quick movement which will allow him still to play forehanded.

PART II

ADVANCED PLAY

7 Expert Essentials

To play badminton really well, to be in your county's (or country's) top ten you need a Gulbenkian wealth of talents.

Just look at the list. A body that has stamina, speed, suppleness and strength. A skill that encompasses not only a wide range of consistent, varied, deceptive, orthodox strokes, accurate both in length and height, but also a number of unorthodox last-ditch rescue ones. A brain that can think calmly on the run and react with lightning reflexes. A character that has the virtues of a saint: equable nature, patience, care and concentration; and determination. To say nothing of less angelic characteristics such as killer-spirit, critical analysis and self-analysis.

If this sounds frightening, take heart. New strokes and new tactics follow but much of what you will need is much of what you have already learnt. It's just a matter of, as All-England winner Ian Maconachie told me when I was on the same quest, 'Keep on doing what you're doing – but do it a b..... sight better'. Top badminton is split seconds and split inches.

Before we look at further strokes and tactics let's look in a little more detail at the above. They are the essential attributes of an expert, of a champion. Each must be worked on, practised to near perfection, for in itself, each is as valuable as any one stroke. So, despite your eagerness to be playing on court, don't skip them.

Golden Rule
There is no Golden Rule that
can apply to all players in all
circumstances. There is only a
Golden Mean

Physical
At least 50 per cent of your effectiveness is deeply rooted in the body. Physical attributes are very necessary for doubles, absolutely essential for singles. (They are dealt with more fully in chapters 4 and 8.) Those of brain and character are equally necessary for both.

Strength In badminton, strength must be applied with speed to become power. 'Timing is all' someone will tell you. Agreed, but timing is the application of power at precisely the correct split second. You will need it to clear when off-balance or with the shuttle deep behind you. You will need it to penetrate a cast-iron Frost Hansen or Chandra defence. You will need it to clear a full length cross-court, 47ft 2in.

Stamina A single can last over 75 minutes. One game alone lasted an hour when Eddie Choong, the Malaysian student, and Joe Alston, the ex-FBI man, tried, cat and mouse, to outlast each other. With rarely more than a seven-second interval between rallies, you will be running, bending, twisting, jumping, lunging and hitting with all your power.

With stamina comes vital confidence. You know you can physically outgun your opponent. You need be in no hurry to go for risky, error-ridden winners. After each long, energy-sapping rally, it is your opponent who is running fractionally more slowly, hitting a little less hard. His is the tortured breathing, his the worry and fatigue that breeds error. Not yours!

Speed in badminton cannot be measured in 'mph'. It is a matter of early starting and driving acceleration. It, and the jumps that go with it, must be explosive. This is the speed you must have if you are to salvage your opponent's near winners; to pressurise him by early takes; to

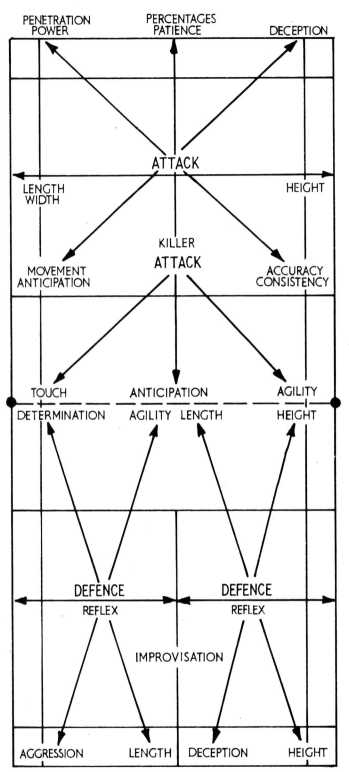

Fig. 27 Expert essentials. Some qualities, of course, are the prerogative of both defence and attack

reach the falling shuttle while it is still above tape-height, still a target for the kill or a wider range of strokes.

Suppleness increases reach, and, ease of movement. It engenders more fluent strokes and more powerful ones.

Mental

From the fore-going, don't get the idea that badminton is solely a game of brawn. Necessary though that is, it won't get you far unless it is masterminded by brain. Badminton is for the intelligent. A degree in classics or science may help but the 'not-even-one-CSE' player can develop a specialised badminton brain too: champions think as they run! It is of equal importance to the smash to be able to spot weaknesses and strengths, to change losing tactics at the right moment.

Self-analysis Perhaps only bridge fiends actually enjoy an acrimonious post-mortem. But after defeat (and even victory) although dissection of your badminton corpse cannot revive it, it can help its triumphant resurrection in your next tournament. Remember what worked. Then look at each phase of your play; look at strokes and tactics: think where you went wrong. Thought is only the first step, so get on court and devise stroke practices, sequences and routines, and conditioned games to strengthen the weak links.

Take note of Ken Rosewall who after winning the US Tennis Open could be seen on an outside court practising the serve that hadn't functioned as well as it might. Or Sandy Lyle, the golfer who, when his drive grievously betrayed him, hit 2,000 balls screaming down the fairway in the next two days.

Equally important is the analysis of your opponent. Dissect him like a butterfly. Keep a card index of players you meet. On one side list strengths to avoid; on the other, weaknesses to attack. Remember to up-date it regularly for, like you, he has doubtless sought to put some steel into the flab.

Always make a point of watching probable opponents in tournaments and matches. Time spent on a systematic stroke by stroke appraisal is interesting and far better than time spent on another cafeteria cup of lukewarm tea. 'Where'

is as important as 'How'. Analyse tactics and positions, rather than technique, under the headings I have already described.

On court, a swift analysis after each rally will tell you the strengths and weaknesses of yourself and of your opponent. Slot them away for reflex recall in later rallies. But don't let them bug you. Be content to learn from experience!

Anticipation Anticipation is the root of speed. It is the source of *early* movement which brings you unhurriedly to take the shuttle high. It becomes second nature, a reflex, as, computer-like, your brain ticks up the known factors and flashes the likely opponent-return to the muscles and limbs concerned.

Anticipation is not just crystal-ball work. It is based on the intelligent observation of six main factors: (i) your court position; (ii) your opponent's position and relationship to the shuttle; (iii) strokes he can't play; (iv) strokes he can play; (v) his favourite or habitual stroke; (vi) the likely return by that player (not by you!) in those circumstances.

A tall order? (Therefore never commit yourself too far.) But you will find that with constant practice, anticipation becomes second nature. It works best, of course, when your opponent is under pressure – the alternatives are fewer.

Confidence Without confidence you have no foundation. This you must have. This you can have if you have digested the contents of a book such as this, if you have trained, if you have practised, if you have played competitively to your limits. Secure in this knowledge, be convinced you are fitter in all respects, that you can win. As unknown Chinese girls Zhang Ai Ling and Liu Xia said to themselves before they beat world champions Perry and Webster, 'There is always the possibility'.

But never be so over-confident as to suggest arrogance or to play casually. That is fatal.

Points Some players are scarcely aware of the overall score; to others each separate rally is important. A good start, 4–0, based on warm-up, knock-up, opponent assessment and careful aggression, can boost your morale, shake your opponent's. First to 8, like the 7th game in tennis, can be important. It's *you* who are in front at the halfway mark.

Plate 29. Nora Perry – at speed – anticipates a winner *(Mervyn Rees)*

If your opponent has a run of points, don't panic. Concentrate on the next point. Put up a wall of consistency so that you regain the serve. Strive too to be first to 13. Now you have a five-point buffer between you and defeat. Moreover, the choice 'to set or not to set' is in your hands. If your opponent recovers from 9–13 to 13 all he might take the next two points for game as well. But if you are able to set he is unlikely to take a further five points before you have recovered your composure.

The last point is often frighteningly elusive. Treat it as just another point that, like its predecessors, will be yours with steadily applied pressure against an opponent who dare not take risks. Avoid equally going into your shell or a mad Light Brigade charge.

Remember: more points accrue to a player through his opponent's errors, forced and unforced, than through his own outright winners. A point lost needs three rallies won to wipe it out: one to retrieve the serve, one to level, one to regain the lead. Take a chance on your serve; be steady on your opponent's.

Strategy This is your overall, long-term general plan; tactics your particular method of achieving that end. So first consider your strategy. But before you can do so you must survey the terrain, in other words, know your opponent. Do this by reference to your card-index, by watching your opponent in play (preferably under pressure), prior to your own encounter, or belatedly, and very much third best, in your brief three-minute knock-up – that is, if you don't knock with your partner.

If your opponent is perhaps 'just over the hill' then your strategy might be long and tiring rallies. If he is just about your own standard but

92

a little slower round the court, play a fast attacking game. If he is faster than you, use deception to hobble him. If he likes hard hitting, slow the speed down with high, very deep clears and lobs. If he is much better than you, a considered all-out attack might surprise him. If the floor is slippery or the light bad, deception again could be the answer.

Any of these strategic ploys could be applied to doubles. There, of course, your first concern is to decide who is the weaker player who will bear the brunt of your attack. This is a two-edged sword. The player thus largely cut out will tend to poach, often leaving himself out of position. And when he does get a chance, will go all out for even a risky winner, so that your attack can't again be switched back to his weaker partner.

Tactics Strategy is long term; tactics, short term. They are the thoughts and actions of the moment. If you wish to slow a game down you employ high clears and slow drops. If you wish to speed it up, use smashes, attacking clears and whip-returns. If the floor is slippery, hold your lobs and drops to the last moment, or use wrist deflections to ensure your opponent is forced to do the maximum amount of stopping, starting and turning on a non-grip surface. If you wish to tire your opponent, drop and clear in long corner-to-corner rallies, or give him plenty of opportunity of exhausting himself smashing against your robust defence.

In the course of a game you will observe a flaw in your opponent's play. Change your tactics to exploit it fully. If you notice your opponent is prone to smash from too deep in the rear-court and is slow to follow in, feed him tempting lobs and play return net-shots. If you notice his backhand drop is invariably cross-court, feed it and move your base nearer that corner for the early take (though not so far that you are totally committed). If you observe he is tiring, prolong the rallies. 'Softly, softly, catchee monkey'. It is this ability to 'read' a game that can sort out the men from the boys.

It is a common saying, 'Stick to winning tactics; change losing ones.' But it is one that needs some amplification. If you can win a game without pounding an obvious weakness, do so. The weakness, thus not strengthened by practice, will still be there if the need arises.

Always have a Plan B in your mind in case your opponent improves or changes his tactics. If his erratic backhand steadies, play the forehand for a while with only occasional attacks on the now more open backhand. If he smashes from a wiser, more forward base, lift deeper still and observe now whether he favours the clear or the drop. If you have won an easy first game don't over-confidently relax. Your opponent can't do worse, may well do better. Or quite probably, as you would, he too will employ new tactics. Can you be ready for them?

The art of switching is to choose just the right moment. Be neither too early nor too late.

Similarly in doubles, you must think out the right tactics to further your strategy of playing on the weaker player. For example, do not play your drops straight to him but a foot or so nearer him. Then he will still have to travel, and partner-poaching and doubt are likely by-products. Don't hammer every smash at him, reserve one occasionally for his now over-anxious or resigned partner.

Often, of course, partners are well-matched. Even so they may well have different strengths and weaknesses. If A is sharp at the net but frail of smash and B is strong in the rear court but ham-fisted at the net, serve low to B to bring him in and flicks to A to force him back. Or it may simply be that A's lobs are hit shorter than B's so A gets the drop; or that B's defence is slightly more lifted than A's so B is the target rather than A when other things are equal.

Character

Concentration is the eradicator of error. At this level, failure to maintain 100 per cent concentration will result in error. You must be able to forget (not even hear) the noisy talker, (not even see) the back-court wanderer, side-line percher, or busty blonde. All your thoughts, all the time, are concentrated on the game.

Some players achieve this by loudly urging themselves, 'Concentrate!' The mind may then concentrate not so much on playing as on concentrating. Others achieve their end by keeping their eyes down, by seeing nothing outside the court; still others by intently watching the shuttle as if to see a mark on its base. And yet some players concentrate by putting the actual score in the back of the mind, and concentrating on each separate rally: it is a point to be won, a serve to be gained. In that way score fluctuations don't flurry them – and that elusive last point loses some of its nerve-wracking doubt. So welcome noisy conditions as a testing ground. One day you may have to play in Jakarta's Senayan Stadium where 10,000 fanatical spectators create constant bedlam.

Determination Think 'I'm going to win' and you may well do so. Think 'I'm going to lose' and you almost certainly will. Clearly shown determination will worry your opponent as much as a barrage of smashes.

Determination wins the 5–0 lead that shatters the less determined. At 4–13, it says, 'This is a good game to win' – not, 'It's curtains'. It drives you (with Leadbeater tenacity) to that dying drop only inches from the floor. It enables you in exhaustion to pull out that unbelievable little bit extra that tips the scale. No shuttle is dead until it's lying on the floor, motionless!

In a crisis, slow down the pace. Don't panic. Be cool and unhurried both in stroke and thought. Breathe deeply from the diaphragm. Relax. Don't let your opponent hurry you. Have guts and be prepared to fight back even if you are physically sick or the pain and effort seem insupportable.

Patience There is no place, particularly in singles, for the wildly impetuous. In mixed, one rash interception by an over-eager lady can be the death-knell of a rally that was so nearly won. In level doubles, with a partner, you may just get away with it. Not so in singles where, on your own, a single rash shot, cross-court or off-balance, can put you deep in trouble. You must be prepared to play endless drops and clears to get just the right opening from which you can make your winner. And if you let that chance slip, you must be patient enough to go back to square one with a high lob or clear – and start all over again.

Don't get me wrong, though. I'm no advocate of badminton pacifism. The next heading proves it.

Killer Spirit The alter-ego of patience is the killer spirit. Patience lays the foundations with drop and lob, killer spirit takes advantage of it by lunging into the net to snap up that inch-too-

high net-shot. It ruthlessly steps up the pressure on an opponent in trouble. With the finality of the Last Trump, it administers the smashing *coup de grâce*. It doesn't try the impossible – but when the real chance is on for a split second, it seizes it. And your opponent, morale shaken, depressed, mutters to himself, 'He never misses a trick!'

Consistency
Consistency is another great virtue to cultivate. Cut out your own unforced errors and you put your opponent under redoubled pressure. To gain a winner he must take risks.

Hit that shuttle over the net and in court 80 per cent of the time and you've won the 'percentage' battle. Chinese brilliance was built on this solid basis of 'nothing given away'. They are a frugal race.

How to achieve Nirvana? Stick to the essentials from the start.
1. Move quickly to the earliest point at which you can intercept the shuttle in front of you.
2. Be on balance; lean into the stroke.
3. Prepare your stroke early and execute it correctly and carefully.
4. Watch that shuttle racket to racket.
5. Control the racket-head at impact.
6. Aim it at the target as long as possible.

Remember: 'There is no short circuit round hard work'.

Discipline Almost invariably when a Chinese team flashes briefly upon the European scene, it is not merely their fleetness of foot and power of shot that momentarily stuns us, it is also their discipline. It is discipline that precludes casual play at any time, be it in near victory or certain defeat. Win by every point you can against a tough rival. It is up to you as a perfectionist never willingly to debase your standard. A crushing defeat is bad for your opponent's morale. Fight for every point to save your own from a body blow. Never give up.

Let me quote Sweden's Ulf Borgstrom: 'Both during practice sessions and matches the Chinese were totally devoted to their task – even if it hurt. Slippery floors, slow shuttles,

Plate 30. Liem Swie King shows essential 'killer' spirit *(Nick Skinner)*

bad lighting brought no grumbles.' So too at the Albert Hall no word crossed their lips in complaint at the infamous drift which bewitched some English players.

Off court they were equally disciplined. They did a fine public relations job, never putting a foot wrong. They were a team – mending each others rackets, encouraging each other at all times. They took the challenge seriously, rose to it – and enjoyed it.

Temperament In top class badminton there is no place for drama-school histrionics, for racket-throwing, or noisy self-abjuration. But that is not to say that we are all born with the same ice-cool temperament. Some are completely expressionless displaying neither weariness, disappointment, nor delighted surprise at a shot's success. A dead-pan expression provides no scraps of intelligence for the opposition. Others do need a safety valve for pent-up emotion. It is better by far to express it 'piano' rather than 'fortissimo'. A sibilant 'Eeeeeh!' does the trick for many. A touch of pre-match tension, like a first night, probably gives you the vital edge. An overdose must be dissipated in warm-up, a mental rehearsal of tactics, or a chat with your coach.

But at all costs avoid altercation and tantrums, particularly in regard to line-calls, umpire's decisions, and service faults. If it's your opponent who is causing the scene, let your mind become a blank. If 'needle' now creeps into the game one player will thrive on it. 'I'll beat the ......!' sets the adrenalin flowing.

Another will rush and overhit. If the latter is you, forget the infuriating personality; instead play the shuttle, net and lines. They are your opponents.

Let's face it, some line calls are bound to be wrong. (Lining is no easy job.) But they will be wrong in your favour as often as they are against you – though not necessarily in the same match. Nothing is gained by argument. The decision remains; it's your 'cool', your concentration, that has gone. With a hot-headed partner, cool him down but with sympathy (feigned or genuinely indignant), or you may merely add fuel to the flames.

If you are service faulted it's no use looking daggers. The service judge can see: you can't! Look for his explanatory signal and adapt accordingly; just don't risk it by serving to the limits.

Like Ilie Nastase, badminton's stormy petrel Kevin Jolly (now happily reformed) once gained an unenviable reputation for dispute. It never won him a match; it lost him several – and popularity to boot. On the other hand, take Lene Koppen. The attitude of the former world champion is completely different. At the 1980–81 Friends Provident Masters Tournament she was service faulted in a crucial game. She said nothing then, played on calmly, and won. Her comment after: 'I have never been faulted before. But I do not like a fuss. What good does it do?' And next time Lene goes on court she has the crowd behind her, not against her. And how it lifts her!

8 Fitness

STARTING OFF

Warming-up is a vital pre-game routine especially in a cold hall. It has a threefold importance:

1. It gently and gradually promotes the full range of movement for joints and muscles, so reducing risk of injury caused by sudden stress.
2. It gives improved performance from the outset of the game. The warm-up should increase the pulse rate from a basic 70 to 120 or so. And it is between 120 and 180 that a body is held to be, sportswise, at its most efficient. Compare this with the performance of a cold car and a warmed-up car.
3. Psychologically too it is helpful. This is action rather than nervous inaction. The adrenalin starts to flow. The mind begins to concentrate on the game ahead; almost a state of self-hypnosis can be induced which blots out all external distractions.

Pre-Game Routine

These exercises should be carried out in a relaxed, unhurried manner while breathing quite naturally. Each should be performed for no more than 10–12 repetitions.

1. *A 400 metre run* (a jog for the not so fit) or running on the spot. Loosely flex and unflex arms, wrists and fingers.
2. *Heel raises*: feet hip-width apart, rise up and down on toes as rhythmically and as high as possible.
3. *Arm circling*: feet astride, circle the arms forwards, upwards, backwards, sideways and down, loosely. *Or*, slowly, with arms straight and stiff, raise arms forwards and upwards. Rise on tip toe and brush ears with arms. Hold for two to three seconds.

Press arms back and lower sideways slowly, pressing shoulder blades together. Lower weight onto heels.

4. *Side bends*: feet wide astride, hands on side of thighs; bend to left and right alternately, with face to the front.
5. *Hurdle position*: sit on floor with left leg bent back, heel to buttock, and the right stretched out forward to make a 90° angle with the left. Push hands slowly and gently forward until they touch the foot, and the head touches the knee. Repeat with left leg forward. Do not jerk.
6. *Hamstring stretch*: standing, cross legs so that left foot is against right side of right foot. Bend gently to touch toes or place hands flat on the floor. Repeat with feet reversed. Do not jerk.
7. *Trunk circling*: feet shoulder-width apart. Hands clasped in front of body. Pushing arms as far away from the body as possible sweep them slowly out to the right, upwards, and then down to the left. Lean back as far as possible. Repeat, reversing direction.
8. *Abductor stretches (Lunges)*
   (i) Stand with feet wide apart. Lunge forward with the right leg, knee bent to 90° and foot pointing forward to right. Rear foot points outward to left. Push back strongly straightening front leg and return to original position. Repeat three times.
   (ii) Repeat with right foot pointing to left.
   (iii) Repeat, lunging alternately, not forwards, but sideways to right and to left. Right foot across both times.
   (iv) Repeat, turning and lunging backwards first to the right and then to left. Again right foot.

((i) and (ii) are the equivalent of playing lobs or net-returns forehanded and backhanded; (iii) blocking side-line smashes; (iv) driving from the backhand boxes.)

9. *Back stretches*: feet wide apart, hands clasped above head. Bend torso fully back twice, then bend forward twice to touch the floor between or behind legs. Reach further backwards with second press.

Some badminton players like to finish with a couple of explosive exercises to raise the pulse rate to the required figure:

Twelve tuck-jumps (knees to chest);

Short bursts of sprinting for 30–35 yards.

It is just as important to 'warm-down' after a game. Essential body heat is lost if tracksuits (hooded preferably because the head is a major source of heat loss) are not quickly donned and some of the foregoing exercises done. This also helps to reduce the lactic acid which accumulates and is a source of fatigue.

SUPPLENESS

Have you ever said to an eager youngster trying to break from your grasp, 'You wriggle like an eel'? Have you ever thought as, entranced, you watched the poetry of motion, the supple grace of gymnast Nellie Kim or skater Robin Cousins, 'They haven't a bone in their bodies'? If you haven't, then you've never admired suppleness.

It is a quality we are all born with. It is retained by women and youngsters. But with growth, increased muscle bulk, and ageing, it is a quality gradually lost, particularly by men.

In badminton it is too often a quality overlooked. Suppleness offers much. To realise that, look at the experts. See just how far supple Karen Bridge can lean to her left to play powerful round-the-head shots. How far forward Lene Koppen can lunge to salvage a drop shot mere inches from the floor. How Nicky Yates can bend backwards to clear the subtle attacking lob that has been flicked over his head. How bouncing Liem Swie King can swing every ounce of his body weight into a sizzling smash out of all proportion to his size.

Increased suppleness offers increased speed, power (you can apply force over a great range) and reach. It enables you to retrieve the impossible (see Sally Leadbeater do the splits)

and to attack the unassailable. In badminton, full of twists and turns, stops and starts, it offers better balance and conservation of energy by lithesome, more effortless movement.

Suppleness then is basically the ability to flex and extend, to increase the range of movement of your body segments at the joints. Fully to achieve this, the joint-activating muscles and ligaments must be equally unrestricted and free in movement.

The quest for extra suppleness must be an intrinsic part of your training. It can be obtained in two ways. First by gradual self-applied stretching, by doing the exercises suggested under warm-up (page 97). These are actually flexibility exercises deliberately incorporated in order to kill two birds with one stone. They will make you supple as they warm you, to prevent possible muscle injury in the knock-up in a cold badminton hall.

Secondly, a far greater range can be achieved by more drastic exercises. These can be of three types:

1. With a partner applying the pressure.
2. By the trainee applying pressure against an immovable object such as floor or wall.
3. By using a weight at the extremity of a limb to give added momentum to the movement.

If this seems to smack of the Inquisition, don't worry! The dynamics of the joint incorporate a stretch reflex mechanism which gives adequate warning of possible damage. Indeed it tends to be over-protective. Use exercises such as the following specifically devised for badminton by National coach Jake Downey in his excellent and detailed book *Get Fit for Badminton*.

The principle in each case is for the trainee to stretch the limb to the comfort limit. Then he presses against his partner in a direction *opposite* to the one in which it is desired to improve flexibility. This pressure is held for six seconds. The trainee then relaxes before the partner pushes the limb slightly farther back to a new comfort limit. Obviously this must be done gradually and not roughly.

1. *Shoulder*: this will give a more powerful overhead action. Trainee kneels, raises right arm vertically, and stretches it back to limit. Then he pushes forward against partner's restraining hand.
2. *Hip*: this will increase the range of lunging

in returning drop-shots or side-line smashes. Trainee sits on floor with legs as wide apart as possible. Partner, kneeling between them, puts his hand on ankles to restrain trainee's inward pressure.

3. *Spine*: this enables you to reach back further to take a shuttle behind you and clear it to a length or to prepare more effectively for a power smash. Trainee kneels upright, then leans back to limit. Partner restrains forward movement by placing his hands on trainee's shoulders.

In this connection points to remember are:

(i) Suppleness, or lack of it, is not overall; it varies from joint to joint.

(ii) As the range of movement becomes greater there must be a corresponding increase in muscle strength to control this increased range.

The village blacksmith performing the same bent-arm hammering action day after day certainly developed brawny arms but became muscle-bound and limited in range. Do all you can to reap the full harvest of suppleness.

STAMINA

Stamina or endurance is obviously essential in

Plate 31. Sally Leadbeater, England's most promising lady, demonstrates determination – and suppleness *(Louis C. H. Ross)*

any strenuous game continuing over a prolonged period of time. It may best be dealt with under two headings, cardio-vascular efficiency and local muscular endurance.

Cardio-Vascular

This in simple terms means that heart and lungs must be developed so that they are capable of supplying the increased flow of oxygenated blood to fuel the muscles into action. When muscle action depletes its store of glycogen energy, lactic acid is produced. This causes oxygen debt or muscle fatigue. Training therefore must be devised to ensure an adequate flow of oxygen to remove the acid and also to train the body to bear with it until that supply arrives.

This can best be done by running. The very nature of badminton is short, sharp bursts of running, jumping, lunging, stopping and turning. Long-distance running therefore should be used pre-season only to build up core-fitness. Even the 'fartlek' system, over different

Plate 32. Sally again – building up core-fitness
(*Louis C. H. Ross*)

types of country, should be varied. A spell of 4,000 metres jogging could be broken by stints of short distance (20–50 metres) sprinting, running backwards, zig-zag running, diagonal running backwards, 5–10 metres sprint and lunge, or skipping, to cover some 4,500 metres in all.

Early in the season this could be reduced to five or six repetitions of 60 metre sprints in three sets. After each 60 metre sprint, first walk, then later, jog back to repeat. A three-minute rest should be taken between each set.

A better alternative for badminton perhaps is 'up and down the clock'. Sprint first 20 metres and jog back; then 30 metres and jog back; then 40, 50, 60 metres jogging back each time. 'Down the clock' would be sprinting diminishing distances 60, 50, 40 etc. Two such sets would be sufficient.

During the season shuttle runs are ideal. Start

3 metres behind the doubles side-line. Run to it, racket in hand, lunge and lob. Run backwards to starting line, there playing a jump smash. Repeat in turn to each of the five lines across court.

If a court is not available mark out 10 metres in garden or drive. Turning, sprint up and down 10 times (ie 100 metres). Repeat this 3 or 4 times, increasing to 8, having a minute's rest between each 100 metres.

Local Muscular Endurance

Just as efficient cardio-vascular training induces 'breathlessness' so must muscular exercises be sufficiently taxing as to induce a 'jelly-like' feeling. Each complements the other. Such exercises not merely thicken and strengthen the muscle fibres but also increase the blood flow to them, and make stored energy more readily available.

I have already outlined specific arm- and leg-strengthening exercises but as the whole body is utilised, other exercises are needed. These are best done in the form of a circuit as this provides its own competitive spark and means of testing progress, both necessary to maintain enthusiasm.

Procedure

1. After a warm-up, exercises are practised to ensure correct technique. Sloppiness must never be allowed to creep in.
2. Next day, count maximum number of repetitions for each exercise done in 60 seconds by man, in 30 seconds by lady. Take a two-minute rest after each exercise in this testing session.
3. Divide the repetition figures by two; these are the target figures.
4. Next comes the timing trial. Note the time of commencement. Perform target figures for each exercise. Note time for completing circuit. Without pause complete circuit twice more. Add up individual circuit times. Reduce this by a third to arrive at your target time.
5. As greater fitness is gained the original time will be reduced until the target time is achieved.
6. Now the trainee must be retested so that the number of repetitions is increased or harder exercises are undertaken. This will bring

his overall time back to between 20 and 30 minutes; less than this is comparatively unproductive.

Home	Gymnasium
1. Sit-ups (abdominals)	1. Trunk twists – weight behind head (abdominals)
2. Press-ups (arms and shoulders)	2. Press-ups – feet on chair (arms)
3. Step-ups – 15in platform (thighs and buttocks)	3. Squat jumps (legs)
4. Dorsal raise (back)	4. Bicep curls – with weight (*see Notes*) (arms)
5. Burpees (*see Notes*) (suppleness and agility)	5. Bench lifts (general)
6. Single leg overs (trunk)	6. Astride jumps onto and off bench – with medicine ball
7. Weight roll-up (wrist)	7. Weight roll-up (wrist)
8. Leg raise (abdominals)	8. Dorsal raise (back)
9. Side bends (trunk)	9. Chins (arms)
10. Squat thrusts (legs)	10. Shuttle runs (legs)

Another useful exercise for wrists and arms is to securely suspend a brick or weight from half a broom handle; with arms extended, using wrists, roll brick up to handle and down.

(Notes: Burpees – 1) Stand upright, feet together, hands in front of thighs; 2) Down to full crouch with hands flat on floor; 3) With hands supporting body, shoot legs out to a full stretched position; 4) Bring legs forward to full crouch again; 5) Spring up straight to starting position. Bicep curls – Stand upright with feet shoulder-width apart, arms fully extended downwards with palms turned outwards. Hold barbell across thighs. Bending arms, raise to chest level, lower and repeat.)

STRENGTH – INTO POWER

At this stage, as you seek magically to change from hutch 'bunny' to club 'tiger', it is salutary to get an international ringside seat. There, almost on court, you really become aware of power.

It may be the grunted effort of a Jolly clear, the sheer physical impact of a Stevens' smash, or the perfectly timed lightning of a Gilks' backhand. Different guises but the same result: a clear from baseline to baseline; a smash that would dent a Chieftain tank. Power is the rock on which much is founded.

How to achieve it? How to change your three-quarters length clear and your pop-gun smash into killers? The answer lies in many things: equipment, strength and power; utilisation of the whole body; pronation of the forearm; wrist flick; timing; practice and still more practice.

Take equipment first. If you didn't splash out on the best when you hesitantly started, do so now that you know badminton is definitely for you. Discard the rigid shaft and shrimp-net stringing of your first buy. Instead, invest in a carbon-fibre shaft that gives added whip, and in real gut stringing that gives extra resilience. Buy a 3½oz racket instead of your old 5oz+ war club. The new timing will take a few weeks to master but then – you'll already have added a foot or more to your clears; mph to your smash, and split seconds to your racket manoeuvrability.

But the best racket in the world can't do the trick on its own. It's muscles you want and mobility. (See page 98.) And you can't buy those. Nor is muscle powered by a 2-star diet. (See page 107.)

Arm Exercises (Using gymnasium equipment)

1. *Chins* Overgrasp, hands shoulder width apart. Pull up on beam until chin just touches it, lower and repeat. Feet must not touch floor.
2. *Press-ups* To make these harder do them on the fingers, not palms, *or* with the feet raised on a chair, *or* with arms placed wide. To make easier (for ladies) push up into kneeling position.
3. *Bicep curls* Feet apart, fingers pointing to the floor, raise the bar (10lb each side) to

chest height by bending the arms. Lower back to in front of the thighs.

4. *Bent arm pull-overs* Lie on bench with feet flat on floor and arms bent behind head so bar is on floor. Raise bar vertically above chest, arms finally straight. Lower back slowly, bending arms.
5. *Alternate dumb-bell press* Lie on bench, arms bent. Stretch arms up (and down) alternately.
6. *Straight arm pull-overs* As in (4) but arms are not bent and bar is lowered onto thighs.
7. *Behind-neck press* Feet astride. Bar resting across back of neck. Extend arms fully and lower slowly.

These should be done a maximum of thirty times. Breathe in as weights are raised; out, as they are lowered.

Leg Exercises

1. *Bench jump* Stand astride bench. Jump up onto bench and down. (Medicine ball can be held.)
2. *Squat thrusts* Crouch on floor. Thrust legs out to full extent then spring back so that knees are just touching arms.
3. *Squat jumps* Squat down with one foot in front of the other; leap upwards explosively to land with other foot forward. May also be done, with hands on floor, without jumping up.
4. *Step-ups* Step up and down onto bench of such a height that when one foot is placed on it knee is at least 90°. (Weight can be held across back of neck.)
5. *Standing long and high jumps*
6. *Kangaroo jumps and hopping for length or height*

Putting Power into Smash and Clear

Make sure you employ this growing strength correctly. Make sure that each phase of your stroke is correctly played and utilises not merely the arm, but almost the whole of the body.

From an alert position of readiness with racket at head height, learn now to delay your backswing but compensate by a faster (and, of course) a fuller one. Watch closely on TV and you will see just how fast this is. How, without pause, it leads straight into the even faster forward swing.

Even in the short space of the backswing, your knees bend, your pelvis rotates, and your shoulder turns strongly. Your arm is bent with the elbow high, your wrist fully cocked, and your forearm is strongly supinated (turned outward).

This you do in a split second, before driving up from the knees and spiralling your body into the stroke. The arm snaps straight, the forearm pronates (turns inward) strongly and the wrist uncocks crisply. At the same time the body turns square to the net, the shoulder swings through forcefully, and the weight inevitably transfers onto the front foot.

In each phase of the stroke you have smoothly accelerated into the next without pause so that your racket-head (like a whip-lash) is moving at its fastest in the 'zing' area.

For the smash, you actually contact the shuttle a full 18in in front of the body. And in the follow-through to knee height pull down strongly on the racket.

It has been estimated that the shuttle velocity off the racket is no less than 180kph and over half that speed emanates solely from shoulder rotation and forearm pronation. It is by no means all arm and wrist snap.

Nor is it always sheer strength. As in other sports (the lazy drive of Colin Cowdrey; the elegant swing of Jack Nicklaus), perfect timing propels the missile just as fast as does a brutal hammer blow. Timing is simply making sure that the racket-head is moving at its maximum velocity at the split second of impact − neither before, nor after. To achieve it requires great patience and much practice.

Bobby Charlton of Manchester United owed his screaming 40 yard out goals to ceaseless practice behind the Old Trafford stands. From 5 yards, then 10, then 15, he hammered the ball ever harder and harder, but without the tremendous physical effort that eventually drains the resources of even the fittest. It was done by timing!

SPEED

Hard experience has, I hope, taught you that other things being equal or even fairly unequal, the faster man always wins. He seizes the

Plate 33. Liem Swie King leaps sideways to shoot down a low altitude attacking clear *(Mervyn Rees)*

attack, has a wider range of strokes open to him, and hurries you into error. You must seek to be ever faster; take the shuttle ever earlier.

In badminton, on a half court 22ft × 20ft, speed as recognised by a sprinter is non-existent. Even a 100 yard flyer such as Alan Wells needs at least 30 yards in which to work up to his maximum. Nora Perry, lightning fast on the 3 yard dash, was unplaced in the Super-stars 100 metres. In badminton the longest sprint is seldom more than the 4–5yds from base-line to front service line – and often less.

Rather than speed, then, it is the following qualities that you must think about. Early starting; immediate acceleration; agility in turning and changing direction; economical braking and driving recovery; balance; and of course sheer strength of leg.

Early starting is based on a mobile, fairly erect position of readiness. This should be relaxed because tension inhibits speed. Watch Lancashire's Rita Heywood: feet always dancing; body inertia reduced. Speed will flourish too on intelligent anticipation and shrewd 'reading' of your opponent's strokes. If poise is important, so too is positioning. Always narrow the angle; always position yourself a little nearer the likely return. Less distance to travel – earlier arrival.

Recovery is speeded up if you are supple and can move early and lightly. Then with short, driving steps your body must be forced into rapid motion. Feet should skim the floor so that maximum floor contact is maintained. Watch Kent's Paul Whetnall. Copy his neat, busy steps. Light and silent; instantly stopping, agilely changing direction: he is always on balance.

In addition to running you must now practise three other skills: (i) lunge, (ii) jump, (iii) scissor-kick. Often you will add one of these to running as a split-second-saving alternative.

Lunge As in fencing, this is a long stride ending with the front right leg, bent at the knee at 90°, the body fairly upright, and the left leg straight or nearly so with only the toes in contact with the floor. To ensure good balance, and therefore quick recovery, keep the hips low and the head behind the front foot.

Recovery can be made either by pushing backwards with the front foot or by first moving the back leg slightly forwards so that body weight then adds impetus to the driving back-wards movement of the front foot.

Jump To intercept a low flying shuttle that would otherwise get behind you, or to gain height and so steepness of shot, or time, you will often have to jump. This will be made vertically or half-sideways. If the shuttle is behind you, you may not only have to jump backwards as well but also arch your back to get at least your racket behind the shuttle. If the shuttle is well in front of you, about to drop below the tape, you may have to leap forward.

Scissor-kick Against attacking clears you may be unable to get behind the shuttle. You will then have to use the scissor-kick. With the last step back onto the right foot push up and land on the left foot. Swing the right foot forward as counterbalance, hitting at the high point of the jump. Recover quickly by pushing forward with the left foot.

Reaching Forward This does not increase speed as such but it saves an extra split-second consuming step. In returning a low serve, by advancing the racket, the shuttle can be taken some 18in to 24in in front of you – earlier. So too with the lunge, advance both racket and foot so that the shuttle is taken early, and there is less distance to travel back to base. In defence too, hold the racket well in front of you; this will give you time to generate more power with a slightly longer swing and encourage you to take the shuttle adventurously early.

Agility
This is the ability to change direction quickly, to twist and turn and still maintain balance: it is an essential part of speed.

Off Court
Skipping will give light footwork. (3–5 repetitions of 1–2 minutes skipping with a minute's rest interval.)

Maze Running Weave backwards and forwards between lines of chairs or skittles set close together.

Shuttle Runs (see page 100).

Timed Runs From centre court run to each corner and back in turn. Repeat five times with one minute rest between repetitions (3).

Shadowing Play imaginary rallies varying them from five to twenty strokes. Allow 7–10 seconds between each rally. *Or* get a static partner clearly (but sometimes deceptively) to shadow strokes to which you 'play' appropriate returns. As well as helping agility this will help 'reading' a stroke.

In both cases it is essential that you drive yourself with fast instant recovery and movement and play strokes fluently.

On Court
In all the following exercises bear three points in mind: Feeders are there to stretch players – not to beat them. Once play to a set pattern has been mastered, occasional variations should be introduced by feeders so that movement does not become automatic. Play must be realistic.

1. A clears, runs in to touch front service line with racket, runs back to clear, runs in, etc, etc.
2. A drops; feeder B plays net-return; A in to play net-return; B lobs; A back to drop etc.
3. A smashes; B plays net-return; A runs in to make net-return or kill; B lobs; A back to smash.
4. Feeder B plays clears to deep corners in any sequence; A clears to B forehanded or round head returning to centre-base between shots.
5. As in (4) but feeder B plays drops and A lobs.
6. Feeder B plays clears and drops to corners in any sequence; A clears or lobs, returning to base each time.
7. A and B play straight half court pushes to each other; between shots they must return to base with one foot over centre line.
8. Player A drives cross-court; feeders B and C play looped straight returns; or A drives straight and B and C play looped cross-court returns.
9. A plays straight net-shots; B and C cross-court *or* A plays cross-court; B and C straight.
10. A smashes, B plays push return; A lobs, B smashes; A plays push return, B lobs; A smashes, etc.

11. A smashes to a specified side; B lobs moving A from side to side.
12. 2 v 1: singles.
13. 2 v 1: feeders return all strokes to player's backhand.

Think out other variations or common stroke sequences for yourself.

Think on your feet: think of your feet.

SURPRISE! SURPRISE!
Deception is a good servant but a bad master. Too many players have failed to make the top simply because they preferred inflicting death by the thousand cuts of deception rather than by one straightforward bludgeon blow – a smash. Never overdo deception.

Nevertheless, wisely used, it must become an integral part of your game. It is the ally of power. Deception creates openings; power smashes through them. And on occasions, deception makes its own winners.

Watch Gillian Gilks' sleight-of-hand reverse cross-court drop leave her opponent floundering; Mike Tredgett, with smash-presaging jump send his adversary tottering *backwards*, before he plays a gentle drop; or Nora Perry taming the eager rusher with a perfectly disguised flick.

Go back a decade and learn of Judy Hashman, ten times All-England singles winner. Nothing fancy here! All honest, down-to-earth stuff, but each stroke armed with an inbuilt deception that hobbled her opponents, that made anticipation a game of Russian roulette.

Deception is not trick shots round the back or between the legs. That is just reflex improvisation when a player has been caught napping, too late to play the orthodox stroke. No, deception is the art of the unexpected.

In basic terms it is the last second change in the speed, direction or trajectory of a shot. It is created partly by the magic that is the wrist. And partly by camouflage, by making kindred strokes (eg all overheads) identical in action.

There are many fascinating avenues for you to explore.

Similarity of Action Overhead strokes (clears, drops and smashes); side-arm strokes (drive, push and drop) and underarm strokes (net-shots and lobs, serves): play all the strokes in these groups with the same basic action from start of backswing to just before impact. You will obtain change of pace by a last-second slowing down or speeding up of arm and/or wrist. Beware though of over-doing it. If your clear or smash is normally played with easy timing don't in your endeavour to fool your opponent do an over-exaggerated, muscle-contorting wind-up accompanied by full facial grimaces; it merely gives the game away.

Change of Direction There are two approaches to this. Either shape to play straight with racket-face square to the shuttle and then belatedly turn wrist and racket to the chosen side. Or, bring the racket-face up to the shuttle angled, say, to the left, then, at impact, turn it disconcertingly to the right.

Serving The low serve to the T-junction is the basic serve. But remember, its placement can be varied with a turn of the wrist to either side-line. It can be safeguarded too by judiciously used flicks and drives which are last-second changes of trajectory and speed. A static receiver in the momentary lull before action has the time to observe your every muscle twitch so each phase of each serve must be absolutely alike.

Remember, too, that in modern badminton 'cut' has now quite an important role. The cut-smash is described on page 111. The cut-drop is also deceptive in two ways:

1. The faster racket-head speed needed disguises the shortened flight of the shuttle.
2. The action of cutting across the shuttle results in the racket head moving deceptively at an angle of about 45° to the intended line of flight of the shuttle. In the reverse cut-drop, taking the shuttle over or slightly to the left of the head, the racket is best turned into a frying-pan grip. By fully turning the wrist outward, the forehand face of the racket can be made to cut down the outer side of the shuttle for a straight drop. A last second turn of the wrist to the right will deflect the shuttle cross-court.

Sleight of Hand In this category include the reverse cut-drop (see above), the double motion return of serve (page 125), the brush-shot (page 125), and the reverse net-shot (page 127). Each

owes its effectiveness to a preliminary movement that momentarily distracts the eye from the final and operative one.

Miscellaneous An occasional covert look, a visual double-think, can be effective. If you intend to serve low, a quick flicker of the eye at the back service line may sow the seed of doubt in your opponent's mind. Similarly, if you are serving from the side-line, intent on the back T-junction, a glance at the far front corner may also unsettle your opponent.

If you are tired, look jaunty; deceive your opponent into thinking you have boundless reserves of stamina.

Deceive also simply by refusing to play to a pattern, by having a wide range of varied strokes and placements, not a limited supply of predictable ones. It is all too easy to become a creature of habit; the backhand drop is always cross-court; the lob, to the backhand; the smash, down the line. So just kick that habit!

Practise and use a full range of strokes, be it in serving, returning serve or defence. Then your opponent is on tenterhooks, never quite sure, a worried man.

Body An *occasional* stronger-than-usual body action in overhead strokes may convince your opponent that you are about to play a clear or a smash rather than a drop-shot. Don't overdo the accompanying facial contortions or you will give the game away. But for a drop-shot to fool, it must have all the trappings of power. The body can also subtly deceive if, in moving forward to take a net-shot, you occasionally sway in the opposite direction to that in which you are going to play the shuttle.

Strokes out of Context Don't *always* play the obvious stroke. Against a strong defensive pair who retreat under pressure, a drop-shot rather than the orthodox smash off a three-quarter clear may be more effective. Similarly, if you have forced a weak reply from your opponent's deep backhand, he is likely to race hopefully for the probable cross-court smash. Don't oblige him. Smash at the spot he's just left.

Use deception when you are playing on level terms but not making headway. Use it, as the thin edge of the wedge, to wrong foot your opponent, to make the opening. Don't use it

Plate 34. Ray Stevens (England's No 1), out-flanked, plays a deceptive backhand cross-court net-shot. Mike Tredgett waits on 'alert' *(S. Perry)*

when you're under pressure because, as a deceptive shot by its very nature is more liable to error, you are now doubly error-prone. Instead, play safe, anything just to keep the shuttle in play. If you are in extremis then a deceptive shot is perhaps your only hope, a do-or-die effort.

But, remember, never overdo deception. That merely takes the shine off it. If there's a clear-cut, outright winner waiting for you, grab it gratefully on the spot, deception is the piquant sauce, not the main course.

SUSTENANCE

The more one studies the authorities the more one comes to three conclusions: They differ among themselves; athletes and sportsmen are beset by fads and fallacies; no one super food which will give immediate extra energy, has yet been found.

Calories remember are simply a measure of the amount of fuel a food will supply. In strict training Mr Average will need about 4,000 a

day to compensate for the 4,000 he will expend in physical exertion. Use a calorie chart to see that a diet well balanced between protein (for body building), carbohydrates (for energy), and fats, gives you this figure.

Simple commonsense is perhaps the answer.

When to Eat

A full stomach is not conducive to eager move-ment. As most foods take at least two hours to be completely digested it is wise to eat two to three hours before your first game. If you labour under the old fallacy that steak makes you strong as an ox, and psychologically, if not physiologically, it gives you an apparent boost, stick to it. But it will take longer than lighter foods to digest. If you favour one of the artificial foods such as 'Complan' it will take you under two hours to digest. You will need food, so eat just before pre-match nerves dampen all appetite. This may help to postpone the mental stimulation and the adrenalin flow that goes with it to more immediately before your game.

What to Eat

Your body and muscles have of course their own built-in store-cupboard of energy. Your meal must help to top this up for the duration of the event. Carbohydrates (sugars and starches) most readily burn up to provide energy fuel. Toast and honey with sweet tea is a simple and effective diet-of-the-day. Other carbohydrates will serve but do avoid greasy fry-ups and too much roughage. After looking at your programme or consulting the referee, plan eating times as far ahead as you can.

What to Drink

As you exercise, the creation of energy for muscle contraction raises the body temperature. At the same time it raises the blood temperature. This in turn stimulates the sweat glands which produce the cooling effect of sweating. This is much the same as the extinguishing action of a sprinkler system which puts out the fire which activates it. In this process you will lose not only water but also salt. Loss of the

latter will result in cramp which may force your withdrawal if you cannot continue to play. It is therefore wise to take extra salt on your food forty-eight hours before the event. Salt tablets taken during the event, without adequate dilution, can cause nausea or even vomiting.

Even though two pints of water weigh 2½lb there is no virtue in not drinking. At the best, discomfort in the form of thirst will result; at the worst, dehydration. This not only creates an energy loss but by increasing the pulse rate, puts extra stress on the cardio-vascular system.

After sweat loss you must take in water to restore the balance. Do so wisely. It is better to drink a little and often rather than in one gargantuan gulp. Equally obviously, avoid very cold or iced drinks or fizzy and gaseous ones. Avoid a surfeit of glucose drinks or an insulin response could be triggered off that would reduce, not increase, the blood-sugar level.

This cheap, home-made drink will counteract dehydration and loss of salt: To a quart of water add a pinch of salt, a glucose tablet, and the juice of one or two lemons.

For players who wish to learn more of diet than can be written here, an excellent book is *Diet in Sport* by Amateur Athletic Association National Coach Wilf Paish.

9 Stroke Production

GRIPS

It will do no harm to give your grip a quick 'service'. Especially if your forehand strokes aren't as wristy as they should be. If that is the case, make sure your relaxed basic forehand grip hasn't degenerated either into an over-tense, full-blown, or even a hybrid, 'frying-pan'. It's so easily done, quite unknowingly.

If all is well you can consider adding two variants:

Backhand In taking backhand shots *behind* you, you will be less likely to 'hit out' if you bring your thumb from flat on the back bevel to almost flat on the top one.

Net-shots Instead of using the basic grip you will get more feel for these very delicate shots if you bring your thumb up onto the narrow bevel between the back one and the top one.

Try them out. See if they work for you.

THE SMASH

This book would have failed dismally if it hadn't already tempted you to dip adventurously into the following pages. Logical development is fine, but to have a crack at the top stuff is finer still. On the other hand not only old proverbs but also wise coaches will warn, 'It's no good trying to run before you can walk'. Stalemate? So let's find a happy medium. First lay a solid foundation of basic strokes and tactics. Only on that will you be able to build the wider array essential at the top.

Be strong-willed. Resist the temptation immediately to have a disastrous 'go' at the lot. Take them one or two at a time. Reach reasonable proficiency with one before adding another to your steadily growing repertoire. And remember that whilst it's fine to have a ready answer to your opponent's every stroke and play, a wealth of half-mastered strokes will lead only to inconsistency.

Let's start with the smash. A highly satisfying stroke, it will, if you can force the lift, be the one most used in level doubles. Like all the other advanced strokes its variants will bring spice and variety into your game – and doubt into your opponent's.

The advanced smashes you must practise are all merely variations on a theme: (i) Round-the-head; (ii) Cut; (iii) Jump; (iv) Steep; (v) Half; (vi) Round arm. For usefulness try them in this order.

Round-the-Head Smash

This is a 'must' and a double delight to play. It has the normal exhilarating smash-power, and gives you also, the triumphant feeling of a man catching a train he thought he'd missed.

Aim: To maintain the attack on shots lifted to your backhand.

As its name implies, its difference is that the racket-head is not thrown straight up over the right shoulder. Instead, it is swung over to the left *round* and *above* the head. Impact is thus made over or even a foot or more to the left of the left shoulder. The height at which it is taken varies from full stretch to just above head height.

Its great advantage is that provided you move smartly, you can play strokes forehanded, rather than backhanded, even if you cannot get right behind them: a considerable gain in control and power for most players. Do not however get the idea into your head that now there is no need for a backhand. There will be times when there is just no alternative.

In doubles, again provided you move quickly, you should rarely have to play an overhead

Plate 35. Supple Gillian Gilks gives a fine
example of a round-the-head smash and kick back
(Mervyn Rees)

(i)   (ii)   (iii)   (iv)   (v)

backhand. In singles, there will be a number of occasions when the round-the-head isn't a viable proposition. Either because you just can't make it, or because although making it, you will be left nakedly off-balance. So a backhand is a necessary insurance policy.

The two main uses of the round-the-head stroke are these: (i) to return a clear or lob to your backhand; (ii) to attack a drive serve from the right-hand court hammered down the centre line.

In both cases you will be squarer to the net than in the basic smash. To maintain balance, place your left leg well to the side. This sturdy, balance-maintaining support is necessary because to reach the shuttle you will have to lean well over to the left. Swing back in the normal way but then for (i) swing the racket up to your left, over or beyond your left shoulder and for (ii) swing the racket back outwards and flat, in an almost circular motion rather than down and up.

Suppleness is a great asset here. The more supple you are the wider is your reach. Not unnaturally therefore ladies should play this stroke well. Sally Leadbeater is an excellent example. Although sturdily built, she will take with ease a shuttle a couple of feet to her left.

In (i) your point of impact should be as high as possible, anything up to two feet or so to the left of that for a forehand shot. In (ii) it will be much lower: at head height. If, as it should be, the drive-serve you are returning is flat, your

Fig. 28 Round-the-head smash. (i) Quick movement to left to play shuttle forehanded – not backhanded. (ii) Backswing; elbow up; body leaning to left. (iii) Forward swing; left foot well out for balance. (iv) Impact over left shoulder, wrist uncocking, racket head coming over shuttle. (v) Strong follow-through and back to base

forearm may well graze the top of your head. The round-the-head smash in this case is an excellent means of allowing you still to smash on the backhand side at a height which on the forehand would be hardly practicable.

Cut Smash
Aim: to add deception to an apparent power stroke.

The only difference here is at impact. In the basic smash you strike the shuttle squarely so that strings and shuttle base are roughly at right angles. In that way you obtain maximum power.

In the cut smash, crisply turn your hand and wrist inwards to the left. This will mean that with a closed racket-head almost at right angles to the net, you will slice the shuttle. This cutting action, played with a really straight arm and a full pronounced follow-through, will contact both the side of the feathers and the cork – not the base alone.

The result is pure deception. The actual spin imparted has nothing like as much effect as that of a tennis racket on a ball. True, it will cause

111

the shuttle to veer slightly to the left and to drop a little more sharply. Its real value is this: Your opponent, seeing the usual strong smashing action will, unless he is a very acute 'reader' of a stroke, expect a shot coming fast to his racket. In fact, if he is defensively dug-in and with his weight slightly back on his heels in defence, he may be surprised by a slower shot dropping 2–3ft short of him. Result: an occasional outright winner; more often, a rather hastily played lob of doubtful length, leaving the striker slightly off-balance, and open now to a full-blooded smash.

The cut smash is a stroke used mainly in singles where a single defender is more likely to be caught out than a pair. Use it when a power smash isn't 'on' or if you are not well-positioned. Its slower flight and the fact that it is taken lower by your opponent will give you fractionally longer to recover. And you have safely maintained the pressure.

The Indian Prakash Padukone is a master of this stroke. With a basic smash relying more on fluent timing and pin-point placement rather than sheer strength, it is doubly deceptive. And deception is a craft in which Indian players excel.

In men's doubles it is purely a mixer. Power smashing sometimes yields no dividend because of a metronome defence. If such is the case then an occasional variant of speed may catch your opponents out as they play too early in expectation of yet another all-out smash.

Jump Smash

Aim: to add steepness to power and to take the shuttle early.

Said Margaret Tragett, England's peerless champion of the 1910–30 era, 'I can only smash well when I jump'. And that in ankle length skirts!

But it was the pint-sized Malaysian champion Eddie Choong who made his name and brought English crowds excitedly to their feet with it.

Eddie had power but lacked the height needed to give steepness. To add considerably more to his stature he jumped vertically upwards two feet or so. Now with the height of a 7ft+ man he could – and did – hit down *steeply*.

At the same time there were two further advantages. With each jump he gained

cumulative fractions of seconds during a prolonged rally so relentlessly harrying his opponent into error. More than that, he could on occasion snatch a quick winner in a gap left unguarded for only a fleeting second.

It was this same ability to take the shuttle high and early that enabled the Chinese, both on their first visit to this country in 1973, and on their second in 1981 to leave English players stranded like whales. It opened wide the eyes of a new generation of badminton spectators who had never actually seen the legendary Choong or Hou and Tang.

Tremendous stamina and agility are needed to jump 2–3ft vertically upwards and then hit both powerfully and steeply down at the feet before swiftly following in almost in the same movement. It was this ability that made China's Jian and Changgjie in a class apart from the top English players. It is an essential skill for top flight today (see Plate 33).

Thrilling and effective it is but also fraught with difficulties. None however are insuperable. Eddie was reputed to have been weaned on rubber latex in the Malaysian plantations. So unless you too have rubber limbs you will have to develop ankle and leg strength out of the ordinary if your jump is to be a matter of feet rather than mere inches.

It must be perfectly timed as well as executed to make impact at the highest point. Being airborne robs you of some ground purchase and leverage for power. Nor, airborne, can the body add so much weight to the matter. Power has to come largely from arm, wrist and timing. Even with 'shuttle away' you still have problems of landing on balance, poised for quick recovery.

The jump smash is also extravagant in its consumption of energy and its sapping of stamina. Overuse it and you may well subside like a pricked balloon. Use it economically to gain steepness; to seize a fleeting opening; to hurry and to demoralise your opponent.

Practise it also jumping out *sideways* to intercept a shot 2–3ft to left or right of you. And if you wish to emulate Tjun Tjun, that great killer of flick serves, practise jumping back to get behind a speeding shuttle.

Plate 36. Dave Hunt uses the invaluable flat round-the-head smash to hammer back a drive up the backhand *(Louis C. H. Ross)*

Steep Smash

Aim: To ensure getting a lift.

A small but all-important variation, this. Steepness is of equal importance with power. A fast, flat smash can be attacked. A steep, slower one must be lifted.

Concentrate therefore on an absolutely straight body and arm at impact and the fullest use of the wrist. Stretch up! Concentrate on pulling down the shuttle as steeply as possible without hitting it into the net. (Conversely, a flatter smash, shoulder high, can just occasionally come as a nasty surprise!)

The steep smash is useful against a pair who, to take pace off fast, flatter smashes, have retreated a little but not so far that a drop-shot would be preferable.

Half-Smash

Aim: to maintain the attack if off-balance or tiring.

This is another variant for occasional use. Play with normal action, but as with a drop-shot, reduce racket-head speed just before impact.

Use it when the all-out smash is making no headway, if the cut-smash has been spotted, if you want to maintain an accurately pin-pointed attack whilst you have a momentary breather. It gives you more chance and time to place the shuttle in the most effective place.

Round-Arm Smash

This is a stroke little used today but it was employed most effectively in the 1950s by English international Warwick Shute. He used it only when he knew the shuttle had outstripped him, that it was too far behind him to be hit down by a conventional smash. Instead of using the correct throwing action, he would use a bowling action.

In other words, he saved the necessary split second by not bending the arm in the backswing. Instead the arm was brought up straight as in a cricket bowl. The smash lacked power but it held surprise and by strong wrist-work it brought the shuttle down from a position in which normally it would be hit up.

Note: A stroke only for an emergency.

Recovery

Never forget the obvious: a fast hit shuttle is always fast returned. If, therefore, you are to maintain the attack you've initiated, you must recover feet and racket quickly so that you're immediately ready to hit down yet again. Seldom smash when off-balance or badly out of position unless you are sure crunching power will give you an outright winner.

DEFENSIVE STROKES

Let me underline yet again that your aim in defence now is not merely to scrape the shuttle thankfully back somehow – though its return, of course, is essential. It is more, much more.

Aim: To return the shuttle in such a way, be it by aggression, surprise or by shrewd placement, that you wrest the attack from your opponents.

To that end you must use not merely feet and head but also a wider variety of strokes: drive, drop-shot, lob, dab.

But first a brief, very brief, digression on 'eye'. Soon you will be up against players who really hit a shuttle. Watch the sheer power of Kevin Jolly; follow if you can the forked lightning of C.H.P. Bacon. Probably no one locally will generate that kind of steam for you to practise against. So your answer is to get the best hitters you can beg or bribe to give you a twice-weekly ration of unstinted smashing aggression. To make up for their lack of 'super killer-power' either use faster shuttles or let them smash from closer range. Whichever it is you must concentrate on four things:

1. Watch the racket-head at instant impact, to pick up the line of flight.
2. Short but early and unhurried preparation – no last second 'snatching'.
3. Play aggressive returns with wrist or forearm only; no time for a long and elegant backswing.
4. Defend off the body. (See Plate 53.)

Digression over! Jack-of-all-strokes is the answer here. No matter how good you are at one return, it will avail you little. With no alternatives to shackle them, your opponents will be lying in ambush, ready and waiting . . .

Drive

Add this to your repertoire first. It is a comparatively simple progression from the push you've already used. Besides with sharper net-players now opposite you, the push will be intercepted. More speed is wanted.

So use your mixed doubles drive – adapted. You won't have the time for the long backswing and the shuttle may well be hit at you more steeply down rather than flat. To counteract the latter, move in a foot or two if you possibly can. Then you can play not only a flatter return but also an earlier return: both hallmarks of the great. To counteract the former you will have to find your power with arm or wrist. Watch Mike Tredgett in particular to see how he can whip back the hardest smash at his body with a mainly forearm action. And whip it back *flat*.

Drop-Shot

Try this next as again it's a fairly simple development of the push. It's mainly a shot for singles but if you've pushed back the opposing net-player in doubles with drive returns there may be a chance for its occasional use in that game too. It all depends on the opposing net-player's base and quickness of reflex.

Simply take the speed out of your opponent's shot by relaxing your grip or by slightly cutting the shuttle. A shuttle on a virtually dead racket should fall only just beyond the net and so force a lift. Remember to keep the racket-head pointing up and also to angle it up or gravity will pull your slow return down into the net. Under real pressure you may have to take the shuttle not in front of your body or even to the side but by use of a flexible wrist, just slightly behind you. In that way you take the shuttle when it has just a little less speed – though possibly at the cost of some lack of control.

Lob

Next, the complement of the drop-shot. The latter brings your opponent in; the lob over his head may unpleasantly surprise him as he hurries in, anticipating yet another net-return.

In doubles, it is a return to be used either when the smasher is not very strong or his partner at the net is very sharp. If the latter is snapping up your net-shots, pushes and drives with the avidity of trout taking may-fly, then the shuttle must be lifted. If the former isn't even knocking splinters out of your defence why not let him carry on? It's a sporting chance that he'll tire and lose his consistency, accuracy, what's left of his power and perhaps his cool. Dan Travers once fired eleven fairly lusty consecutive smashes at the Stevens-Tredgett defences. It took a lot of steam out of him and nothing out of them. His last despairing effort – into the net – was little more than a fast drop.

And what better example of the lob defender than Indonesia's big Ade Chandra. In the 1980 Friends' Provident Masters tournament he revelled in it. Taking up a backhand stance, he lifted cheerfully and deep with a strong upward sweep of the forearm, smilingly challenging even the Stevens-Tredgett combination to a battle royal – which he won handsomely.

The Chinese Jian and Chenggjie had developed an explosive return of almost pure wrist that extricated them, even deep in court, from the direct trouble.

Dab

The lob return if short, forces the defender to retreat almost to the doubles service line to avoid annihilation. (You can afford to do so only if you are quick off the mark, or have an agile partner like Christian, ready to nip in and take the drop.)

On the other hand when the defender plays a crouch defence dab he must move cheekily in almost to the front service line. It can be, but seldom is, played by men. Basically it is the very difficult shot which the man nevertheless expects his lady to play in mixed doubles! Her only consolation is that it is played against the longer-travelling, slightly slower-moving, cross-court smash.

To play it, move forward to, or just short of, the front service line. There, well on balance, crouch a little. Have your racket up at tape-height, just to the right of or directly in front of your face. With the racket slightly angled back in a frying-pan grip you have only to dab forward at a flat smash. And, with a little wrist, you can score a winner. If the smash is angled down, you will have to crouch a little lower and play upwards. Even so, with the racket turned away from the attacker, you can still be in business if he is a little slow to recover. If your opponent is smashing very steeply or very fast there is little to be done except retreat gracefully.

There is no better exemplar of this stroke than Gillian Gilks. Tall though she is, her wide stance permits her to get down to it. And her eagle eye and split-second reflexes enable her miraculously to snatch nonchalant winners out of thin air.

For the defender such successful dab returns are a morale-booster: the smasher smashed. For the attacker, a morale-deflater.

Close Range Body Defence

The other form of defence that you must practice is equally important: the return of short range dabs made into your body by the opposing net-player.

Now you have less time than ever to prepare your defence. If possible, still on your toes, sway sideways rather than remain square; this will help to eliminate the body and allow you a little more freedom of stroke. With shuttle travel-time virtually nil, observe the racket-head at impact. Time only for a bent-arm push. Seek to skim the tape, to hit the shuttle through or angle it away from the all-embracing predator at the net. And, of course, make the shortest of follow-throughs to enable the quickest of racket recoveries to counter further quick-fire dabs to the body.

This defence is easy to practise with a long-armed friend who delights in 'pin-cushioning' you from just the other side of the net. Fight your way out of that one!

In defence, as in attack, the difference between 'good' and 'best' can clearly be seen. To succeed at the best level you have to be impregnable when you have hit to a good length; even when your length has faltered a little. So practise constantly to build the essential eye and reflex movements. You are dealing in split-seconds!

It is good to play practice games in which you seldom lift; it is equally good practice to put yourself deliberately on the defensive and then slide yourself neatly off the hook. Satisfying too.

'Take it early' and 'Keep it flat' are two maxims to remember in match play.

It is equally important to defend aggressively against drop-shots. There is little future in merely scraping them with the dust from between the floor-boards. By agility and eager anticipation take them early – no more than 2ft below the tape. Then lob fast and flat down the side-lines, especially in singles, to speed up the tempo. And with super agility and anticipation

you can jump into a semi-lunge position to take the shuttle *above* the tape and dab it down for a decisive winner, or just *below* it to play a tight upward net-shot.

DROP-SHOT (FAST)

This stroke, second cousin to the smash, is a useful one and simple to acquire.

Aim: To hit the shuttle downwards fast and steeply enough *to by-pass the net player*, yet slowly enough to force the mid-court player to move in.

It is used largely in mixed doubles by the man, and sometimes in singles. It is an excellent pot-boiler maintaining the attack but with little expenditure of energy. For full effect it must be struck deceptively and with a nice judgement of speed.

It is played from deep in the rear-court when a smash isn't 'on'. The action however should be just the same as for a smash. The only difference is that the racket-head must be slowed to half-speed. The wrist must be brought over for crisp steepness.

Hit too gently and the shuttle will be intercepted by the net-player. Hit too hard and you will not force the man to travel the maximum distance forward so out-positioning him and forcing a weak return. Hit inaccurately and you risk interception.

FLAT CLEAR (ATTACKING)

Although hit up, the flat clear, if used in the right situation is, like the smash, an attacking stroke.

Aim: To surprise an advancing opponent with a fast, flat shot hit just out of his reach.

This is an easy-to-play variation of the high clear. To change a strictly defensive shot into an attacking shot is a simple matter which yields good dividends.

Trajectory depends on racket angle at impact. Therefore strike the shuttle fractionally earlier, that is, just in front of the head. Uncock the wrist less than for the smash. As a result of these two actions the racket head at impact will be angled only slightly upwards. The shuttle therefore will travel just high enough to elude your opponent's racket and give him little time to recover.

It is a deceptive shot. If it bears all the hall-marks of a drop-shot or smash, it may achieve either of two results. If a drop is anticipated your opponent may well move forwards; if a smash, he may well 'dig in'. In either case, he will be hard-pressed to recover – and there is open court behind him. Even if he does recover, a well-played (fast, flat, deceptive) attacking clear will leave him off-balance and with little option but to play a clear that, taken behind his head, is likely to be short. You have achieved your aim – a weak return of which you must take full advantage.

The flat clear is best used after a sequence of drops or smashes has proved unavailing. Played in such circumstances instead of yet another drop or smash, it comes as an unpleasant surprise.

Used mainly in level doubles, it can also be employed effectively in singles if your deceptive drop-shot or accurate net-shot has left your opponent stranded in the fore-court. It can be almost staple diet if you wish to speed up the tempo, constantly hurrying him. But you yourself must be very fit if your opponent decides to play you at your own game!

DRIVE-LOB
Another point-saving shot by the top players is, for lack of more definite nomenclature, a drive-lob – and all strokes in between!

To make myself clearer: If you are wrong-footed and the shuttle is falling low in the deep forehand corner, things look black. But, as this is a situation in which you may not infrequently find yourself, you must find the antidote.

Turn quickly, facing the back of the court, and lunge with the right foot to the shuttle whilst taking a full sideways backswing. If it is a desperate situation with the shuttle only inches from the floor, then with strong arm and stronger wrist action whip it upwards fast and straight down the side-line. Speed and a rising trajectory are the keynotes if you are to avoid an optimistic net-raid by an advancing opponent.

If the shuttle can be taken higher, then if you use the same strong action you may get away with a flat drive or even a drop-shot. This will depend largely on whether your opponent is now more circumspect having already suffered two or three of the surprise shots outlined above. But you'll have to recover quickly.

The drive-lob is a frequent Kevin Jolly shot. He is a young man who can generate amazing

power in the most unpromising circumstances. Sitting courtside when he plays it, one becomes a little less sceptical about initial shuttle speed now allegedly scientifically checked as 180kph off the racket.

LOW SERVICE VARIANTS
I have underlined that the basic doubles serve is the low one. Played well it has no equal. And although now I am going to suggest a number of variants, that advice still stands rock-firm. Variants are the hidden weapons, held in reserve, which threaten and curb, at least momentarily, the most rabid attacker of the low serve. Play them deceptively; use them thoughtfully and sparingly. Complementing your low serve, they will make it more effective.

Aim: To unsettle your opponent with varied low serves.

Before I describe these variants let me remind you of a too often neglected truism. '*There must be a reason for every serve*'. Never let serving become merely a matter of hurriedly hitting just another shuttle over the net. And that reason must be founded on shrewdly observed details.

Does the receiver stand too close in, or too far back? Too much to the right, or to the left? Does he hold his racket too high, or too low? In other words, 'Where is there a gap?' or 'Where is he weak?'

Which serve does he thrive on; which causes him trouble? Which serves of yours are mainly effective? What was your last serve to this player – and the four before that? In other words, 'What succeeds? What will be a surprise?'.

Vary your serve more in the first seven or eight points than you will later in the game. In this way you can probe your opponents' strengths and weaknesses. When you find such a weakness don't hammer it mercilessly. If you do, not only do you lose the element of surprise but you may play your opponent in, and so have no weakness to play on when in emergency it is most needed. He may learn how to deal with the problem you've handed him.

If, and at this advanced stage it seldom happens, your opponent appears incapable of

(*Overleaf*) Plate 37. Coolness, length of lunge and power of wrist get Liem Swie King out of rare but desperate trouble *(Mervyn Rees)*

finding the answer to one particular serve, then keep the pressure more firmly on. Constant failure in return of service can sap confidence not only in receiving but also in other branches of the game.

As I said earlier on, the serve to the centre line narrows the angle of return, forces the shuttle back within your or your partner's reach. If, as it goes direct to your opponent's racket, it is constantly rushed, you must obviously use other low serves before you desperately resort to panic-stricken high ones.

Pin-Point to Centre
Still serve to the T-junction area. But now with pin-point accuracy direct it to your opponent's backhand, or body, or forehand. This may result, if you are lucky, in your finding a weakness or a strength; or it may result in your being able to gauge the return more certainly. A tight, deceptive serve to one side or the other often elicits a *cross-court* reply that you can then anticipate. A serve to the body, some players find difficult to return accurately or they are caught in two minds.

Altered Serving Base
If there is no joy there, then take a leaf out of Ray Stevens' book and move your serving base a couple of feet or so off-centre. This leaves you, admittedly, with further to travel for a return to the distant net corner. But it does break your opponent's rhythm and present him with a different angle of receipt and return. It may also lure him into too frequently making the obvious return. I have seen this ploy used successfully even in singles. Derek Talbot conned points with it from young Andy Goode, over-eager for the kill.

Serve to Side-Line
Or, yet again, retain your central base and with a well-concealed last-second turn of the wrist, deflect the shuttle away from the receiver's hungry racket to the far corner. The action must be crisp in order to by-pass the danger area immediately within the receiver's reach. And yet not so fast as to overshoot the side-line. Remember though that the cross-court shot has further to travel than the straight, so hit it a little harder.

You've certainly cut down the possibilities of

the receiver getting an outright winner but the angles are wide open, the receiver's options increased: straight net-shot, push or attacking lob to the backhand, or cross-court drive or lift to the forehand.

So here again it's essential to have a discussion with your partner. He is the one who will have to bear the brunt of fast attack, withheld to the last fraction of a second, to either deep corner. If, without a bullet-proof backhand, he likes to take up his stance a little towards the backhand side then you may have to opt to hang back a little to intercept, with a Gillian Gilks snap reaction, the cross-court shot. Such failure to follow in does then leave the straight net return a likely runner. The options are unpleasantly numerous, but at least you're forcing a lift and not being pounded. You can't have it all ways! With luck you may find that your opponent has but one answer, as pre-ordained as the Saturday visit to the local.

Another deceptive variant worth occasional consideration was one cheerfully employed by fifty times capped Warwick Shute. Slightly altering his stance in the right court, he made it appear likely, but not too obvious that he was going to have a go at the outside front corner. A covert look there (or as a double-think, a quick glance at the deep backhand corner) then . . . The forward swing is seemingly aimed at the outside corner but a sharp turn of the wrist to the right sends it skimming straight down the backhand, half drive, half flick. An outsider, yes. But fun – and you *may* find a sucker just now and again.

Reverse Cut Serve
If your forehand low serve is making no impression then there's always the backhand variant already described (see page 69). In addition, of course, there is also the Sidek 'S' serve described on page 135.

RETURN OF LOW SERVE
In chapter 5, I mentioned dab, net-return and lob as useful service return shots. In this chapter let's see how to make those basic returns yet more effective and how to add to them other attacking variants.

Aim: By hitting down, flat, or very accurately to the net, to obtain the attack by forcing a lift.

First a quick reminder about court positions.

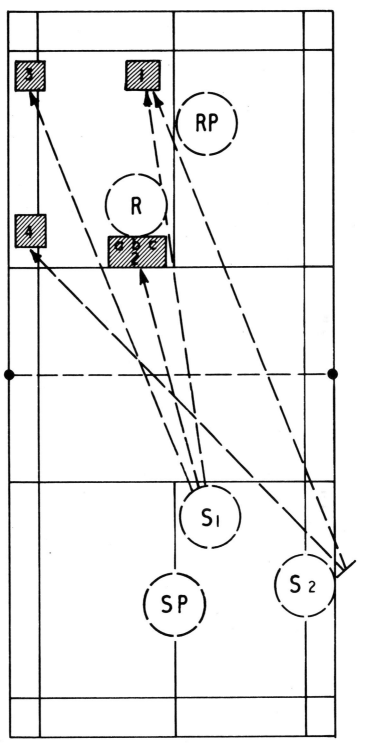

Fig. 29 Placement of serve (from right court).
(1) Drive or flick. (2) Low (a. forehand; b. body;
c. backhand). (3) Flick. (4) Low

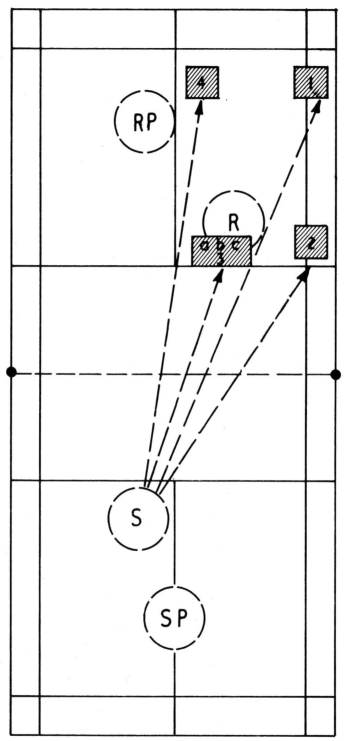

Fig. 30   Placement of serve (from left court).
(1) Flick. (2) Low. (3) Low. (4) Flick or drive

If you have edged forward an inch each week you should now be standing no more than 1ft back from the front service line if you're a man; no more than 2ft if you're a woman. Only from such a forward base will you be able to meet serves, as you must, within a foot of the tape. Besides the nearer the net you are, the more intimidating you are to the server – and this is a point never to be overlooked.

Your opponents will now be serving correspondingly better; the shuttle (if it's from Nora Perry's racket) will be dropping to below tape-level as it crosses the net. With less brilliant servers, it will have dropped within 12–18in of doing so. Unless, therefore, you can meet it in that region you will have little chance of really attacking it.

Three Essential Skills
Your ability to move that little faster will hinge largely on three things. First, your ability to read your opponents' intentions more clearly; a task, however, rendered more difficult by their greater skill in concealing them. It is vital you do so. Look for every faintest hint in mannerism or action until you develop almost a seventh sense.

Secondly, speed up your reflexes so that *as*

the shuttle leaves the strings – not as it crosses the Great Divide – you are leaving your starting blocks. This is where the split-second is saved. And it is achieved only by constant practice.

Thirdly, develop the leg-power that drives you forwards with the initial velocity of a bullet from a gun: one short driving step and a stride or even a jumping lunge. Instant, powerful action is the answer.

Like Tjun Tjun you must develop the same speed in moving backwards to kill the flick and, almost as important, recover your balance instantly to counter a quick return. Seek to gain such an ascendancy over both low and flick serves. Then your tail will be up; your opponent's between his legs.

Placing the right shuttle in the right spot won't make you any faster. But it will be almost as effective in making your *opponents* move further. Just as you carefully position yourself, so carefully note your opponents' positions. A backward serving base invites a net return. A forward base, with partner standing well behind, cries for a half-court push. If the server is too far forward, then a dab into the body is

Plate 38. Jack-in-the-box Tjun Tjun bounds back to kill *(A. C. Taylor)*

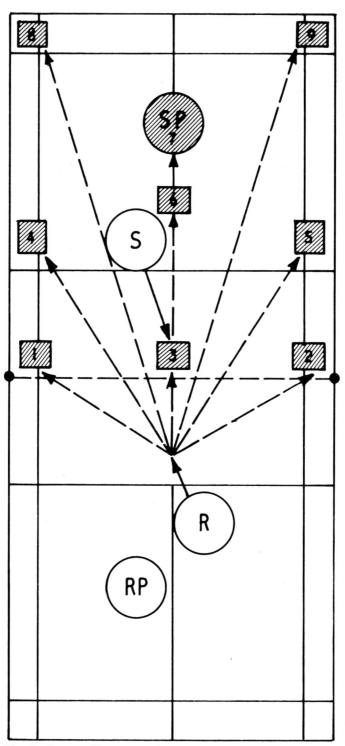

Fig. 31   Return of low serve. (1), (2), (3)=Net-
shots. (4), (5), (6)=Half-court pushes. (7), (8),
(9)=Fast rushes

required or a brush-shot just through him. If it is the server's partner who is too far forward then even the much-maligned lob to the backhand may have its day, provided it's fast and low. Shrewd observation will pin-point possible targets – but don't try for the right target from the wrong serve. Know your options.

So, to the cry 'Move – and make move' also add new strokes with which to threaten your opponent's serve and to hold him back.

Brush-Shot

This is used when a shuttle is taken right on the tape, or perhaps an inch or two below it. To dab will mean hitting the net. To avoid this fault move your racket in a firm, semi-circular sideways action along the net. It can be from right to left, or left to right. The shuttle, thus brushed rather than hit, will drop just over the net. If the shuttle is only inches below the tape, no more, you will have to crouch a little to get under the shuttle and thus add a little upward inclination to your rotary action. This latter plays a part in dragging the shuttle down quite steeply once it crosses the net.

In addition to enabling you to attack serves (or net-shots) right on the tape without faulting, it also adds a useful touch of deception. The server, observing the rotary motion of the racket, expects the shuttle to travel cross-court. That swift and slightly confusing action may stop him in his tracks, momentarily puzzled. In actual fact, unless you have angled the racket, the shuttle will fly straight.

Half-Court Push

This is a simple and delightful variant of the dab. Earlier, I have advocated if not brute strength at least a crisp dab into the server's or the server's partner's body; or an even crisper 'rush' into the back boxes. This if played fast enough will lead to an uncontrolled shot, restricted replies, or outright winners.

The dab must be placed with real accuracy. An experienced player will be able to defend fairly effectively against a shot aimed at the stomach. Therefore place the shuttle still further to your left, to his right. The target now is the right side of the body, rather than the centre. If your opponent defends this backhanded also, you will have to pinpoint your return still more precisely. So aim now still

further to the right until you reach that nice point where a backhand return is nearly impossible and a forehand one difficult. Under such extreme pressure there can be little clever placing of a return so make sure you are poised to hunt down the likely cramped reply. Alternatively, play an almost dead racket return that drops the shuttle only just over the net, in the tram-lines, away from the server.

Back to the half-court push. This you will use when the shuttle is tape-high – too low for a dab down. In itself its innocuous appearance – a mere push – belies its real worth. Its true value lies in its safeguarding deception and delicate placement.

Meet the shuttle early. Threaten with arm action (and face!) to fire a fast dab or 'rush' to the corners. At the last second, slow the action down and push the shuttle quite gently down between server and partner to the tram-lines. Added camouflage is a last moment turn of the wrist to angle the shuttle away to the opposite side of the court.

Its advantages are twofold. If played with just the right power, it by-passes the server. But tempting him, it draws him across court, half-turned away from the net. With the shuttle behind him, even fractionally, his return, if any, is likely to be out or uncontrolled. At the same time, his partner, doubtful as to whether the server will intercept the shot, also moves hastily across. If it is the server's partner who makes the return, it is likely to be strictly defensive, from near the floor.

Thus, with one simple stroke, two advantages are obtained. Both players have been brought close together thereby opening up a vast acreage of untenanted court. They may well clash rackets or leave it one for the other. Doubt – and possibly dissension – have been sown. Either is likely to make a weak return. A gem of a shot!

Double Motion Return

Deception is even more the mainspring of this stroke. Eighteen inches before possible impact, play a feigned push to your, let's say, left. Instantly recover the racket and hit the shuttle in the opposite direction – to the right.

Some receivers are suckers for this stroke. Obligingly they move in the direction first indicated. Thus wrong-footed, it is either

impossible for them to recover or recovery is so scrambled that only a weak return can result.

Others quickly spot the feint and unmoved (in both senses of the word) can play a sound return to your possibly inaccurate stroke. So try it out and note results. If one receiver isn't volunteering to be your 'bunny', tuck it away in cold storage for another who will. Jack Warwick of the RAF and now of the Badminton Association of England was a master of this stroke. His crisp 'one-two' action mesmerised many a player – leaving them not only tongue-tied but also foot-tied!

Reverse Net-Shot

Here again is a stroke relying largely on deception. It is particularly effective from the right court. Play it only after you have 'set the scene'. In other words you've returned three or four low serves directed to the centre, backhanded to your right hand corner of the net. This has drawn the server quickly across to his left in anticipation.

Now, having lulled him into the entirely erroneous idea that this is the full extent of your meagre repertoire, it is now the time for a change. Shape to play the same shot yet again. Then, just before impact, with your opponent well under way, dip the hand down and move it through 180° to the right. Now, you are able to sweep the shuttle flat to the left, still backhanded, to your opponent's distant right hand post.

If you are too late to play a net-shot just the same action can be employed to play a deceptive attacking lob to outwit the receiver's partner in the same way. But, as with all deception, a milli-second change of pace or direction, and an opponent who is ready to play Trilby to your Svengali is necessary. Also, for your part, you must have the accountant's cold ability to cut your losses – and there will be losses – immediately. Always count the total cost of that moment of fleeting, deceptive glory.

Flick Lob

Just occasionally change the slow, careful netshot action into that for an attacking lob with a last second flick of the wrist. Remember your opponent may be a Chinese fire-cracker so give it just enough air to avoid a spring-heeled interception.

FLICK SERVE AND RETURNS
Flick Serve

In service variation, this is your first priority. If your only alternative to the low serve has so far been a straightforward, obvious high one, there has been no real deception – unless your opponent is singularly obtuse. The flick will remedy this lack of surprise.

Aim: To hit a *medium* height serve with a *low* service action thereby deceiving your opponent.

So, up to 6in before impact, the flick must look exactly like the low serve, or there will be no deception. And deception is all.

Imagine your opponent is a badminton sleuth, searching with Holmesian acuity for the faintest clue as to your next move. A longer backswing or a faster forward swing, just because you have to hit the shuttle further, are old hat to him. He is looking for something far less obvious: a covert glance at the base-line, a fractionally longer (or shorter) time taken in preparation; hitting the shuttle earlier or later; a different racket angle; a bent knee or a dipped shoulder. It is all too easy to make a slightly different move that gives the game away. So think through each phase of your low serve – and make your flick an exact facsimile of it. Better still, get a tried and trusted friend to do it.

Back to the action then. The flick serve is just like the low serve until within 6in of impact. Only now do you crisply uncock the wrist to get height. No faster *arm* action, please. That does give the game away! And push through in order to get a reasonable length.

Not too much height either; that will give your opponent time to recover from his surprise. You want just enough to beat his upstretched racket, plus a foot or so extra because he may well jump to intercept. (Target area and follow-up action, we'll discuss under 'Tactics', though you could give the latter a bit of thought for yourself right now.)

Occasionally, you have the very real satisfaction of an outright winner. (Even the nicest of us can't repress a triumphant smirk after a bit of skilful fooling!) Not often though. So be thank-

Plate 39. Skovgaard gets down to it to play a delicate upwards push. (But oh! those background feet) *(Mervyn Rees)*

ful for small mercies if you elicit only floating drops or short clears – and be ready to deal with them summarily. They are the first stepping stones to a rally won. And if they don't come your way, remember the difference between the expert and the journeyman. It lies in holding back the wrist a fraction of a second longer. Surprise, zip, exact height and length, are what you're after.

You will hear much of the metronome-accuracy of Nora Perry's low serve, little of her beautifully concealed, crisp flick. And yet it is the constant hidden threat of her flick that makes her low serve the more effective, her opponents less eager to 'rush' it.

Return of Flick Serve

Unless you can make this as lethal as your return of low serve, you've let the server off the hook, given him an escape route. He may still have to suffer your scourging his low serves – but not so often, for now he has a viable alternative and you will have lost a little heart for the hunt.

Your answer is in drive, in speed. Speed based on thoughtful positioning. If you're just not getting back, then, for the time being, you must surrender the vainglory of toe-to-line. After all, that 6–12in retreat may not nullify your attack except against the very best of low serves.

Your anticipation must be more finely attuned yet. You've got to out-do the shrewdest detective. You've got to 'spot the lady'. Reaction time has to drop to nil.

Leg strength for drive and jump has to be improved. A flick serve, because of its lower trajectory, can be intercepted early. If you want a fine example watch Tjun Tjun: Back with a bound – airborne – two point landing – instant recovery – renewed aggression. A human Catherine wheel.

Notice where server and partner position themselves after the serve. Is it defensively sides? Optimistically back and front? Or a compromise? Upon this and upon whether the serve is to the centre or the side-line, depends your return. (Its exact placement we can discuss in tactics). Practise movement backwards straight and diagonally across court. You will need them both. A dignified walk will allow the shuttle to ingloriously outpace you. The only

result of trying to hit a shuttle that is to the rear of your head is to mishit it, or spoon it steeply up. And, for bad measure, you will leave yourself reeling backwards hopelessly off balance.

If you are 'away with the gun' and can get behind the shuttle to smash, do just that. If it's touch and go, settle for a controlled drop-shot played firmly downwards. Even an almost dead racket shot – servers are notoriously pessimistic and often don't follow in. If you were slow off the mark and the shuttle is behind you, there is nothing for it except a defensive clear, desperately seeking length.

Remember of course the big difference between playing these shots off a high serve and off a flick. Now, you're under pressure. You're playing whilst in full flight. You're error-prone. So play it with extra care and regard for the margins. But still attack.

And, also, your landing is likely to be more off balance. Recovery will be slower, so place the shuttle with greater care to ensure it cannot easily be whipped away from a still-reeling you.

DRIVE SERVE AND RETURNS
Drive Serve

This is another surprise up your sleeve, but one even more difficult to conceal than the flick, so use it sparingly.

Aim: To hit the shuttle *fast and flat*; to hit it into a gap or straight at the face; to hit it crisply and with surprise – all to force a weak return or even a complete miss.

The action must be like that for the low serve (and the flick) until the last possible split second. Then with a speeding up of the forearm forward movement, jab or punch the shuttle. This time it's all arm for if you use the wrist, the shuttle rises and a rising shuttle is too often a dead duck – it can, just as swiftly, be shot down.

The drive serve's most effective use is from the right court. Use it against players of slow reflex, who stand well up to the front line, or 2ft or more away from the centre line. Then the vulnerable backhand is often gloriously exposed. (See Figs. 29 and 30.)

It can also be used from the left court if the receiver leaves a gap down the centre by standing too far to the left in order to cover a weak backhand. In this case it is still more important for the shuttle to leave the racket crisply, to get it behind the player quickly. Then, even if it is returned, it is unlikely to be a controlled shot away from the server.

But beware the very real danger of over-shooting the back service line. The drive needs nice judgement of power: hit crisply enough to outspeed the receiver but not so hard as to fly out at the back. It needs surprise, accurate placing and a flat trajectory. To achieve the latter, impact should be only just below waist level and the wrist kept cocked back. But do keep the racket-head down. It is all too easy for it to creep slowly into the horizontal entirely contrary to Law 14(a)(ii).

Angled Drive There are two other 'drive' possibilities, useful at least up to advanced club standard. To get much more angle, position yourself with your right foot almost on the side-line of the right court. Hold the shuttle as far outside the line as you can without loss of balance. After a long look at the *back* centre T-junction, hit the shuttle flat and fast there to your opponent's backhand. Such a drive if accurately played will come into the receiver's reach only much later, much nearer the back doubles service line, than one hit from the conventional, central base. He is therefore tempted to play round-the-head smashes whilst off-balance.

It can also be played backhanded from the left hand court to a left-hander. A variant seldom used – except by the author.

Advantages? It attacks still more sharply a weak backhand. It puts pressure on the round-the-head man who can't resist a challenge. And, if after error, he does retreat, it opens up the fore-court for a fast, deceptive tape-skimming serve to the outside forehand corner. Ong Poh Lim and Ooi Teik Hock, the great Malaysian champions of the 1950s used it with great success. Experts at crouch defence, they counter-attacked the ill-balanced, over-optimistic smasher.

Disadvantages? All too obvious. Your partner is left to cover a frightening area of open court. It is therefore absolutely essential that you and your partner have a plan. Basically it will doubtless be for you to follow in to kill off the expected weak return to the net; for him to cover wide drops or the lift straight or cross-court. He must be on his toes for this. If the receiver has still other ideas, your plan will have to be quickly rethought. But if the serve is played well there isn't a lot left for him but to lift.

The round-the-head receiver will be forced by the angle to smash at the server. So here you must be instantly ready to turn his shot back sharply short across court. Off-balance, he will find it hard to recover. If your return is played crisply it should safely evade the receiver's partner who will have had to move very quickly to by-pass his partner and reach the net.

Return of Drive Serve
Success here stems from racket manoeuvrability rather than foot reaction. But again all depends on acute observation. Drive serves are generally from the right court, unleashed like cross-bow bolts at your left cheek or a fine gap down your backhand.

If the drive is too straight you may be able simply to play the shuttle just in front of the head with a controlled dab or block to the corner of the net. If the shuttle is wider and your reactions are gun-slinger fast, then use the more aggressive round-the-head smash.

Remember that with the latter it is all too easy to hit over the sideline and out if you are a fraction late, if the point of impact is behind your left ear. Remember too, you may be left off-balance. So take early and place your return shrewdly right into or right away from the body.

Return of Angled Drive If the server changes his serving base to the side-lines you too will probably have to change your strokes, tactics or even base. If the serve is badly played you will still be able to play a round-the-head stroke though you may well be a little more off-balance. If it is well played it will not come within striking distance until within a foot or two of the base-line. From such a position it is difficult to smash accurately or powerfully. If that is so, don't let misplaced pride force you into a losing duel.

Alter your tactics. If he is prepared to alter base, so are you. Drop back a pace and take up a backhand stance. A wide range of straight-forward backhand placements are now open to you. These are lifted strokes admittedly, but this is more than compensated for by the tatters

129

in which he has left his defences, especially if server and partner have no concerted plan of attack for dealing with your return.

Notice his partner's position. Go for the corners, away from him. Lift deep to the corners if he is close in; drop to the net away from the incoming server if he is hanging back. Outright winners are probably not on, but a lifted shot by your opponent is. Now it's your turn.

Oh, remember to keep your weather eye open for the low, cross-court alternative. You'll feel such a ninny if you're caught by it!

CUT NET-SHOTS

You have already learnt to play the dab and the straightforward upward net-shot. The dab still reigns supreme both in simplicity and effectiveness for a net-kill. The upward net-shot, however, should now be Mark II, one of the cut variety.

These are a comparatively recent innovation. And as such are played by the experts in slightly different ways to achieve slightly different – and sometimes unexpected – results. By their very nature they are rather more difficult to control accurately, especially on the forehand.

Basically a cutting or slicing action, with the head of the racket parallel to the floor, is applied to the base. This causes the shuttle to tumble over its own axis, cork base over feathers. Sometimes as well, to spin around its own axis. The result is that the receiver has to let the shuttle drop until it has righted itself and is falling base first.

Stab or Jab

In this stroke the racket, top-edge of the frame first, is stabbed or jabbed flat or angled slightly under the base. If the shuttle is met high near the tape, the stab must be limited or the net will be hit. As a result the shuttle will do little more than just drop over but very close to the net. If met more vigorously a little further away, the shuttle will somersault disconcertingly and if it hits the tape, will drop down almost vertically. Played at full stretch in front of you, it ensures the earliest possible take but is not easy to control. Some players feel they get greater control playing shots backhanded.

Cut

This is an alternative to the stab. The racket, with bent arm, is sliced strongly under the shuttle with the side of the frame leading. A much more vigorous tumble will be achieved at the expense of a slightly later take. It can be played forehanded or backhanded.

Derek Talbot, a recent English international, uses a slightly different action coming down the side of and across the base of the cork in an action he likens to 'peeling an orange'. As a result the shuttle both tumbles and spins.

To return a spinning shuttle take note of the cut imparted. If you play against it, the opposing actions will take way off the shuttle and cause it to jump up slightly. If you play with it, spin will be added to spin, causing a faster and tighter return.

For real effectiveness, the shuttle should be taken high but really skilled players can still control such a shot almost from floor level.

These strokes well repay the intensive practice necessary. In singles particularly, games can be won by the player who can tumble the shuttle most vigorously resulting in a drop so tight to the net that any return, and certainly one of good length, is virtually impossible.

BACKHAND STROKES

I have stressed that the best way to play a backhand stroke is not to play one at all – but instead, to play a round-the-head stroke. But this obviously is not always possible. Any attempt to do this when you have been wrong-footed or out-manoeuvred would only result in your tying yourself in a knot and being completely off-balance.

It is essential therefore, whilst taking as much in your deep backhand corner as possible round-the-head that you also develop overhead backhand strokes as an insurance, as well as a full range of other backhands.

Danish Wipe

This (page 69) doubtless has so far served you reasonably well. I recommend it, as do the Danes, because using arm, body and wrist rather than largely wrist, it is easier for most players to learn it as an initial stop-gap. It has however, disadvantages:

1. As the shuttle is allowed to drop, the wipe,

130

or any variant, must be hit up rather than down.

2. By virtue of the same reason, you lose – and your opponent gains – a second of time.
3. The wipe does not have as many variants as the overhead backhand clear.
4. It is more physically demanding and tiring.

Use it to return a shot played deep into your backhand corner. Remember, shape as though to play a backhand drive. Then in your forward swing instead of hitting flat, bend the knees slightly, sweep the racket down and then powerfully up and under the shuttle in an arc to lift it high with a strong follow-through forward and up.

If a player of the brilliance of Denmark's Lene Koppen can use the wipe so successfully throughout her career, it is a stroke that some ladies may be happy to stay with. Most girls and all men, however, should move on to the overhead stroke.

Overhead Backhand Clear

The five guide points we laid down on page 67 still apply of course. In fact the overhead stroke is virtually the same stroke as the drive but played in a vertical rather than a horizontal plane.

The backhand grip will certainly help to give you power through thumb leverage – and also greater control. If, however, you are taking the shuttle behind you, it helps to alter your grip slightly (page 38). Place your thumb along the top bevel rather than flat on the back one.

Turn your body to face the backhand corner. Your right foot, in advance of the left, points into it. The back, not the side of your shoulder is facing the net. It is therefore important that you turn your head to keep as much of the court in view as possible. As the right foot goes down, lift your elbow up almost to head height so that it is pointing into the dropping shuttle. As a result your racket head is down at about stomach level. Bend slightly at the knees.

The forward (or upward) swing utilises body, arm and wrist but it is the latter which predominates. As you snap your bent arm straight, also turn your forearm strongly to bring the back of your hand facing the net at impact. At the same time, straighten your knees, and spiral the body upwards to utilise the latter's weight as

Fig. 32 Overhead backhand clear. (i) Quick movement to backhand corner. (ii) Back of shoulder to net; elbow up, racket-head down. (iii) Arm snapping straight – wrist still cocked. (iv) Impact, over shoulder, straight arm; wrist uncocked. (v) Quick turn to regain base

(i)   (ii)   (iii)   (iv)   (v)

much as this stroke permits. Punch upwards with your elbow as the arm straightens. And in the zip area, uncock your wrist strongly to make racket–shuttle impact high above the right shoulder. The follow-through is only a foot or two as this is basically a snap stroke.

Wong Peng Soon, the greatest of many great Malaysian players, was a small man. Despite that, he had the perfect, seemingly effortless clear. His power lay in his steely wrist and his perfect timing. David Hunt, a former English international, uses a fast arm as well as wrist action. You will need to experiment with both. Beware equally of almost forgetting the arm and seeking to clear simply with a flicking motion of the wrist. Use both.

It is essential, of course, that your clear has a full length. That, initially, may seem a distant and almost unattainable goal. It can be achieved by regular practice, use of shuttles of correct speed, hitting straight, and forearm- and wrist-strengthening exercises; above all, by concentrating on *timing*. It is so easy to uncock the wrist fractionally too early or too late – the racket-head speed has been dissipated uselessly or never fully generated instead of utilised fully exactly at impact.

Backhand Drop-Shot

This is obviously a much easier stroke to master as the shuttle is hit only just over half the length of the court. But unless you can clear well it loses much of its effectiveness. Your opponent, knowing your clear presents no threats, can safely move in for the kill when he has forced you to play an overhead backhand. So the stronger your clear, the more effective your drop-shot.

As with the forehand, actions for clear and drop must be similar. Here too the arm and wrist action must be slowed down. To hit down, the point of impact must be further forward and the wrist rolled smoothly over. Though a crisp shot is essential don't overdo the wrist action or the shuttle will be hit down too sharply – into the net!

Beware too of over-playing the *cross-court* backhand. It is indeed the natural swing. So natural, unfortunately, that many club players unwittingly turn it into a habitual shot, one that is soon spotted by an observant opponent. It is therefore accorded the doubtful honour of a ready-and-waiting reception committee.

Much more frequently, control what comes all too naturally. Force the racket-head straight through for a straight drop. Ray Sharp, Kent and England representative, was a master at both.

Emergency Overhead Backhands

So far you have doubtless thought of clears and drops as being played at full stretch and with a straight arm: the classic Gillian Gilks or Prakash Padukone action. Quite often you will find this not to be the case. If you have been wrong-footed by a deceptive attacking lob or clear, you will find the shuttle over your head and making tracks for the back-line. All appears to be lost.

Not so! Watch Sven Pri for example. He turns, runs and then crouched and with back to the net and a nonchalant snap of the wrist, plays a good length clear or a deceptive drop-shot. No time for the purist's straight arm, for the shuttle now is sometimes only a little above head-height. And yet it is amazing what power a strong wrist can generate even in these most difficult circumstances.

Similarly you may find yourself with the shuttle not so much behind you as wide of you towards the sideline. Here again you must adapt and learn to play the stroke with the arm and hand away from the body instead of, desirably, close to it. Again wrist and arm compensate for lack of body–arm co-ordination.

And it is in those kinds of shots as well as the more leisurely ones that you must learn to play your backhands effectively. This is the difference between the good player and the very good. The former has no answer. The latter has a stroke that extricates him from the deepest and darkest of holes to fight again.

Backhand Smash

Who hasn't heard of Flemming Delfs? Not just as a former world champion but also as the possessor of the world's most powerful backhand smash.

A more than useful shot: at best it makes an outright winner from an unpromising situation;

Plate 40. Sign of a master. Sven Pri (Denmark), deep in rear-court trouble, still plays a deceptive backhand (*Louis C. H. Ross*)

at worst, it maintains the attack. In the former case it is morale-shaking and disconcerting to learn that there is little change or respite to be found in a quick lift to the backhand. Finally it is a means of snapping up a fleeting opportunity, especially in singles and mixed where there is more open space than in level doubles.

In actual production it relies on quick reflexes and a strong wrist. It is very largely powered by a wrist flick, aided and abetted by some forearm. Take it as high as you can, forward of the head. Initially restrict its use to that from mid-court; later it must become effective from rear-court too.

Backhand Serve

The basic version of this stroke I described way back on page 69, a tribute to its usefulness and simplicity.

Now, there are still useful variants of it for you to learn. The basic stroke had its roots back in the 1920s; those that follow are very much products of the keener thinking of the Open badminton of the 1980s.

For 100 years, the shuttle has been held by the feathers, base down. For 100 years it has been the cork base that was hit — most certainly not the feathers. Our variants here stand badminton on its head.

Torpedo Serve One of the snags of the backhand serve was that it was not as easy to serve backhanded to the corners as it was forehanded. Thoughtful experiment showed that if you held the shuttle horizontally like a torpedo and not vertically, you changed the shuttle's direction. Try it like this.

In the right hand court, hold the shuttle thus with the cork pointing to the right. When you hit the shuttle, most of the impetus is taken by the side of the base which then veers to your left and so to your opponent's right side-line. Properly mastered, the stroke sends the shuttle very crisply across the receiver to the side-line although the racket-head direction is deceptively straight ahead.

Alternatively, the shuttle can be held with the cork pointing to your left. If you then turn slightly and aim your racket as if to your

Plate 41. Swedish maestro Sture Johnsson illustrates a powerful backhand smash *(Mervyn Rees)*

opponent's right corner, the shuttle will fly instead to the central T-junction.

From the left-hand court, a shuttle with its base to your left will fly to the tramlines. With base to the right, it must be aimed to the right for it to fly safely to the centre.

Very intriguing, but there are snags: an observant receiver will doubtless note the torpedo hold, then deception is lost. Against the unobservant and the unversed, however, it may well mystify if not overplayed. Even against the observant, it can be tried as an occasional mixer with possible surprise effect.

The other snag is in holding the shuttle. Holding it by the feathers presents no difficulties. Holding it by the base is not so simple as the hand tends to get in the way. But with practice you won't rap your own knuckles.

Reverse Spin Serve Pioneered in 1979 by the youthful Malaysians, the Sidek brothers, it caused first a furore and then a storm. When used initially it took leading England players by surprise. A little later in the 1980 All-England Championships it led to the defeat of a disgusted Swedish No 1 pair, Thomas Kihlstrom and Bengt Froman, former All-England title holders, a pair who would normally have beaten the young Sideks ten times out of ten. Such was the efficacy of this new serve.

The storm came when the legality of the serve was questioned at the International Badminton Federation Council meeting. As the rules stood it was certainly not illegal. After discussion, the Council proposed on two counts to make it just that.

First, on the score of shuttle damage: a new shuttle with really stiff feather plumes and quills takes more spin than one in which they have been softened by play. There is therefore a tendency for spin-servers to want frequent change of shuttles, the feathers of which must obviously have been damaged or weakened to some degree when struck in this way.

Secondly, the Council found the new serve gave the server too big an advantage. This despite the fact that only a year before the same council had considered legislation to make the receiver stand back from the front service line in order to lessen *his* ever-growing dominance over the server! As in war, answers are already being found to this new weapon.

135

Plate 42. Kenya-born Dipak Tailor demonstrates a Malaysian speciality, the reverse spin serve, at Wimbledon *(Louis C. H. Ross)*

Place the racket with its face slanting slightly away from you. Hold the shuttle by the base and point it downwards slanting into the racket at a slight angle. Swing the racket to the left and then to the right. The strings will now cut crisply against the firm lap-edge of the feathers and spin the shuttle.

The shuttle then veers and wobbles in an S flight and also dips quickly to safety below the tape. The result is twofold. Its erratic flight may cause an eager receiver to miss or mishit the shuttle. If he hits it cleanly and attempts a net-shot, the spinning shuttle may well fly 'out' from his racket or down into the net. There is nothing for it but to let the shuttle drop until the spin is not effective, then lift.

The server, by sweeping the racket up as well as across, can also play a very useful flick.

Ray Stevens, England's No 1 and a thoughtful student of the game, studied and practised the serve assiduously. He used it with mixed success in the Men's Doubles in the Friends' Provident Masters Championships. But three months later he used it effectively throughout his English National Singles final against Kevin Jolly, thus generally forcing a lift. A revolutionary ploy, for seldom if ever can an entire singles have been played on a low serve — and a backhand one to boot.

Author's note: The proposal gained a majority but not the two-thirds needed to amend a Law.

Thus, the backhand is just as richly prolific in strokes as the forehand; and at this level you must play them all just as efficiently. Set aside a fair share of your practice stint for backhand strokes. Use them to the full in practice games where winning is a minor consideration. Make your backhand fire-proof!

10 Advanced Tactics

ADVANCED SINGLES

Singles have long been the darling of both the paying and the playing public. In the big-time tournaments it is the singles which attract the greatest individual prize money. It is the winner of the singles who gains prestige, who becomes the World's No 1. In tennis everyone knows Borg and McEnroe, Navratilova and Evert-Lloyd; but how many times do they know the doubles finalists and runners-up?

So too with players. 90 per cent of the young men want to play singles. Why? First, for the greater exercise: it's a test of gruelling fitness. Secondly, it's uncomplicated by a partner: in victory or defeat, you alone call the tune. A clear-cut man-to-man battle!

Court Positions

By now I hope you have played and enjoyed a weekly single. If so you should have mastered the basics. Now you are ready for a faster, more varied game.

In chapter 6, I suggested you make your base on the centre line about 5ft behind the front service line, a position in which you are roughly equidistant from the four corners.

Now you must learn automatically to vary this base slightly to suit the situation. Your aim is to narrow the angle of your opponent's likely returns so that you most effectively cover them without leaving a vulnerable gap.

If you serve from near the centre-line to near your opponent's centre-line, a base astride it neatly bisects your opponent's angle to either side-line. If you serve to your opponent's side-line, the likely straight and therefore shorter return will take less time to arrive than the longer cross-court shot. So, move your base 12–18in nearer the side-line. Thus you are equidistant from the two possible replies – not

in distance but in time. Apply this precise siting of your base not only to serves but also of course to other strokes in the course of rallies. It saves that vital split second.

In the same way, it can pay you to move your base slightly backwards or forwards. If you have played a really good length drop-shot, your opponent will be able to lob effectively and safely only by hitting very high. This means you can edge in 18in for the alternative net-shot and yet, because of the lob, have plenty of time to get back to it.

So too with net-shots: having played a really tight one, it would be folly to retire to your base. A return net-shot is hopefully inevitable so stay in on the front service line ready for a chance to make a lunge net-kill.

Now too is the time gradually to advance that general base by a foot or two. This will ensure you can take drop-shots early and yet, because of your increased mobility in running backwards, still get behind any lobs or clears and be on balance. The faster you are backwards, the nearer you can base yourself to the net. Ask Han Jian!

You can also narrow your opponent's angle by your own thoughtful stroke placement. If, slightly off-balance, you are playing, let's say, a clear from deep near the right side-line and your opponent is well placed centrally, it pays to play straight rather than cross-court. By doing this you need move only to within 18in of the centre line not 18in beyond it as you would have to, to cover the straight reply to a cross-court shot: 3ft less to cover. Your length should be better too. And the better your length, the narrower your opponent's angles.

Cross-Courting

The natural swing is cross-court. This means,

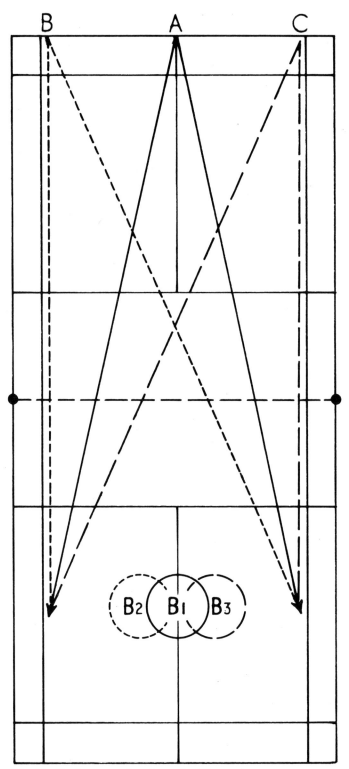

Fig. 33 Singles: narrowing the angle. When
shuttle is hit to A, B1 is base; to B, B2 is base; to
C, B3 is base

138

under pressure, you are more likely to play cross-court than straight. So let's have a closer look at the pros and cons.

Pros: (i) A cross-court smash *crosses* the defender's line of vision and is harder to pick up; (ii) a cross-court shot, judiciously played, has a surprise element; (iii) it may make your opponent run a greater distance and change direction with more difficulty.

Cons: (i) From a central base they are easier to intercept; (ii) they take longer to reach their target so giving your opponent longer to reach them; (iii) the length of the ideal clear increases from 44ft to 47ft 2in; the drop-shot from 22ft to 27ft 9in — error creeps in; (iv) it opens the angles.

The balance seems to be slightly with the 'cons'. Nevertheless there must be a place for cross-courting. But it must be used at the right moment or it will rebound. And that moment is when your opponent is out of position or off-balance — and you are neither.

Then there is the chance of an outright winner. Even if he scrambles the shuttle back, you've had the extra time to position yourself effectively. Open the angles in attack; narrow them in defence.

Cross-court only if you feel you can be 'bouncing' on your correct base before your opponent plays his return. If you are still moving, he will probably switch his return to the spot you've only just hurriedly left.

Serving

For simplicity I recommended the high serve for almost full-time duty with the low serve getting just a cursory mention. So first let's look at the former in more detail, and then at necessary variants.

High Serves In top class badminton 75 per cent of serves are still high. And of these, 80 per cent are very high to the centre. This leaves you with 20 per cent occasional 'not so high' serves to hurry your opponent backwards and break his rhythm. As you vary the height, so too vary the target area. Serves to the centre narrow the angle of return; to the sides, open it. What you lose on angle with serves to the side-line you can regain by opening up the court. Some players who don't move so well diagonally, fail to get back fully behind the shuttle with a resultant weaker clear.

It's a question of swings and roundabouts. Experiment. See what suits your game, what irks your opponent. But remember if you vary your serve too frequently you may not only break your opponent's rhythm, but also your own. If length and accuracy falter, stick to the

Plate 43. Two vital singles qualities shown in a single photograph. Alert Prakash Padukone (India) has played a tape-hugging net-shot; aggressive Morten Frost Hansen (Denmark) is racing in for the net-kill *(Mervyn Rees)*

very high to the centre. The advantage of this serve is that it drops vertically not in a gentle parabola. Feathers and side of the base must be hit, often less cleanly. Timing too is made more difficult.

Constantly check your length. If the receiver's back foot isn't behind the base-line or his smashes seem unusually sharp, you're probably way off target. So, get length!

Low Serves Once seldom if ever used, they are now in frequent evidence.

The high serve, if of good length, certainly pins back the receiver. But it is he who has the attack, who has had the lift presented to him. Instead of such quixotic generosity, a low serve to an opponent who must stand 2–3ft behind the service line *forces a lift to you.* To make full capital out of this you must be able to move quickly: back to smash or drop any lob, probably directed at the backhand; forward to attack any net return with dab, a return tumbler, or a flick lob. You'll certainly need a really strong backhand too.

The low serve is generally and best delivered with the normal action. It can however be played deceptively – a 'flick' in reverse so to speak. The high serve action is slowed down at the last moment to fade into a low serve. Ex-international Ray Sharp is a master of the art: with it he gleans a point or three from the inexperienced and at the same time dents their sang-froid. So slip in one or two low serves early on. Unwelcome surprises.

Yet another alternative successfully used is the reverse spin. Its spin makes it difficult to return accurately to the net; the receiver therefore has little option but a definite lift. Andy Goode has won more than a few singles partly thanks to his disconcerting, very powerfully cut serve.

Flick Serve Always regarded hitherto as a doubles stroke it is today in singles vogue. Now that the low serve is in frequent use, it is essential that you have a safe-guarding complementary flick serve. With the receiver 3ft back it may appear vulnerable. But as ever there are compensations. Too often the *doubles* flick goes out over the back service line, so there is little trouble in deceptively flicking the full length of the court. And, 3ft back, the receiver

fed a sequence of low serves, tends to commit himself perhaps a little too fully, forwards. This serve is best used after a gruelling rally when energy is at low ebb.

Drive Serve Seldom used at top level but a useful occasional mixer on the lower rungs of the ladder. Hitting flat and fast out of a high serve action, you can surprise a slow reflexed or over-ambitious receiver, or find a gap against a badly positioned one. Beware the quick return!

Returns of Serve
With more varied and aggressive serving, consistent and varied returns are a must. Again, with added experience behind you and low serves to cope with in front of you, a rather more forward base should be assumed, about 2–3ft from the front service line.

Some of the 'tops', Flemming Delfs is one, take up a much less-threatening stance than in doubles. Admittedly far more often than not you will have to dance backwards but I would advise an aggressive, if more upright, stance.

This is your first vital stroke, your chance to gain the initiative. You have time on your side, so no indecision, no hurried errors. Play, initially at least, to safe margins for you cannot afford to lose a point so easily. Your return depends on the depth and direction of the serve. It depends also on what base your opponent takes up, so use your peripheral vision. Varying your returns, be alert for a weakness.

High Serves Now that you have both a full-length defensive clear and a deceptive attacking clear, these, together with drops, straight or to the corners, provide a dozen instant answers. But use clears sparingly (and more often make them flat, attacking ones) or you will lose the attack as soon as you are given it. Even off good length serves, provided you are well-balanced, fire the occasional fast smash. Use it as a ranging shot, a deterrent that shows your metal. Cut smashes or drops are an excellent alternative. Keep the attack!

Low Serve You will seldom get so loose a serve that, from a rather deep receiving position, you can dab it down. Beware the tempter, one an inch above the tape – it may be a Trojan Horse. Push it flat and a keen-eyed receiver may intercept it and flick it over your head. Ray Stevens is a master at this.

Generally, therefore, meet it as near the tape as you can. A really tight return is essential if you are to get a short lift. The more you can cut it, the longer the receiver must delay his return.

If the receiver is slow following in, you may have time to give the shuttle a little air in a 'hair-pin' net-shot dropping vertically down the net. Alternatively you may with a flick of the wrist, play a fast, attacking lob to the backhand.

Again a word of caution. Receiving what seems to be an innocuous low serve, it is all too easy to relax, so practise until no return finds the net, and no lobs are hit out.

Flick Serve From your base 3ft back you should be able to bound back in time to smash if it is at all short. But if it is of good length you must be on balance, more, be actually moving in as you hit or you will be left stranded by a net-return. If in doubt, settle for a threatening drop that momentarily has the receiver rocking on his heels, or a half-smash that enables you to regain your scattered wits and footing.

Drive Probably seldom attempted, this should be dabbed down if still rising; blocked gently down to the corner of the net if flat.

Reverse Spin Net returns are fraught with error if played while the shuttle is still spinning. They may well be hit out or into the net. There is little option but to let the spin abate then lift fast and low, not too low, to the corners.

General Play

The modern game is generally a fast, attacking one. But it is useful to be able to play a defensive game too. This will enable you to get a 'breather' if necessary or to break up the game of an opponent who thrives on attack.

High, deep clears and slow drops are the order of the day to move your opponent or to force him into error. The backhand may be harassed repeatedly or the shuttle kept largely to the centre of the court to narrow the angle, cramp returns or upset the opponent's length.

The attacking game of a top class player will not differ greatly from yours in general outline but enormously in detail.

He will move so much faster and earlier; seldom wrong-footed, he will always be on balance; quick in recovery; neat in change of direction; dynamic in acceleration, jump and lunge. He will hit so much harder and be more powerful in smash and desperate recovery alike. He will use a wider range of strokes (all strong) and an in-built deception; have an 'early eye' that makes defence look child's play; be consistent in length and accurate to an inch; be resourceful and cool under pressure.

To particularise, let's look now (as we shall in chapter 11 at other greats) at Liem Swie King – no mean player on whom to model yourself!

Attack This, not defence, is the bed-rock of his game. His aim? To outspeed you, outwear you, and out-hit you. With the shuttle high in the rear court he has the same options as you. Even from deep in court he will play blistering smashes into the body or find the gap inches only from the side-line. As a variant he will play perfectly concealed cut-smashes to draw you stumblingly forward. If your length is impeccable, he will play bullet-like attacking clears to send you reeling backwards or delicate cut drops to draw you falteringly forward. The floating drop disappeared with the advent of the fast net-raider as swiftly as the whale with the coming of the factory ship and the harpoon gun.

There will be no chink in his backhand armour. Generally, of course, he will be fast enough to maintain the pressure round the head. Occasionally he will resort to a backhand – a steely second best that can clear, smash or drop with power and precision.

Your attacking lobs or clears will be countered with winged-footed jumps sideways to maintain the attack. Your defensive net-returns of his smash will be given short shrift by a lunge-jump; net-killed or countered at the tape with a cut net-shot that gives you little option but to lift high and short.

Neat dancing steps, a jump, a steep smash . . . These are the hallmarks of Liem Swie King.

(Overleaf) Plate 44. Ray Stevens' early take – a net-shot or flick-lob – has Japan's Zeniya in two minds. Plate 45. Despite a perfect lunge, Zeniya's late take causes Stevens no hesitation *(Mervyn Rees)*

His deep serves will have a metronomic regularity of height and fall within mere inches of the back-line. His tape-skimming low ones will draw you forward to lift to the net, then make a darting early take; or draw you to the backhand corner to be met by round-the-head or backhand attack. The initiative is his – he will maintain it if he possibly can.

Defence Defend he must sometimes. The blitzkrieg attack is replaced by a Rock of Gibraltar defence. Rocket-gun smashes, robbed of speed, will be returned tape-caressing just over the net to bring you racing forward. Or, if you are too eager, they will be whipped over your head into the most awkward corner. Drops will be anticipated and returned at near tape-level with interest as net-shots, or wristily, deceptively, flick-lobbed over your head. Too-low attacking clears may well boomerang as his dancing feet position him to jump and intercept. Defence, all too soon, becomes attack.

No man is perfect. Assume that at last you have out-foxed him. Your clear is behind him in his left-hand corner, not perhaps as deep as it should be. Back turned to the net, knees bent, arm not straight, he plays a backhand half-smash or drop. Even from that position there lurks the threat of a clear if you are overbold. Driving feet are forced into instant recovery. He's back on level terms, or better.

A better length, deep in his forehand corner? Jump not possible. He turns, runs, then lunges towards the shuttle he has let fall well behind him. Secure in his power of wrist, he lashes it high and deep for temporary respite, or deceptively strokes it just over the net. There again is that instant recovery, that uncanny anticipation that sends him homing in on your reply.

No joy in the rear-court. Is he vulnerable in the fore-court? A tight net-shot will be countered with one tighter still or a lunging kill. Occasionally with discretion for once the better part of valour, he lets it drop a little before with arm, wrist and forceful follow-through he lobs it high enough to gain every last possible inch of length.

For once he hasn't read your tightest drop. Shuttle low, inches from the floor, your hopes are high. He bends low to play a still perfect net-shot straight or cross-court.

All men are mortal. Where then are his weaknesses? Prakash beat him by deception: by drops and lobs and attacking clears that got the shuttle behind him. China's Han Jian's implacable defence and threat to his World No 1 ranking made him lose his cool and lapse into error. Indonesia's Hartono, whose mantle King took up later, also beat him. Unaccountable lethargy and mistakes dogged his game. Ugly rumour whispered he had been given his orders.

You will learn much by watching the experts. Do not fall into the error of watching everything and seeing nothing. Study one facet of the game at a time: feet, and movement; positional play; serve; smash; drops; defence; tactics. Such skill is not observed in a single sitting. Steel yourself to forget the game; to observe only the player and the shuttle. Make notes. Draw up suitable analysis sheets for each phase.

ADVANCED MEN'S AND LADIES' DOUBLES

Men's doubles have long been the highlight of top class international matches and tournaments. Here, from the first drop of the shuttle, the emphasis is on attack: aggressive receiving; power smashing; and quicksilver net interceptions.

Necessarily there is another side to the coin, defence: the fiercest smashes parried by seeming sleight-of-hand and lightning reflex; the impetuous receiver curbed by deceptive flicks; drop-shots whipped up into play again from the very floor boards.

Long fluctuating rallies are the order of the day. No fewer than 103 strokes were played in a match between David and Eddie Choong, and Johnnie Heah and Joe Alston. Attackers are thrown back into defence; defenders, against all odds, seize the initiative. Movement and power are offset by the subtle delicacies of tape-hugging low serves and net-shots.

Ladies' doubles on the other hand have until recently, long been the black sheep of the doubles family. At one time they were derogatorily known as 'glassy eye'. Not because the players were so aged and infirm as to need such props, but because of the effect of their play on the few brace of spectators remaining. Lengthy rally after lengthy rally of defensive clears, of unadventurous stalemate, produced a glazed look in the eye of the beholder.

Not so today. By no means. Not all badminton ladies are be-shorted, athletic Amazons, but up-and-coming youngsters who, probably teething on a racket, are a pretty tough lot. RAF physical education instructors, no less, put top squads through paces strenuous enough to make the average man blanch. As a result they move with speed and grace and hit the shuttle with the crack of a whip. Glassy-eye is dead!

A modern ladies' doubles can be nearly as exciting as a men's doubles. See our English world champions in action against a challenging Japanese pair and you have high drama indeed. Dour, left-handed Jane Webster smashes with relentless precision; blonde, glamour girl Nora Perry like some avenging angel, sweeps in to the net for the kill.

And on the other side of the net scamper two diminutive Japanese girls still with breath enough to twitter shrill instructions to each other. Tom-boyish Saori Kondo launches herself into the air like a rocket; Mikiko Takada dives to take a shuttle inches from the floor, inches from a point against Japan. They fight with the tenacity of samurai.

Don't be deterred. Such absolute dedication and fitness are only for champions. But given a reasonable modicum of those qualities, your game too will be aggressive; a delight to watch and a delight to play.

Partners
Before we move on to see how your tactics and skills must be extended for you to become an expert, a word about partnership. A real partnership will always have a distinct edge over two individuals.

To that end, partnership at this level is much more than merely playing with someone you like. Certainly you must have rapport, and a similar burning enthusiasm that will not only result in playing and practising together and in entering tournaments, but also in constructive discussion.

It is important that overall you are of roughly equal ability. If your styles and attributes are too similar, you will pose fewer problems and spring fewer surprises. If they are complementary, the opposite may apply. (Scotland's No 1 pair are at their best with powerful smasher Dan Travers at the back and brilliant interceptor Billie Gilliland at the net.) Between you there must be all the outstanding qualities – but no real weakness.

You must each have confidence in the other. Seek to encourage and protect your partner if he is going through a bad spell. Try then to raise your game and somehow fill the gap he leaves. Grins, not groans, raise morale.

Together you must improve your game: real severity in the rear-court; rock-like defence mid-court; deadly anticipation in the fore-court; nearly invulnerable low serves; crushing service returns – and everywhere apply the early take! These are the experts' ingredients. But without the right shot at the right time to the right place, without tactics, they will be to little avail.

The 'in and out' (or 'back and front') formation is used almost 100 per cent. When defenders are playing attacking, cross-court lobs off smashes, there is a growing tendency for the opposing net-player to drop back to maintain the attack, and, of course, for the smasher to take over at the net. Quick reaction and partner-understanding is necessary. But it does obviate the danger of the original smasher being caught off-balance in one corner unable to maintain the attack in the other.

Court Positions
Server Try now to serve from a little nearer the front service line. This will give you two advantages: (i) the receiver has less time to move in and attack; (ii) you will be fractionally quicker in to nip net returns off the tape.

Server's Partner Realise that this is a highly skilled role. If your partner's serve is having an off-day or he is facing a rapacious Eddie Sutton, you are the last back-to-the-wall line of defence. Scramble it back somehow; then you're still in with a chance. Resignedly watch it go, and one hand down, you're in deep trouble. So it's a dynamic defensive position, eyes watching the receiver's racket at impact, ready for instant movement of feet and racket – a vital skill too often left unpractised.

In defence, learn to defend off the body with limited swing, or to eliminate it by a quick pivot. In attack, seek the early return and accurate placement of half-court pushes. Be prepared to jump to intercept any attacking lobs.

145

Receiver By now you must be perfectly poised no more than a foot from the front service line, able to go back as fast and effectively as you go in, attacking all serves.

Receiver's Partner This, as when you are the server's partner, is no two-bit minor role. The former was mainly defensive; this must be attacking – so adopt a dynamic stance from which you can maintain the attack, not lose it through a moment's sluggishness of mind or foot.

Change of Position This is as described formerly (page 77) but like everything else speeded up and precisioned. You must learn to adjust to balance even the slightest move by your partner; to cover gaps created by his movements; to anticipate; to seize the initiative; to move when he moves – not just when he plays his stroke. Only then will you be unhurriedly and soundly on base before your opponents even hit the shuttle.

In attack, as net player, you should now be able to make your base some 2ft behind the T-junction. From there you can better intercept drives and pushes. But you must still be quick enough to dab down even slightly errant net-shots.

And from this position you must also be able to bound back to the backhand rear-court to maintain the attack. Your opponents may have whipped your partner's smash high, cross-court, while he is still in the forehand rear-court.

In defence, don't position yourself exactly alongside your partner. If you are cross-court to the striker, move a little forward and nearer the centre line.

Serve and Return of Serve

Neither the low nor the flick serve are particularly difficult to produce in themselves. It is the threatening conditions under which they have to be played that can be the difficulties. Quiet confidence must overcome them for at this level the best servers generally win. Try not even to think of the possibility of your serve being 'killed', though be ready for the weak return.

Although you are faced by a 5ft net and a rampant receiver just beyond it, try not to be

intimidated; be calm, consider. Remember:
1. You can take your time – even five seconds after you have taken up your stance keeps the receiver on tenterhooks; calms your jangled nerves.
2. Don't look at the deterring, threatening, uplifted racket; look instead at grubby shoes or knobbly knees. A shabby tiger indeed!
3. There are open spaces, small admittedly, behind, in front, or to the side of the receiver into which you can place the shuttle.
4. Nerve, coolness and confidence can counter intimidation and *must*.

If you follow this advice then despite restrictive laws, you will regard the serve as an attacking shot, one that can tame an attacking receiver, force a lift. In this chapter you will add considerably to your fire-power, to your surprise quotient, by learning a wider variety of serves.

Serving

Low Serves In this league, 2–3in clearance of the tape is suicidal. Now, you must have a serve that planes down from its upward flight just *before* it crosses the net, or literally skims it with scarcely space between it and the tape for a cigarette paper. Only then is it directly unassailable.

How to achieve it? Dare I say yet again? 'Practice' and under match conditions. Add to that the slow almost inching care of a Ray Stevens. Look at the close-ups on television. See the concentration.

From near the front line, the low serve to the centre is still king. But now pinpoint your placement – to the forehand, into the body, to the backhand. Somewhere you will find a slight flaw or a more predictable return. A really tight, deceptive serve to the forehand often leaves the receiver with no option but to follow his natural cross-court swing and return to the forehand; so too on the backhand.

Make your follow-in more effective too. Threaten in order to force a lift to your partner. If your opponent is made of sterner stuff and plays a net-shot, be there to 'knock it off'. Look too for the subtle half-court push. Crouching slightly, controlling it carefully, steer it back to your opponent's half-court target. Success here can leave opponents with no option but to lift and prevents your partner being unpositioned. And even that lift if it is a low, attacking one, can sometimes be intercepted with the help of radar-anticipation.

If you just cannot serve from centre-line to centre-line because of an aggressive receiver you have two more low-serve options. (1) The delayed turn of the wrist (remember you must hit a little harder on the longer diagonal) to place the shuttle between the side-lines. This certainly moves the shuttle away from the receiver's racket-head. But you've opened the angles, cutting yourself out to some extent and putting your partner under backhand and cross-court pressure unless you achieve real surprise. (2) The change of serving base 2–3ft near the side-line. It leaves you further still from the far net corner but the new angle may upset the receiver's rhythm. Ray Stevens has found it useful in times of stress. In both cases, partner consultation is called for because they are 'roundabout and swings' strokes.

Flick Serve Your next alternative is the flick. Don't be panicked into using it too early, until your low serve has been well and truly collared. Then, when your opponent is leaning eagerly a little too far forward, comes the right moment to sow doubt in the receiver's mind. Remember serve *just* high enough to beat the racket plus a possible spring-heeled jump.

Two problems: where to place it – straight or cross-court? Is the follow-in necessary?

As to placement, the pros for cross-court seem to have it. (1) The receiver is forced away from his base and is possibly weak on a wide forehand. (2) A longer distance to the target area enables that stronger, crisper flick which gains vital initial surprise but now does not overshoot the back service line. The cons? The angles are opened.

To follow in, or not? The optimist, confident of an effective serve, moves in to kill the enforced weak drop. The pessimist, fearing the worst, drops back to sides and loses his chance, but is much more happily positioned if the drop becomes a smash.

If rule of thumb isn't for you, can you immediately assess serve effectiveness? Going in if you've got the shuttle behind the receiver, dropping back if you haven't; knowing your opponent's limited or likely returns. None of this is easy and needs both partners alert and ready to adapt.

Drive Serve As one more imponderable for the receiver, why not make an exploratory drive or two? Its virtues and vices were dealt with on page 128. Hugh Forgie, of *Badminton on Ice* fame and eleven times World Professional Champion, suggests the sharpest power is generated by the long backswing server with a steely wrist. Speed and surprise are all. Nevertheless at very top level it is the quick-reflexed receiver who generally holds the balance.

Backhand Serve You have, of course, alternated forehand with backhand serving just to see if the receiver 'has a thing' about the latter, or if it's working more smoothly today than the former.

Very High Serve All that remains is the very high serve: the forlorn hope, the silly option, but one which may have the receiver rolling in joyous but *careless* rapture. Hit very high and dropping vertically, it can cause error of timing or clean hitting. Its sheer cheek may cause over-hitting. Try it if shuttles are slow; your defence is very strong; your opponent's attack weak; or, simply, if nothing else goes. Use it very sparingly, it may just break their rhythm by its apparent quixotic fecklessness before you slip it back into cold storage.

And do remember, have a reason for every serve.

Return of Serve

Important at any level, return of serve is vital at this advanced stage. Success ratio in gaining a winner or a lifted return must be 80 per cent plus. Put a Gilliland hoodoo on your opponents. Break their essential concentration and confidence. Take a calculated risk from the outset to gain the psychological edge.

Return of Low Serve Return serve at the earliest possible second. This not only gives you a better angle of return but it also forces the server into a hurried reply. You and the shuttle have roughly equal distance to cover to the net. So make sure you meet the shuttle as near the tape as is superhumanly possible.

First make sure you have in your mind's eye a

147

precise picture of your opponents' formation before they serve and immediately after. The shuttle must be returned to the most awkward spot possible; often there is a half-court gap.

If the serve is very tight to the tape you have only a split second in which to decide to use attack or attacking-defence. Be prepared to change your stroke to an upward one if you cannot dab down. Change the pace and direction. Play a brush shot or, if need be, bend your knees to get under it rather than hit down and inevitably into the net. You cannot afford to lose one point with a single stroke.

Avoid the flat or even slightly rising push return. Speed does not always mean success. The half-court shot must threaten − to avoid interception − and be hit down into the gap. The rush must be equally precisely placed, into the chest not onto the racket. And if lob you must, make it a deceptive fast 'flick' lob.

Return of Flick Serve You must be 'reading', using agility to the full, jumping if necessary to raise the mortality rate of your opponent's flicks. But remember placement and recovery are both vitally important. Hit straight or you may be outpositioned; hit steep or you may be counter-attacked. To cause confusion, hit down the centre; to force the shuttle back to you, hit into the inner side of the directly opposite defender if they have dropped back to sides. Sometimes a half smash or a carefully placed steep drop-shot is the better part of valour; a wristy one if you are in trouble. Even then, recover instantly. Move feet and racket so you are ready to attack a half-court push or drive into the body. Both must be taken early and high if you are to maintain your attack with net-shot or push.

Return of Drive Serves These you hammer back into the server's body. If you are off-balance your shot will be flat. Your opponent can then deflect the shuttle away from you to the right and your partner may be unable to help you because your wide round-the-head action has hampered his moving in. A down-ward block to the corner of the net is the alternative.

Return of Very High Serves Treat these with a little suspicion and a lot of care. Accept them gracefully rather than greedily. It is all too easy to mishit a steeply falling shuttle if you're trying to pound it spectacularly through the floor-boards. Besides, such savagery gives you no extra points.

Return of Reverse Spin Serve All depends on the amount of shuttle spin. If it is only average, a careful rush or net-shot into the body is still possible. If it is really veering and dipping, a rush invites a miss and a net-shot may be ill-controlled. The only answer is to let the shuttle drop. If possible play a looped half-court shot but if your opponents are likely to move in exceptionally fast then you will have to settle for an attacking lob. In both cases use all the deception you can to blunt the back-players attack and do all you can to return the inevitable smash *flat*.

Middle Game

By now you realise the vital importance of serve and return. Are you yet equally aware of the importance of the middle game? These are the next three or four strokes, often played by the main protagonist's partner.

Each player from the outset must be alertly poised, keenly observant. As receiver's partner you must maintain the attack; as the server's, more often, you are the last line of defence, or dominance may still be swinging in the balance. Early tape-high takes pushed flat or dropped with deceptive delicacy just over the net, or skilful attacking-defence off the body, are the answers.

Think out and practise the middle game. Jump to it!

Attack and Defence

In this context your attack must be the 'irresistible force'; your defence, the immovable object. One of you at least should be withering overhead; both of you sound in defence.

Attack − at the Back Here the accent now must be on sheer power and the speed of foot and recovery to maintain it.

First, it is important to probe to find which is the weaker defender. The attack should then be centred on him but not if this involves cross-courting over-much or playing the wrong shot − an optimistic smash instead of a sound drop.

Note too on which flank your opponents defend less well.

Next, note the defensive formation. Where are the gaps? If centre or side-line, then smash. In the forecourt? Then drop. In the rear-court? Then an attacking clear.

From the centre, probe down the middle with your smash to seek indecision. This also brings your net-player into the game with a chance of interception. Alternatively, blitz the weaker player or the one that is stumbling back to base after a desperate lob or clear.

From the side-line, smash at the inner side of the player opposite to obtain a cramped return back towards you. If, as is often the case, a player adopts a predominantly backhand defensive stance, then attack the forehand side. But where this involves hitting to the side-line beware of over-shooting it. Such a defensive stance may leave a gap down the centre.

Adopt such a general, though not pre-ordained, pattern of attack, then, not guessing in the dark, your partner can move accord-

Plate 46. Seeing double. A down-the-middle smash causes Japan's Yonekura and Tokuda to clash (S. Perry)

ingly, hopeful of intelligent interceptions.

Variation of Pace If the defence holds out, other tactics must be applied. First try varying both the pace and steepness of your smashes. Whilst a succession of flat smashes at chest height invites fast pushes, an occasional still flatter one at the right shoulder may surprise your opponent — especially if he has moved in. Secondly, vary your regular pace, which tends to produce a metronome reaction, with the occasional half-smash or cut-smash. It may break his rhythm. Provided you can still hit into the body, a rapid switch from forehand to backhand and back may be equally disconcerting. Find the weaknesses.

Drops and Attacking Clears Still no breakthrough? Then bring your other attacking shots — the drop and the attacking clear — into

149

operation. In these days of attacking-defenders, only the most skilfully camouflaged slow or 'floating' drop is likely to survive.

The cut drop may supply this cover. It can be deceptively played cross-court. It looks as though it will travel further and faster than it actually does. The nearer defender therefore makes no bid for it. The distant defender finds it falling short and has to make a hurried rescue effort.

Generally drops are played to the centre. If you play them nearer the weaker or slower player you may force a weak return from him or lure his partner into rash poaching. If you play slightly nearer the stronger, his very speed may lure him to play a net-shot. Then, if you can return this to rear-court, you now have the weaker player at the back, the stronger at the net.

And as a complementary shot, the punched, flat, attacking clear will catch the defender racket down and too far committed to take yet another drop, badly off-balance. Having moved your would-be victim up and down the court, the smash should be used again. If your smash is really powerful it is worth using it even from near the base-line occasionally, not optimistically but certainly disconcertingly, just to show you can never be taken for granted.

At the Net

Tactics here are much more limited, more basic. What must be improved is the number of interceptions. You must constantly pose a threat that harasses the defenders. But remember the controlled short-fall dab can be just as effective as the more error-prone all-out kill.

A slightly deeper base helps but for the rest there is no magic formula. Lively feet and watchful eye are a good basis. But it is only constant practice and experience that can speed up your returns into reflex ones. Add too a dash of take-a-chance.

Obviously in a match, dash is tempered with discretion. Even the most eye-catching side-line interceptions lose their sparkle if you are left facing the line as your opponent turns your uncontrolled shot right away from you.

Standing further back for half-court interceptions you may not always be able to nip down net-returns by the defenders. When the latter are still mid-court, a return net-shot is the answer.

If your partner misguidedly smashes straight down the side-line be prepared for a cross-court drive or lift. If the latter, provided you have an understanding with your partner, bound back to maintain the attack which he is unlikely to sustain, having the whole width of the court to cover. In either case, move your base a little to the left or right of centre.

A round-the-head smash applied to a shot speeding past your left shoulder is a desirable, optional extra. Ask Gilliland or Pri. So too is a crisp backhand kill. Ask Nora Perry.

Defence

In your early days, you probably heaved a sigh of relief if you returned one smash in three. Now you sigh if you don't return five out of six, and as often as not regain the attack.

Watch Christian and Chandra. You'll be staggered how easily they return the hardest of smashes. Watch Tjun Tjun and Wahjudi. You'll be even more amazed to see how they drive them back with interest, follow in and nip the return off the tape to stand the game on its head!

How do you acquire a Stevens–Tredgett defence? The answer depends on several factors. (i) The strokes that put your opponents on the attack. (ii) Your positional play. (iii) Your stance. (iv) Your reflexes improved by constant practice under heavy fire. (v) Your returns. (vi) Your placement of those returns.

Lifting When you lob, presumably you are under pressure. Nevertheless, you must make the best of a bad job by lifting high to give you time to regain a sound defensive position. Even more important, your lob must be deep to minimise your opponent's power and to maximise your chances of switching to attack. In addition, lift either to the weaker opponent, or so that the more effective and likely straight return will be to whichever one of you has the strongest defence. Blunt their attack.

Positioning Now, the early days' strictly central sides-positioning must go. If you have hit to the corners (lifting to the centre leaves the centre gap vulnerable), you must position yourself to narrow the angle. In addition, against smashers of moderate ability, move your base forward for the early take, high, that enables you best to push and drive. Against really powerful smashes your only hope of survival may be to drop back within a foot or two of the back doubles service line. You dare do this only if you can dart forward to deal adequately with alternative drop shots. Your chances from here of snatching the attack are lessened but at least you have taken speed off the shuttle and should survive.

Stance This must be dynamic, enabling you to retreat or advance quickly. It must be such that you can pivot quickly to eliminate the body if, as is likely, that is the target. Some players like to be square to the net, racket across the stomach, ready to cover either side easily. Some, stronger on that flank, like to defend with a definite backhand stance.

Such a stance is often more effective because strokes can be played with a shorter swing — there is no time for a long one. It also precludes too much switching from one side of the body to the other. In the right hand court it makes any attack on your forehand dangerous in as much as shots inaccurately fired there may overshoot the side-line.

On the other hand it tends to leave a central gap. If your partner moves across to cover this, it leaves his backhand flank a little more vulnerable. And it does leave you open to accurate attack on your forehand.

The answer then is not to commit yourself too completely and to learn to defend back-handed not merely on the backhand but on the body and even a foot or so to the right of your body. Anything wider than that, then you will have to pivot quickly and take the shuttle not in front of you, but to the side or even fractionally behind you.

Whichever of these two stances you choose, always try to advance a little from your base. Even a foot or two once your eye is in, carries the war into the enemy camp. Several feet forward into the crouch position against a flat smasher is even more disconcerting. But beware sudden attacking clears over your head.

Practice This alone will sharpen your reflexes. If you know no one with a whizz-bang smash get others to smash from well in front of the back service line or provide them with fast 83speed shuttles. In practice games un-ashamedly lift. You'll lose initially but the proof of your improvement will be shown by steadily better scores. And in tournaments if you meet C.H.B. Bacon or Ray Stevens or some other thunder-bolt merchant, rejoice. Here's the acid test!

Return of Smash No masochist now as you play in deadly earnest; your aim is to wriggle off this sharpest of hooks as speedily as you can. Therefore play flat, or off the flat smash, play down. Much depends on the positioning of the net player, your main threat. If he tends to cover the cross-court at the expense of the straight, or vice versa, play accordingly. If he hangs back, play net-shots. And follow them in so that you can threaten his return net-shot to force a lift. Your partner must now drop back.

If your opponent is well in, then play a fast push. If he gobbles this up too, you'll have to use all the reflex God gave you: drive, and follow in. If that's not one of your skills (yet!) you'll have to lift and still be in trouble. If your opponents have no pile-driver smash however then this can be a useful ploy for you — a fatiguing and demoralising one for your opponents. (And, incidentally a favourite one of the great Choongs who could probably have returned a shooting star.) No time often for a long backswing — now it's a perfectly timed wrist flick or strong forearm sweep.

Placement Where to place such returns? Permutations are endless according to the strength and weaknesses of all four players. As a basic precept, lift to the weaker opponent, or so that the likely straight return will come to the stronger half of your partnership.

If, as is generally the case in top level play, all four players are armour-plated, the latter does not arise. Play net-shots to the corners. Follow them in and if a return net-shot is played, keep it just there, on the net. Play lobs too, to the corners. Both will move your opponents and open up the court: high and airy, if you are ultra-confident; fast and low if you are intent on forcing error and fatigue. But with net players hanging back these days, ready and eager to bound back, see that the low ones conform to safety regulations.

151

Play drives straight into the smasher's body before he has recovered his racket and poise. Cross-court only if that 'backward' net-player hasn't the usual eagle eye. And do follow in or the momentarily seized attack will be as quickly lost.

Return of Drops and Dabs So far we have thought mainly in terms of returning the enemy's main thrust, the smash. What of his skirmishing probes, the drops? At all costs, by agility and anticipation, seek to take them early and high enough to play an attacking cut net-shot. An outright winning dab at this level is a rare luxury but a tight net-shot can be there for the playing. If your opponents' skilled deception and cut strokes hold you back momentarily, a push, risky if lifted too high, is the least you can do; another lob which merely returns the status quo, the worst. Probe the backhand by all means but at this level attack will be maintained round-the-head. The best you can hope for is to hurry the striker off-balance. Then seize your chance.

The other less clear-cut form of defence (which you will have to master equally well) is against a series of attacking dabs into your body by an opponent. This may be the attacking net-player or an opponent seizing the attack while you are still at the net. Here the answer is the manoeuvrability of a light racket and reflex reaction aided by keen observation of the racket at impact. Short arm swing, instant racket recovery and flat returns are as obviously essential as using every endeavour to angle the shuttle away from the human octopus opposite. Do all you can to avoid slugging it out toe-to-toe if your opponent is a better Bronx brawler than you are.

When this threat is first apparent you must think under pressure. Decide whether you have time to drop back or whether you will stay in under cover and leave, hopefully, a better placed partner to cope. Don't retreat too far or you will be vulnerable to a deceptive stop drop-shot, and try not to be still moving as the attack is launched.

ADVANCED MIXED DOUBLES

Mixed doubles have long been the most played branch of the game in English clubs. And from such a vast reservoir of mixed talent have risen players and pairs who were world-beaters.

In the 1930s it was Betty Uber, partnered initially by her husband then by agile, hard-hitting D. C. Hume. In the 1950s it was craftsman Tony Jordan, first with trim but lethal June White (perhaps the greatest net-player ever), then with Jenny Pritchard and Sue Whetnall. In the 1970s, tall and powerful Gillian Gilks, partnered in turn by zippy Roger Mills and eager-beaver Derek Talbot. Today it is the inimitable dead-pan Mike Tredgett and vivacious Nora Perry combination.

With the Danes (except for a one-against-the-book USA win) England shared the All-England title for thirty-two post-war years. It was only in the late 1970s that the all-conquering Indonesians showed any interest in mixed. And in 1979 the completely unorthodox Christian and Imelda Wigoeno at last broke Europe's stranglehold.

Today, with the threat of Chinese emergence from the badminton wilderness, England must look more keenly still to her laurels. What then are the outstanding qualities that must be added to the basics given in chapter 6? For ease of comparison let's take them in the same order.

Lady's Role

Once play is under way, her base is never static but constantly shifting fractionally. No longer can she afford just to bestride the T-junction. With so little time in which to play her shots she must cut down the distance she has to move.

So, if her partner is attacking down either flank, she must move a foot or two towards that side hoping to make a controlled interception. Then she'll be nearer the likely straight return but not so near that the centre of the net is left unguarded against a cross-court shot. If her partner is stranded or off balance on that flank or if he lifts, then she may be wise to move unobtrusively just to the other side of the centre-line to defend against the probable cross-court drive or smash. She must develop a sixth sense for these shots.

Normally her base is just in front of the short

Plate 47. The focus is on well poised and positioned Karen Chapman (England); close behind is long-armed Billie Gilliland (Scotland); aggressive receiver is Skovgaard (back view for a change) *(Mervyn Rees)*

service line. If her opponents are playing very tight to the net she may have to advance it a little; if they are constantly and successfully passing her with half-court pushes she will be wise to move back 18in to 2ft, though never so far that she can't nip off net returns.

Serving No pair can reach the top without the lady having a nearly fireproof low serve. Most points are scored off her serve as her partner is then more ready to maintain the initiative won than when he himself is serving.

Such a serve must have an almost metronomic regularity. To be secure it must be dropping as it crosses the net. Even then it will only be safe if she has a complementary, perfectly disguised threatening flick that holds the raider in at least momentary check and denies him the early take. Such a low serve will be achieved only by endless practice under pressure, relaxed concentration, confidence and refusal to be intimidated.

She must also add to the effectiveness of her 'return of return'. To this end, she gradually advances her serving base, right up to the line if possible. To counteract the steeper trajectory caused by this advance to the net, she can try two remedies. Both result in the shuttle being struck at a higher level and so achieving a flatter trajectory: (i) Rise up on tip toe – no wobbling though; or (ii) shorten the grip or bend the arm still more so that impact once again is higher (beware faulting!).

If, despite this, the new base results in a rising serve, the retreat must be sounded. The serve itself is of prime importance. If it doesn't, then several advantages accrue. First, she is rather less open to the push to the body, and, moving in less hastily, she is less tempted to 'snatch' at shots. Secondly, her opponent has a shorter time to move to the shuttle or to decide upon what return to make. Thirdly, and vitally important, she will threaten more effectively and be able to counter her opponent's net returns *at or above tape level*. It is an immense help to her partner if she effectively cuts off brush shots or gentle half-court pushes. The initiative is maintained.

See what I mean? No? Then watch Nora Perry throughout a tight match play these strokes. Nothing else. Then you'll learn!

The low serve to the centre must now be pinpointed more accurately: to the body for a cramped reply; to the forehand for a return to the forehand, or to the backhand for a return to the backhand. If the serve is tight, quick and deceptive, leaving the receiver with little time or opportunity for anything but a reflex return, it will often be played cross-court. Find out then which flank produces the weaker return. Try also to read the wrong-footing, deceptive return.

Occasional serves to the side-line deflect the shuttle away from a destructive racket, sow a seed of doubt, and bring her opponent well away from base. On the other hand they open the angles and, if served from the right court, they leave her partner's backhand very much exposed. The ability to switch to a backhand serve may sap the receiver's confidence.

Flicks are probably best played when the receiver, eager after successful forays, is leaning too far forward and best played to the corners. With greater distance at her disposal she is less likely to overshoot the back service line. In addition she can use greater crispness and so gain foot-rooting surprise. She is practically on base to defend unhurriedly against the cross-court smash; and the opposing man's rear-court is more widely opened. And why not test out the opposing lady's ability to cope with flat, fast drives down the centre – especially on her backhand. Weak returns must be snapped up.

Return of Serve Again counsels of perfection. Just as her low serving must gain the lift, so must her return of serve. She must be menacing from as forward a base as she dare risk – not more than 2ft from the line. It must be a base from which she can now meet every low serve chest high in front of the service line. Then she should be able to play delicately judged half-court shots away from the server to the 'divorce' area, even gain the occasional triumphant outright 'rush' winner. Fractionally slow in, she will touch the shuttle delicately down and wide of the server, or she will play tight upward netshots to the corners. Gone for ever are wide-eyed lifts. And, as with the serve, she must cultivate the immediate readiness of eye, hand and foot to kill off the weak return she's just forced. Let there be no respite for the servers!

A round-the-head smash must be cultivated to counter drive serves.

Return of the flick may still present some problems. Now, of course, the lady will have much less difficulty in getting back to hit down. After all, why, nimble, light and observant, should she be slow? It's getting in again to maintain formation and the attack that is still the difficulty.

Assuming her opponents take up a triangular defence formation there are three possible returns at her disposal: First, a straight slowish drop to give her time to regain the net and to bring the opposing man off base. Secondly a smash (see page 46) for an outright winner. (But if it isn't a winner or thoughtfully placed, a quick return will put her in trouble.) Thirdly, occasionally an attacking clear as a surprise packet – especially after a number of drops.

The success both of her downward return and of her speedy recovery will depend initially on getting back swiftly *behind the shuttle*, and on balance. Then only can she hit down accurately and be moving in again almost as she hits it.

How much of the net can she cover? It depends on her speed and her partner's willingness to be drawn in. They must discuss this together. Her return should seek to negate her opponent's aim of a counter to the distant net corner. But if the opponent succeeds in this there is nothing for it but for the man, doubtless reluctantly, to come in. Few women, not even the winged-footed Nora Perry, can be expected to cover more than three-quarters of the net's width. She should beware also of snatching wildly at her opponent's deliberately tempting return as she hurries to the net, unless she is sure she can control the shuttle.

If the girl is very strong, the less need she has to feel she must, even off-balance, race in on her very first stroke. As long as she controls the game with attacking shots she can wait for the ideal moment to come in. But she should not be tempted into deciding she can stay there and slug it out for ever; few ladies can. A call of 'back' can give her forward-looking partner early warning of her return to the net – and his retreat.

Attack If the lady is constantly on her toes, racket up, threatening, she is attacking without even hitting the shuttle. She is forcing a lift that might not have been played with a less menacing player at the net. To this basic principle she

should now add the often deterring movement of stepping only a foot or two towards that precise spot to which the opponent is hoping to play, or is only able to play.

For the rest, there is not a lot to add to the catalogue of virtues listed on page 86, except: take early; don't lift, hit down steeply away from the racket or into the body; cross-court only when the opposing lady has been moved from the centre; play the 'divorce areas' with touch and accuracy – the key shot.

Apart from her superb serving, Nora Perry's other great virtue is her ability to make quick reflexed interceptions, backhanded as well as forehanded. If the lady can snap up more half-court pushes and fast drop shots the man's work-load is eased. Not being drawn in and having to scramble back, the man can more effectively police the rear-court. On the other hand he must still be able to save the day if the chance is missed. The lady's interceptions must be controlled, hit down, or the initiative is lost. In practice games, let ambition exceed grasp; in matches, temper aggression with discretion.

Remember that the opposing man forced into the deep backhand corner is most likely to play drops. Straight or cross-court? That is the riddle to be solved by observation of action and habit. If he plays round-the-head straight, a crisp cross-court return may catch him off balance.

In returning net-shots near the post, the lady should never get nearer the side-line than the shuttle or even just stand opposite the shuttle. She must expect a cross-court return or it will leave her ignominiously standing. So, she must edge 2–3ft towards the centre so that the straight return is still well within her reach and the cross can be intercepted.

Defence Not so long ago the strictly-net lady did not have to worry about defence. Her partner was happy to show what a hell of a fellow he was by taking the lot. Today, stronger more athletic ladies and a less chauvinistic male outlook have in most cases radically altered things.

Now, ladies are expected at least to adopt the triangular defence formation, dealing with cross-court drives and smashes whilst the man takes the straight ones; at most, to drop back to a full sides defence. In the former case, it is a

matter of crouching, racket up, eye riveted to opponent's action and racket, to spot early the type and direction of the attack. It is a matter too of much practice in playing dabs away from or straight at the attacker. Few things more upset the male ego than having his winning drives and smashes ignominiously cut down in their prime!

In sides defence, she must be as quick in to return the drop with an early take net-shot as she is to dance back to hit down the attacking clear and follow in. There is also the substantial difficulty of returning the man's smash. Generally directed at the body, it should be whipped away flat and fast. Then, following in, with intuitive anticipation, the scrambled return is neatly nipped off, Perry-wise. Despite such heady success the lady must not be drawn into a single with the man.

Man's Role

What's sauce for the goose . . . The man too must adopt a more attacking position by edging steadily forward. This will narrow the gap between him and his partner and also the size of the vulnerable 'divorce area'. As a more positive bonus he should now be able to attack (not merely parry) his opponent's half-court pushes, to be constantly playing them down and so forcing an off-balance lift. Watch Gilliland and Skovgaard using their reach to do just this. Grovelling for near-floor returns, opponents are likely to come off court with grazed knees! For safety, you must have developed the agility and backhand power that will enable you still to punish any hopeful or desperate lifts to the rear-court, now more exposed.

Serving If the man too can move his serving base forward, the gains are worth having: A more effective flick; improved domination of the half-court push return; and less time for your opponents to attack your low serve. But, as before, a backhand fast drop or smash is essential.

Attacking the lady, now an athletic Amazon not a hobbled housewife, will be more difficult.

She will probably give as good as she gets. But it is worth trying her out especially with flat drives, or well-disguised flicks that, pushing her to the back, at least break your opponents' strength formation. The man must seize eagerly on her return to place it well out of her incoming reach or to draw in her reluctant partner. As a nonplussing variant, he should play an occasional lift back to the spot from which she has just hopefully raced.

Low serves to the centre to the opposing man are still the order of the day. Occasional low serves to the side-lines have their merits and demerits. From the right-hand court, the server's backhand is vulnerable but his partner is right on the spot for the straight net return or push. From the left court, it is the receiver's backhand which is under some pressure but the server's partner now has a little further to travel to attack a net return taken early. If flick he must, it is best done from the left-hand court when his lady is right on the spot for the cross-court smash.

If he plans to force a return to his own backhand, it may pay him to serve with the right foot forward. It is then easier to pivot smartly across to intercept. And it may pay him to shorten his follow-through so that his racket is more quickly in the ready position to snap up a fleeting chance. He should not attempt these if they interfere with the accuracy of his serve. That is his absolute priority.

Return of Serve Here again the man will probably wish to suggest a tactical positional change. If he is confident of his ability, even when drawn right in by a tight, low serve to make a thoughtfully placed net-shot or push that gives him time to recover to his base, he will keep his lady in front of him.

If he is not so confident and he has a hard-hitting, agile partner, he may ask her to stand near the centre line, 1–2ft behind him.

If his 'rush' is fully effective, well and good. If it's not he can confidently stay in to hunt down the weak net-return. His partner should be just as lethal to a half-court lift. To cut down the

Plate 48. Aggression answers aggression. Nora Perry, in crouch defence, prepares to dab down Gilliland's cross-court smash. Karen Chapman, racket down — a dead duck? *(Mervyn Rees)*

(*Overleaf*) Plate 49. A perfect divorce-area push; Pri, cool and balanced; Gillian Gilks, sensing trouble; Tredgett and Nora Perry on their toes for the inevitable lift *(Louis C. H. Ross)*

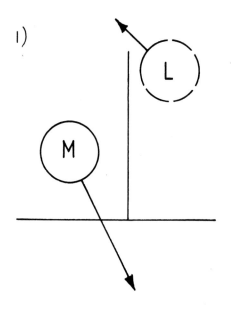
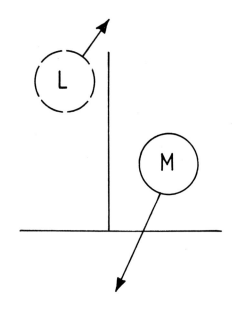

Fig. 34 Mixed doubles: opening positions. Man receiving; strong, agile lady behind him. (1) Right court; (2) left court

risk of more searching returns to her, the shuttle should have been pushed into the opposing man's body to cramp his reply.

If the man's return of serve does not warrant his staying in, he will, if he has so placed it as to force at least a cramped or belated reply, drop back and his partner quickly nip in again. Experience and understanding between partners are very necessary.

At this level the opposing lady will certainly be no easy target, but it is worth making an early attack. Sharp pushes straight at her or a deceptive, wrong-footing turn of the wrist are likely to be more morale-shaking than a very tight net shot. Even if the man isn't 6ft 4in he should try to be a punishing Billie Gilliland, the Scottish 'Servers' Scourge'.

Attack Here, as with the lady, it is very much 'the mixture as before'. But once again the whole tempo must be faster, stronger, more accurate. And the wrist must play a more *deceptive* part by the constant threat of a last second change of pace, trajectory or direction.

Speed is particularly necessary in getting across to take half-court pushes whilst at tape level. If only the man can do so fast, he is in a position not only to hit down and cross-court but also to play deceptively. He can threaten the wrong-footing cross-court drive and play yet another straight push, in addition to the two probing ones he's already played, preferably past the girl's backhand. Then if his opponent, sensing yet another push, edges in, he can 'hold' the wrist late and play a wristy flick to either back corner. If the shuttle is above tape height and the opposing lady has also been drawn across, then now is the time for the cross-court drive. If played at the right moment, it is an admirable shot; at the wrong one, or upwards, fatal.

If his push is intercepted with a dab by the lady who may well have had to face the side-line to reach it, then a cross-court net-shot is an effective counter. But it should be remembered that whether it is a drive or a net-shot, the stroke must be crisp, flat, through an unguarded centre and into the opposite tram lines. Only then is the opponent really stretched.

Shots to the net against a really nimble lady will have to be played very accurately or

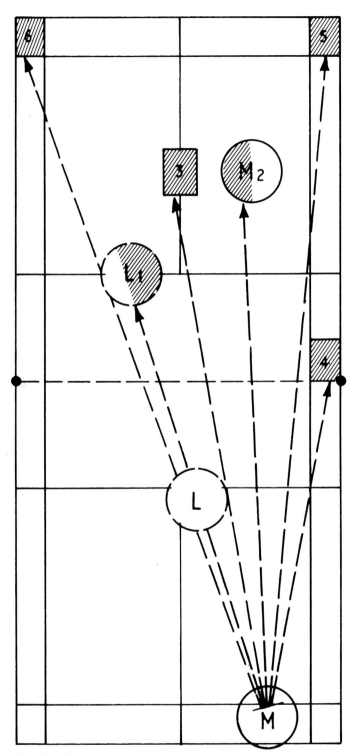

Fig. 35 Mixed doubles. Positions and attack areas
for triangular defence: Smash (1) at lady; (2) at
man's right side; (3) between the two; (4) straight
drop; (5) and (6) *attacking* clears

deceptively. If they are not, then it is the man who does the 'grovelling'.

When the opponents lift and adopt triangular defence formation, the man has a number of possibilities. If their clear or lob is deep, the straight drop is favourite. This may elicit a shorter lob. If it is short, there are four alternatives. (i) A straight smash at the inner side of the man's body; (ii) a really steep cross-court smash at the girl; (iii) an attacking clear straight or cross-court, preferably to the backhand; (iv) a smash between the opposing pair, behind the lady. See which works!

If the opposing man 'holds the bridge' on his own, steep to the sidelines or the body is the answer. If he is very old-fashioned or ultra-modern and likes his partner alongside in times of trouble, then the girl should be engaged in a 'singles' to see if she is vulnerable. Women's defences are strong these days so a drop or two, even an attacking clear if her position warrants it, may be needed to force the really short lob or clear return needed for a winner.

As in singles, the man must develop round-the-head shots to maintain the attack. And a crisp backhand smash is equally essential to snap up half chances too far to his left and ensure there is no Achilles heel.

Defence If the lady is in trouble in the forecourt corners, the man will have to come to her aid. She will do the same for him with cross-court interceptions when it is he who is on the run. There is little alternative then but the last resort – a lift. A straight lift (it's the girl who lobs cross-court) will mean he has the minimum distance to travel to take up his triangular defence position. A deep lift, and to the corner, makes his chance of survival better than evens.

In triangular defence, he must be alert to move in quickly for a straight drop, or back (and across) for an attacking clear. If only he can play his opponent's smash or drop early and straight to the net and half-smash any flat clears, the attack may be regained.

Co-operation

Finally, the man and woman must always try to be a real pair. Fast driving by the man, especially down the wings, tends to cut her out of the game. Smashes into the man's body will bring her into it. Such co-operation does not stem solely from shots played. Equally it comes from calling, encouragement and collaboration.

The famous Perry 'smile and bottom tap' must be worth two or three points to Mike Tredgett. So too are their calls to one another; unintelligible to spectators but meaningful and positive to them in a game where opponents seek to plant indecision and doubt.

For this same reason and because the ebb and flow of the game are less clear-cut than in level doubles it is essential that partners have a full understanding of each other's capabilities and weaknesses, of their positional interlockings, of 'who takes what'. A call, 'Yours', helps.

So much depends on speed of eye, hand and foot. With it comes the ability to play down serves and net-shots, to win the vital 'divorce area' battle. Almost equally important is tight serving, a strong male backhand, and using the full width of the court.

PART III

THE EXPERTS' WAY

11 Top Thirty

CHANDRA (Indonesia)

No more, no less: a name as squat and solid as the man himself. He and Christian won the All-England Men's Doubles title in 1972 when they beat Tredgett and Stevens 15–5 and 15–12, and again in 1973 when they brutally crushed the up and coming Tjun Tjun and Wahjudi 15–2, 15–7, an affront they were perhaps to regret when the latter scourged them three times during their run of six titles in seven years. Consolation prizes were the 1980 Friends' Provident Masters and the World Championship title which they annexed when a Tjun Tjun back injury kept the latter pair out of the lists.

No one can reach such heights without a sound all-round game. But Chandra may well be remembered for three strokes that etch themselves on the mind: his smash, his serve and his defence.

Big man that he is, he would take off vertically with the controlled power of a shuttle-plane. He did it on the run; he did it tirelessly. For him a shuttle in the air was anathema; it had to be chopped down in mid-flight. The powerful body played its full part.

To serve, villainous crew-cut above impassive face, he stands square to the net, right up to the line. Shuttle to strings – a momentary pause, then a sudden, short waft of his racket to send the shuttle skimming the tape or zooming up shallowly in a deceptive flick; and with surprising agility, a neat cut-off of any attempted half-court push is made.

And in defence, a positive no-nonsense backhand stance is his style. Dug in, time and again, almost robotic, with bent arm, he lifts back the fiercest smashes. Obviously relishing the duel, he seldom actively seeks to gain the initiative and is content to lift.

CHRISTIAN (Indonesia)

Christian Hadinata – Hadinata Christian? The changes have, like other Indonesian name vagaries, been rung time and again; but to most enthusiasts this slim, even-tempered, good looking young man is simply, Christian.

He is a player whose anticipatory eye has perhaps robbed him of the full quota of fame which so often attaches itself to spectacular display. Moving early, spectacular last-second dashes and leaps are unnecessary for him.

Indonesian men tend to be single-game specialists. Christian deserves a niche in the badminton halls of fame because he was a champion at both doubles games. In men's doubles, he and the bounding Chandra, who gets an occasional nod of tacit approval, were seldom beaten. In mixed, he and petite Imelda Wigoeno fought it out with England's Tredgett and Nora Perry for world supremacy.

Leaning slightly away from the shuttle he produces a sound low serve and a flick veering slightly to the right. As part of a usefully unorthodox combination with Chandra, he sometimes follows his own smash in to the net if played from not too deep; and frequently glides into his partner's forecourt gracefully to dig out the short drops which Chandra, that man of action, seems not to regard as quite worthy of his note. The forecourt is Christian's forte.

Christian has a superb eye and matching reflexes. In defence he nonchalantly takes the pace off the shuttle. At the net he is lethal but without ostentation unless you consider forked lightning ostentatious. No excited bouncing; no racket waved menacingly on high. Instead, cat-like, he treads softly, slightly adapting his position to the ebb and flow of battle behind him; racket held almost still at shoulder-height.

Then, at just the right second, he makes a leap and a smash, or a leap and a delicate stop volley.

Christian, with trim little Imelda Wigoeno, was the first Asian ever to break the years-long European domination of that branch of the game. He did it with as little orthodoxy as a Royal Academician scrawling a portrait in school crayons. It was Christian who was at the net 50 per cent of the time, and very effectively, partly because of his own quickness of foot and eye, and partly because of his partner's dash and pin-pointed smashing from rearcourt which forced the lifts of which he took full advantage. Such play won them the World title in 1980.

In the 1981 All-England he and Wigoeno played a much more orthodox game – and lost on the more subtle delicacies of half-court and net placements. In a last ditch stand in the third, an unhappy Wigoeno was given her head at the back. The slide was halted, but too late.

FLEMMING DELFS (Denmark)
One of the world's greats, in style, success and size (over 6ft in height and well-built to boot), Delfs dominated the court in his hey-day. Despite this, his smash doesn't pack the knock-out punch one might expect. Rather, he relies on height, wrist and a positive follow-through to gain steepness. That said, of course, 'Delfs' and 'backhand smash' are synonymous.

Packed with more power than most of us have in our forehand, this backhand smash is one of the attributes that helped him reach the top of the singles tree: All-England and first World Champion in 1977; European Champion 1976, 1978, 1980. Partnered by still bigger Steen Skovgaard he is a force to be reckoned with but he has never quite been 'tops' at men's doubles.

His attack is augmented by drops deceptively delicate for so big a man and by a sudden effort-lessly punched attacking clear. In defence he rides smashes to the body with easy disdain and counter-attacks pushes aimed at his body. In the forecourt, drops met early are tumbled over the tape or, with the merest hint of wrist, flicked tantalisingly down the side-line. In serving, slowly, deliberately, in rapt concentration, he eases rather than hits the shuttle over the net.

With his blond good looks, easy smile, imper-turbability and impeccable court manners, he is surely badminton's Beau Ideal. But perhaps it is his very virtues that have become his vices.

Delfs is great indeed when he is dominating the game. But in 1978 and 1979 when he lost to Hartono and Swie King respectively in the All-England he seemed unable to raise the tempo, to generate the fire-in-the-belly that is the champion's hallmark. A semi-final 5–15, 8–15 defeat in 1980 by King suggested that the fires were still damped down.

In 1981, the reigning European champion was unseeded because of erratic form. And, by black coincidence, he was drawn against none other than World Champion Rudi Hartono in the very first round. Delfs, almost disdainfully succumbed again 8–15, 4–15 in a game that even then could not fan any slumbering fires in him into vengeful blaze.

GILLIAN GILKS (England)
The 'Golden Girl' of English badminton in the 1970s – tall, leggy and blonde, Gillian hit the headlines when she was only 12 by winning her first All-England Under 15 Junior title. Even before she had run the gamut of Under 15 and Under 18 titles she was playing for England. And from there it was but a short trip to All-England titles.

A warm favourite with English crowds she has played for her country on over seventy occasions. Can she be the first woman ever to notch up the coveted century? At thirty-one her singles appearances are likely to be rarer but time has taken little toll yet of her doubles skills. She is still in the inflation-hit prize money, but most of her estimated £20,000–£30,000 income surely comes from endorsing equipment that must range from hair products to shoes. Retirement, hopefully, is still just a thought.

But without doubt in the 1970s, Gillian was the world's finest all-round player, capable of virtuoso performances in singles, ladies' doubles and mixed alike. In 1975–6, she was Triple Champion in the English National, All-England and European Championships: the record of an indisputable champion!

In singles, deceptive round-the-head drop-shots or a beautifully timed backhand clear make her fire-proof in that deep corner. At the right time, she uses a powerful smash to force a winner or a weak return. And she has the speed and aggression to follow in like an avenging angel to snap up a split-second winner or to play tumble net-shots with rare delicacy of touch.

Hardly of conventional petite build for mixed, Gillian uses her reach with blanketing effect; uses it too in return of serve to give opponents no semblance of respite. Lightning reflexes, sound positioning and uncanny anticipation make her a by-word as an interceptor of withering smash and cross-court drive alike. Upright in attack or crouched in defence, Gillian's racket is always high, a threatening sword.

Her success lies not solely in skilled technique and a natural eye. To these she adds in full measure the champion's essentials of an almost fanatical urge to fitness, to success.

At the other end of the scale lie nerves and lack of confidence which in moments of stress dull the sharp edge of her skills; nerves that should have no place in one so thoroughly prepared.

Upset emotionally, she could not give of her best in 1979–80 and was a shadow of her own greatness. Shattered by a first round All-England Singles defeat at the hands of rank outsider Kirsten Larsen (whom Lene Koppen later annihilated 11-0, 11-0) the English idol tottered on her pedestal.

But, with cheerful Nora Perry as her doubles partner, greatness returned. Towering head and shoulders over other pairs, after losing the first game, they summarily dispatched Japan's best, Yonekura and Tokuda, to bring Gillian's tally of titles to nine.

Then, with the world at her feet, sadly, inexplicably, she announced her retirement. Like many another such retirement it came to nothing. But one of the world's strongest-ever pairs was split.

In the 1980–81 All-England final, Gillian, now partnering Paula Kilvington, faced Nora Perry and Jane Webster, who in renewed partnership had won the World Championships. With three victories behind them, Gillian and Paula were eager to show the English selectors once and for all who were No 1. But it was not to be – and it was Gillian who faltered under a whirlwind attack, not Paula. Still at loggerheads with the Badminton Association of England she did not accompany the English Uber Cup team to Tokyo. (Although she was restored to the Association's fold in 1982.)

MORTEN FROST HANSEN (Denmark)

World title honours continue to elude this tousle-headed, unassuming Danish champion. But, only 22 years old, his error-free play and thoughtful approach to the game must surely pay off. Lithe and wiry, singles are his game. As he says: 'It is fun to play doubles with Fladberg – not *too* serious, you understand.' As to mixed: 'I'm not old enough yet,' he teases. 'Besides three events is too much.' So Hansen who for three years was the Danish junior champion has now assumed the mantle of Flemming Delfs as Denmark's No 1.

In 1979 he gave eventual All-England singles winner Liem Swie King his nastiest moment in a close semi-final encounter; and beat him in the 1981 World Games semi-final, though losing in the final to China's Chen Changjie.

He is a firm believer in the essential need for physical fitness, and that tactics go hand-in-hand with technique.

He displays few flamboyant leaps or jumps. His skill in reading his opponent's shots, his neatness of balanced movement, reduce the need for them; reduce too the number of easy points, of unforced errors given to his opponents, for his philosophy of 'practise, practise – results don't matter', has brought him steadily to the pitch where 'chances must become certainties'.

It is heartbreakingly difficult to put the shuttle on the floor against Hansen. 'A little defence,' he says, 'then sudden attack'. But even in attack Hansen is not flamboyant. What his smash lacks in power, it makes up for in precise placement, to the right side of the body, to within inches of the side-line. It takes more subtle forms too: a silken touch at the net. ('The best on the net wins.')

If the sound and fury are not there, the fighting spirit is. 'You must have fight, have determination. You must never know when you are beaten,' he says.

Hansen is as modest and unassuming off court as he is controlled and well-mannered on court, an excellent model for any young player aspiring to the top of the championship ladder.

RUDI HARTONO (Indonesia)

The idol of Indonesia, the man who won the All-England Singles title a record seven consecutive times (1968–74) and a record eight

in all (1976). The man who, almost written off, was brought back after Indonesian defeat by China to crown a glorious career with the 1980 World Championship title. A man who will be remembered too for his unfailing sportsmanship, modesty and courtesy.

Anticipation is allied with agile footwork. The resulting early take always seems to leave an unhurried Hartono with a bewildering variety of shots open to him: attacking shots mostly, for he likes to play an aggressive game.

His pile driver smash (long swing, shoulder and full follow-through), even from the base-line, goes straight into the body. A net-return – and he's there to rat-a-tat-tat it into his opponent's body. Half chances seldom get a second chance. A lifted return to his backhand – he is there again with a ballet dancer's leap, and, airborne (shorter swing now) smashes again round-the-head.

No champion ever flourished on power alone. Drop-shots and tape-climbing net-shots, exquisite in their delicacy, are essential parts of his game. Attacking clears are played with the same deceptive ease of stroke.

The low serve is meted out with similar treatment or, taken early, suddenly and shrewdly pushed through the over-anticipatory server.

His own high serves he cracks up with a long follow-through. But the racket-head is quickly dropped down across the stomach. Crouched, he leans across to the side-line to tame the fiercest smash with a velvet touch or, if it is carelessly placed, with lancing cross-court drive.

At close quarters too he is dexterity and reflex personified. And he has the ability, when the pace gets too hot, to lift body-probes disconcertingly over his opponent's head.

There's an answer too when he's in deep trouble. The tumble net-shot is allowed to drop below the net, then, with long follow-through, steepled to a height that gives some safeguarding length. Even the shuttle left as dropping 'out' may suddenly be salvaged with a precise flat drop-shot to the net.

Like all champions he can raise his game to meet a crisis or a bold nothing-to-lose challenge. A champion of champions!

Plate 50. Impact! Which is just what Frost Hansen makes as he smashes *(Mervyn Rees)*

SUN AI HWANG (South Korea)

This almond-eyed South Korean girl with impassive face closely framed by jet-black hair could metaphorically, but never literally, be called 'the joker in the pack'. Rarely does even a flicker of emotion cross her face, neither of delight nor disgust. Her nearest approach is an apparent cry of satisfaction, almost of triumph. 'HAAA!' Not so, says her coach; it is simply 'to boost the spirit', though she seemed not to need it at the 1980–81 All-England Championships when she overthrew the established queen, Lene Koppen by an incredible 11–1, 11–2.

She was certainly the No 1 surprise. Kept out of the badminton eye for four years of arduous training, she hit the high spots on her first major outing. She took the Japanese and the Taiwan titles against a field that included the world's best, except for Lene Koppen. Then, although inexperienced and only nineteen years old, she forced her way into the All-England No 2 seed position – and more than justified it.

Her reported life style made dramatic reading. Rumour was rife: she had trained in a convent; was slapped if error broke the rhythm of her sequence practices. With her father dead and her mother incapable of work she had been 'mothered' by an elder sister. Playing from the age of seven, she caught the eye of ambitious Korean coaches and was swiftly taken to the Korean Athletic College, there to be housed by the State – without pay!

With 300 other potential sports champions, preparing for the Los Angeles Olympics, she was subject to rigorous training for technique, concentration and to build up a dedicated determination that didn't count the cost. This amounted to six hours each day (and only two hours of that actually on court), six days a week. Small wonder therefore that she needed a 5,000 calorie elite diet and 'had no time for other interests'.

Broad of shoulder and strong of thigh she has a mannish figure and hits with a man's power. No dancing feet for Miss Hwang; no impression of whirlwind speed. There are few early takes at the net; no lunging kills. Indeed she much prefers playing the deep corners with probing attacking lobs to keeping it on the net. There is deception too in her drops: a brush stroke and a last second turn of the wrist.

Her game is built on power and pertinacity,

169

on care and concentration, and on deception. At the end of a successful rally, there is the hint of a lilt in her footsteps as she takes her time in a circuitous route back to base. No one is going to hurry Miss Hwang.

Her high serves are as much a model of concentration as the slow down-swing is of care. Even though subtly varied in height, they are implacable in squeezing the last inch of advantage out of length. Her crouch too bespeaks refusal to be beaten as much as do the acrobatic splits to reach a drop. Retrieving is certainly one name of the game!

But her real power is overhead. Strong round the head, she seldom needs to employ a wristy backhand – but it's there. Her smash wins its way by sheer speed; her cut smash nearly chops the shuttle in two! And if its her turn to be pounded, that same strong wrist whips the shuttle away from even the most awkward of spots.

Something of an implacable machine, Sun Ai Hwang gives nothing away. Her name means literally, 'beautiful mind'. You could have fooled us! We thought it meant 'beautiful physique'.

ING HOA IVANA LIE (Indonesia)
A long name indeed for this slight, pony-tailed twenty year old Indonesian, as dainty as each syllable of her name.

She burst into the very top flight in 1979–80 when in the semi-finals she just edged home to put paid to Lene Koppen's fond hopes of becoming World Champion. But in the final it was the majestic Verawaty who triumphed (11–1, 11–3).

In 1980–81, the Danish champion turned the tables on her as she swept through to win the Friend's Provident Masters title. And Ivana had no better fortune in the All-England when in the semi-finals she met another Amazon, the much heralded but little known Hwang. Ivana's fleetness of foot and delicate drops swept her to 11–5. And beaten 7–11 in the second, she could find no answer at all to the big, rampant and fully confident Korean girl; an unhappy and untypical 0–11 defeat, explained perhaps by the fact that she had a very heavy cold.

Lacking reach and the ability to hit down really powerfully, Ivana jumps to intercept early and to smash when a winner is on the cards. A very supple back enables her to play round the head and to reach far back for clears to which she cannot jump. An equally flexible wrist enables her to place porcelain-delicate cross-court drops with crisp deception, or steep half-smashes to maintain the pressure. With little weight to carry she is dancing quicksilver despite a rather upright stance. In defence, against unadventurous opponents, she relies on a hair-pinned net-return to force the short lift she needs.

Blue-shorted, pony-tailed, golden-skinned and with a wide smile, Ivana is becoming a warm favourite.

HAN JIAN (China)
As Sun Ai Hwang brought fame to South Korea in 1981, so did Han Jian to China in 1980. Comparatively unknown, he defeated Liem Swie King, twice All-England Champion and then rated as the best in the world.

5ft 7in Han Jian started his sports career as a footballer. He took up badminton when he was sixteen. Within six years he had come second only to Liem Swie King who defeated him roundly in the Bangkok Asian Games.

How then, a little over a year later, did he beat him? Planning and determination are the answers. He studied video-tapes of his conqueror. And having seen them, worked out ploys to curb the bounding Indonesian: clears and lobs deep to the base-line and corners; awkwardly placed defensive returns.

And since it was to be wearing-down tactics, making his opponent work for each and every point, he trained: 3,000 metres a day in the stifling humidity of a 28°C diving hall! When others had finished their training assignments, it was Jian who asked for still more time.

Han Jian, now confident and very determined, played his own game – not the typical non-stop, all-out Chinese attack game, but more one of defence interspersed with sudden sharp counter-attacks. What he lacked in inches, he made up for with agile footwork and jump smashes once he had painstakingly forced a short clear.

At 15–17 down in the rubber game, still no thought of defeat crossed his mind. A rock-like defence caused the usually stable Swie King to hurl his racket disgustedly into the net. Another King smash into the net and a cunning Jian

flick lob saw the latter home and dry for the victory of the year.

But it was another Jian who was seen at the Albert Hall in 1981. Though the talk, as ever, was of friendship and learning rather than victory, it was a vibrantly aggressive Jian that we watched open-mouthed.

It was a repeat of the Chinese visit in 1973 when Tang Hsien Hu and Hou Chia Chang had made England's best look like bemused cart-horses. Against such speed and agility, our players gleaned only a handful of points.

As fast backwards as forwards, Jian made the conventional lift to the backhand tantamount to signing one's own death warrant. A towering jump and a round-the-head smash of unprecedented speed was shared, with nice discrimination and accuracy, between forehand and backhand. And, if he was a foot faster he was also a foot higher, with a resultant smash a couple of feet steeper, down at the floor.

Plate 51. Sun Ai Hwang, South Korea's bombshell, shows how to defend the right side of the body *backhanded (Mervyn Rees)*

No returned-with-compliment lifts for Jian. Knowing his ability to leap upwards to make interceptions and leap backwards to smash, he set up base only 2ft behind the front service line. From there, restless feet enabled him to play tape-high pushes and net-shots to the corners that gave his opponent no respite.

On occasions an airy backhand clear and seemingly leisurely recovery brought his defence into play. Sudden wristy lobs from deep, and flat fast pushes from closer in, were interspersed with superbly controlled stop-volleys that dropped a mere 2–3ft beyond the tape.

Unforced errors were few. Although Jian played to the lines, seldom was a shuttle hit out. 'Relentless concentration' was the watchword.

Jian proved beyond doubt that modern singles are based on agility, stamina and power. Above all in the ability ceaselessly to jump, to gain steepness and time for the killer stroke.

Jian v King? What an All-England final that would make!

KEVIN JOLLY (England)

Let it be admitted Jolly has no major championships to his credit yet. But he is worthy of inclusion here for reasons other than a string of titles.

A junior of rare talent, he might well have been European Junior Triple Champion in Malta in 1977. But an unnecessary leap for an easy semi-final smash resulted in a twisted ankle – and dashed hopes.

Heir apparent to Ray Stevens as English National Champion he now has Steve Baddeley and Nicky Yates snapping at his heels. Can he make it alone to the top, or will he be overhauled?

In two other respects Jolly is unusual. He is one of the first juniors who, with the Open horizon before him, has taken up the challenge, has opted for a career in badminton. Daily training has made him one of the fittest men in the game; will it make him one of the most skilful?

Relying on that fitness, his game tends to be a war of attrition. He has the ability to play long rallies to grind down his opponents. On occasions, too rare perhaps, he'll slip dramatically into higher gear, and then with speed of foot, jump smash and net-lunge, the heat is really on.

And yet such an approach is not in keeping with his stormy petrel image. Hassle on the court; dissension with the umpire, dark glances and darker words thrown at the linesmen: Jolly too often was the man behind the trouble.

Today, all credit to him, this is a thing of the past, a relic of his behavioural immaturity. Now, Jolly curbs Jolly. Let's hope that his fiery nature will be shown in faster action, not in fiery words.

THOMAS KIHLSTROM (Sweden)

Sweden's No 1 player, he has assumed the mantle of Sture Johnsson. A good singles player who has never quite hit the top, Kihlstrom is a brilliant men's doubles player who certainly has. ('There is more satisfaction in doubles; in singles you must be very, very fit or it is not funny.')

In 1976, he and Bengt Froman, playing fast and flat, beat the Indonesians Tjun Tjun and Wahjudi at their own game to tumultuous applause in the All-England Final. It is the only occasion in the last ten years when the title has not gone to Indonesia.

An intelligent student of the game, he watched and analysed the play of champions Erland Kops, Rudi Hartono and Sven Pri. In singles, he is a firm believer that the only way to break Indonesian domination of the men's singles is to clear very high, to slow the game down, to take the pace off the shuttle. Speed is the catalyst for still greater speed.

Watch the slow concentration of his serve and you see why he says 'You must forget the receiver. See only the tape – and skim it. And still be ready to cut off the pushes through you or to the side-lines that such a serve forces'.

In receiving, his eager stance exemplifies the aggression he preaches – and practises: 'But you must vary your returns so your opponents cannot anticipate. Steen Skovgaard is a fine example of this; Sven Pri too, but sometimes he tries to be too clever!'

Lacking a really powerful smash he is a staunch advocate of thoughtful placing: 'Into the body so that you narrow the angle and force a cramped reply!'

The other side of the coin – defence – is his forte. Few men can fight their way out of seemingly lethal body attack more effectively than he does. 'Pushes are easier to play if you follow in,' he says. This, using natural aggression and anticipation, is just what he does, to turn a loser into a winner.

And, although a hunter of the shuttle, he urges, 'It is essential to keep calm under pressure.'

LIEM SWIE KING (Indonesia)

One of the world's great singles players. Seemingly made of india-rubber, Swie King will bound high to smash, then sweep in to kill the loose return, or set up a winner with millimetre-accurate cut net-return. Superbly trained and equally consistent, he can run less fit opponents into the ground.

Swie King disappointingly lost to the legendary Rudi Hartono in 1976 in an All-

England final that critics felt to be 'arranged'. The following year he lost again, to Delfs's backhand smash. In the 1977 World Championships, he lost surprisingly in the third round to Thomas Kihlstrom.

In 1978, however, he at last assumed the mantle of Hartono who now held the all-time record of eight All-England titles. And he held on to it firmly in 1979, but only to have it snatched surprisingly and shatteringly from him by a brilliant Prakash Padukone, in 1980.

A crumb of comfort must have been that he had established himself also as a world-class men's doubles player by fine wins in the Thomas Cup and against China.

In September at the Royal Albert Hall, he cut Hartono to ribbons. And in March 1981 at the Wembley Arena, he gained satisfying revenge over Padukone.

To see this ace of the Indonesian pack in play, turn back to page 95.

MICHAEL KJELDSEN (Denmark)

One hardly expects a string of battle honours from a seventeen-year-old. Not so with Kjeldsen.

In singles, he has beaten one of England's 'top ten', Andy Goode; with little real resistance, cut his European contemporaries down to size in the 1981 Junior Championships; and forced Prakash to setting.

In doubles, partnered by dour and burly Mark Christiansen, he has gone a step further. He has defeated some of the best in the world: Jolly and Sutton, then Delfs and Skovgaard of Denmark before losing narrowly to Sweden's Kihlstrom and Karlsson.

For a seventeen-year-old he carries a wide range of armaments: a disconcerting left hand, a wise head on young shoulders, and a surge of destroyer-speed that almost seems to leave a wake behind him.

In singles, his speed from base-line to net to snap up unconsidered trifles gets him off to a flying start. Suppleness enables him to maintain the attack with a wide range of round-the-head strokes from the backhand corner. And he has a blistering smash that he delights in using, often from the baseline, where it can still pierce all save the toughest armour by sheer speed, generated by arm, wrist and body, rather than accurate placement.

In doubles, it's blitz-krieg tactics for Kjeldsen. An accurate low serve, aided and abetted by a shrewdly disguised flick, gains the attack. So does his aggressive receiving: he is a firm believer in the 'meet the bird early' maxim. Once seized, the attack is maintained with bull-dog tenacity but whippet speed. In this, an almost sixth sense enables he and Christiansen to interchange effectively from net to rear-court, and rear-court to net, so the quarter-chance at the net is snapped up, the quick cross-court lob attacked, and the gap in defences instantly plugged.

Wisely, perhaps mercifully, he seems to eschew mixed doubles.

To say 'Will do well' is dated; to say 'Should reach the top' is a not too-difficult forecast.

SAORI KONDO (Japan)

In 1977 another star rose in the East. To the names of Ueno and Yonekura, Tokuda and Takada was added that of Saori Kondo. For a young, slightly rotund student, quarter-final appearances in both the All-England and World Championships showed unusual promise.

This promise, alas, seemed destined not to be fulfilled when she appeared in 1978 at Wembley, unseeded. Nevertheless such is her determination that she reached the final, as she did again in 1979, losing only to Gillian Gilks and Lene Koppen respectively.

Saori has the rolling gait of a sailor, the looks of a cheerful tomboy and the ceaseless industry of her race. She makes the most of a limited range of strokes by sheer hard work. Hers is an engaging roll-up-your-sleeves, spit-on-your-hands approach.

Vertical take-off smashes are accompanied by stertorous grunts; nose-dives for a desperate retrieval, by an engaging grin.

Rather off-the-boil in 1980–81, nevertheless defeat sits lightly on Saori Kondo's shoulders. Within minutes she's back in the players' stand, restringing compatriots' rackets.

LENE KOPPEN (Denmark)

The darling of the Wembley crowds, she's the only dentist you'd ever positively enjoy visiting! Lene has charisma. Dark hair cut square, a finely boned face, lively brown eyes, trim figure and (what else in a dentist?) a ready smile.

For almost a decade Lene has been

Denmark's indisputable No 1: a winner of innumerable titles in all three branches of the game in both Open and Closed championships. Winner too of no fewer than twenty-two Nordic titles; triple champion for the last two years and World Champion in 1977 in both singles and mixed (with Steen Skovgaard).

And yet a Wembley jinx seemed to keep her from a coveted All-England title until 1979 when at last she regally usurped Gillian Gilks' singles crown. She held on to it in 1980 when having dropped only nineteen points in four matches, she routed the challenger, Amazon Verawaty, 11–2, 11–6.

In 1980–81 it might well have been 'three in a row' but for the startling emergence onto the badminton stage of little-known South Korea's even less-known Sun Ai Hwang. Against an inexorable badminton machine, Lene pitted all her skills – consistency and speed, length and determination, strokes backed by a decade of tactical experience – to no avail.

Lene is no stylist and flaunts no particularly outstanding strokes. She has however an athleticism and speed of foot that, allied to great determination, make it a Herculean task for her opponents to 'ground' the shuttle. Her consistency ensures that there are few easy points for the taking. With such qualities she is happy to wait for the right moment to go for the kill. A slightly cut defensive stroke takes speed off the shuttle. Drops played with an almost wristy flourish draw her opponents in that extra vital foot which often leads to a shorter lob and a slower recovery. Then she employs a smash barbed with accuracy and steepness, rather than power.

Watch her feet rather than her hands and you will see the lightest in the world. Her footwork is pure dance, not stilted ballet, but the thistle-down epitome of easy grace. Her feet are never still. With short, perfectly balanced steps she runs, almost glides backwards. Even as she hits she is on the move forwards with the eager acceleration of a skittish filly. But the dancing feet can stop with disc-brake suddenness; direction neatly changed in a flash. In trouble in the forecourt: a long lunge, a push of the hand

Plate 52. Tomboy Saori Kondo jumps, belatedly, to intercept a 'flick' *(Mervyn Rees)*

(and a toss of the head – in disdain at being so pressed?) and she is back dancing on her base. The lightest of perpetual motion!

Her temperament and sportsmanship alike are impeccable. No histrionics or tantrums here. ('It is not good to argue; besides you only lose concentration'.) Against brick-wall Hwang she stuck at it to the last point. And it was Lene who showed the impassive Korean girl how to raise aloft in salute to the cheering crowds, the trophy that had been hers. So it was too in 1977 when her smiling hug for Hiroe Yuki, who had snatched a possible first All-England title from her, made it hard to tell victor from vanquished. Modest in victory; smiling in defeat, Lene's 18ct genuineness won English hearts. And she's kept them ever since.

Now married to Hans Ropke (a player for Gentofte B.C., one of the leading Danish clubs) on court she is still Lene Koppen.

NETTIE NIELSEN (Denmark)

Just seventeen, with a ten-year badminton career behind her, and a reputation still to make, Nettie is included in the Gallery of the Great, because hers surely will be a name to conjure with. She's the heiress-apparent to Lene Koppen, not merely in looks but in speed of movement and eager attack.

Nettie has drive. Drive in instant recovery and drive in an all-out attack smash. Her body and her heart go into it and it has venom-tipped accuracy – into the body. Nettie has youth's eager good looks too, fair hair that curls, a fresh complexion and a warm and ready smile.

She varies her singles serve. The usual 'steeplers' are interspersed with lower ones to break the rhythm, and low ones suddenly setting new problems.

Caught occasionally in the forecourt she has Lene's lunge and instant recovery, perhaps even that same toss of the head. She has more – the ability to play the tightest of net-shots inches only from the floor. In doubles, the Nielsen motto is again 'Attack'.

Nettie Nielsen has a future: European Junior Championships Ladies' Doubles winner and Singles runner-up; Denmark Uber Cup player at sixteen. Perhaps she will spearhead a back-to-greatness drive of Danish ladies to rival the golden days of Toni Ahm and Kirsten Thorndahl, and the Rasmussen sisters.

NORA PERRY (England)

England's blonde personality-girl – indisputably the world's finest mixed doubles net-player, to say nothing of being the 1980–81 All-England and World Championships Ladies' Doubles Champion with left-hander, Jane Webster. She frequently wins a very becoming Triple Champion's crown but would be the first to admit that doubles are her forte. 'Besides, two events in a major competition are enough for anyone,' she says.

Just for good measure and to prove overall skills, after being in the lead at the halfway stage, she took the bronze medal in the 1981 TV 'Superstars' contest. She took like a duck to water to win the swimming; showed Robin Hood accuracy and nervelessness in archery, and turned a very fast pedal in the cycling. But 100 metres and assault courses in a Scottish deluge weren't for her.

The 'Barking housewife' (as the Press oddly insist on calling her) catches the eye – and ear – with her partner-consoling bottom-tapping and shrill cries of encouragement and warning. And on the not infrequent occasions when she walks up to receive the trophy, there's a charming, old-fashioned curtsey to match the warm smile. A good loser and as modest off court as on, Nora is pure gold – one of the few badminton personalities who comes across to boost badminton's TV image.

Her champagne years have been 1980 and 1981. In 1980 she joyously snatched back her All-England Mixed title from Indonesian usurpers Christian and Wigoeno, and, with Gillian Gilks, stormed through strong Japanese opposition to show that without a shadow of a doubt, they were the finest ladies pair in the world. This partnership was sadly to be immediately sundered by Gillian. Later in the season, with her new and comparatively inexperienced partner Jane Webster, Nora won the World title in the stifling heat of Senayan Stadium in Jakarta.

In 1981 at the All-England it was a face to face confrontation for Nora and Jane with Gillian Gilks and Paula Kilvington. On their mettle they swept through 15–8, 15–4 to expunge memories of three recent defeats at their hands. And she and Mike Tredgett carried on the good work in the Mixed to retain their title from the challenge of Christian and

Wigoeno – the sixth successive appearance in the final since she first won the title in 1975 with Elliot Stuart.

In both games her strengths are best seen at the net with a powerful partner behind her. There she effectively allies gossamer delicacy of touch with ruthless dabs into the body; uncanny anticipation with speed over the measured three metres! Despite an ebullient nature she is seldom tempted to take what she can't effectively control. But in times of trouble, she will drop back not so much for passive defence as for active attack, with sweeping cross-court drives that have wiped the smile from the face of many a chauvinist male opponent.

It is for her low serve that she is best remembered. Completely unruffled by the fiercest or longest-reached receiver she gets the lift with an economical action, delivering metronomic, tape-skimming serves.

Perhaps only the purists give equal praise to her flick. Elegantly identical, it not only keeps the eager receiver champing at the bit but it wins, even at this level, a few joyous points.

Occasionally there are signs of incipient madness. The feather-light touch to the net changes to a crisp lob. Aghast one watches her follow in to the net danger-zone only to see her, like some homing-devised missile, unhurriedly pick off the resultant smash!

Some girl, our Nora!

LUIS PONGOH (Indonesia)

Luis Pongoh must surely be heir apparent to Liem Swie King and the All-England Singles title which the Indonesians have made almost their own prerogative since 1968.

A typical Indonesian in appearance: dark hair, slight, but a slightness stiffened with whipcord, he is typically Indonesian too in graceful speed and deceptive power of shot. Paradoxically straight-legged in receiving stance yet slightly crouched as he serves high, Pongoh also serves deep. Time and again the receiver has to dance back that extra 12in which forces his back foot behind the line.

Instantly, the delightfully named Pongoh adopts a wide-legged, slightly crouched stance

Plate 53. For sheer grace Koppen is irresistible; a fine example to ladies of *attacking* the serve
(*Mervyn Rees*)

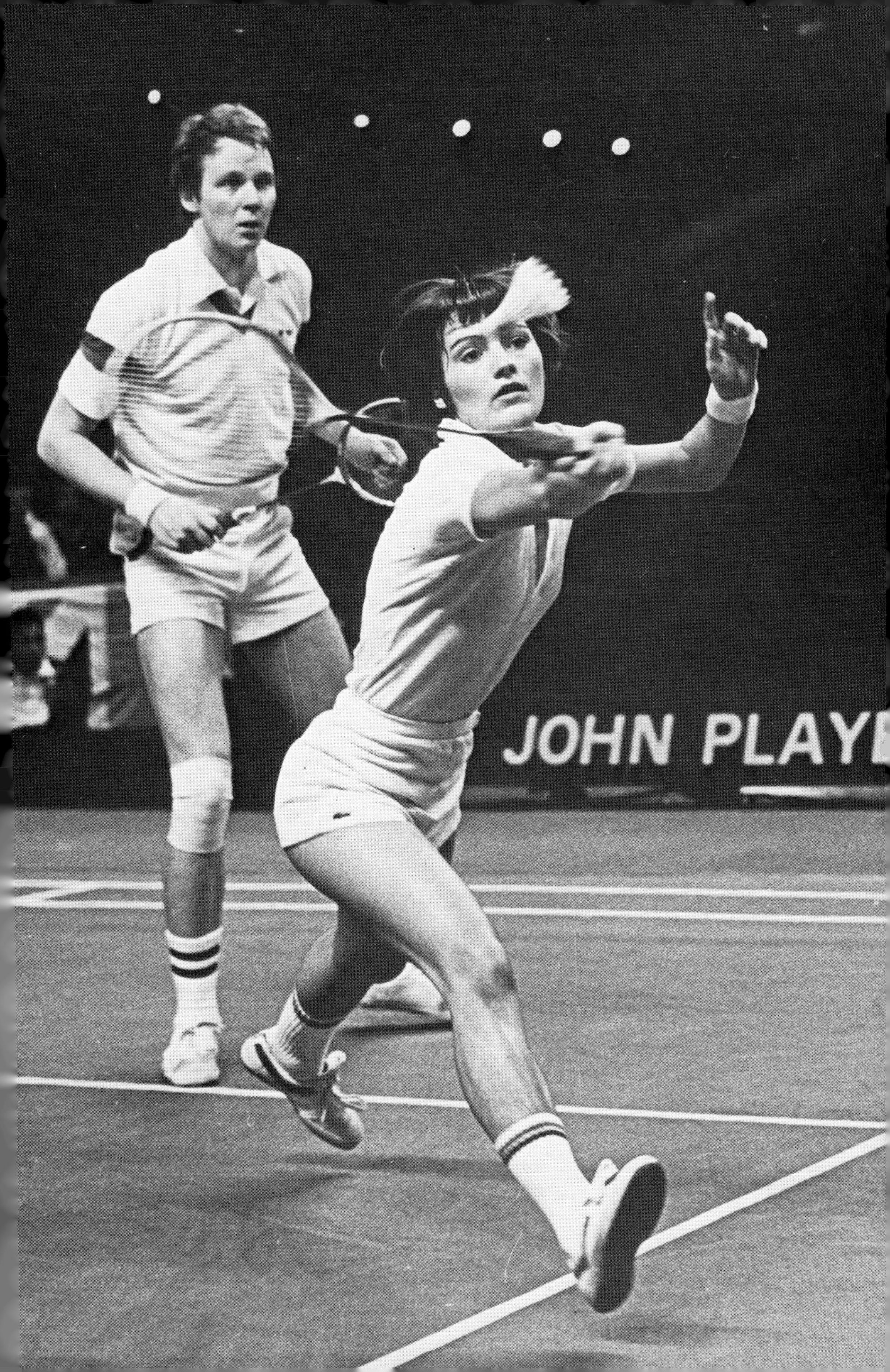
JOHN PLAYE

astride the centre-line. Crouched because aggressive in defence, he constantly edges forward to take the flat smash early with a dab or a straight arm fast punch. The steep ones he whips up wristily from the floor. Drops are countered with body-wracking lunges.

But defence is turned to attack with cobra-striking speed. A deceptive cut drop played with a caressing follow-through, softens up his opponent's defences. Then follows the blitz-krieg. On balance, he jumps to make up for his lack of inches; even with the shuttle slightly behind him, his supple body bends like a bow and as racket strikes shuttle he is moving after it, almost as if to overtake it. Stroke and recovery are one. Deceptive suddenness and placement are the cutting edges of his smash, though no one would say it was lacking in the matter of sheer speed.

The low serve he returns with seeming casualness, but inbuilt deception: a sudden, wristy flick-lob or the apparent straightforward net-return that can suddenly fizz into a fast, flat punch down the line. And if his net-return is countered with another net-shot look out for trouble. Pongoh snaps up trifles: a leap, and in mid-air the shuttle is killed stone dead.

Holder of the Copenhagen Cup in December 1980 he was seeded No 3 in the 1981 All-England where eventual finalist Prakash's uncanny anticipation negated even his speed of foot and shot.

PRAKASH PADUKONE (India)
'Bangalore Torpedo', once the name of a fire-cracker, would not be an inappropriate nick-name for Prakash. He moves with aerial grace, and fireworks sparkle from his wristy style.

A graduate of Bangalore University and now a bank employee, he plays a thoughtful and exact game. Nothing is given away!

Primarily a singles player, this quiet, good-looking young man won the Commonwealth Games title in 1978 and beat world champion Flemming Delfs in the Wembley 'Evening of Champions' in the same year.

1979–80 was his highlight. Having effort-lessly removed 2nd seed Frost Hansen, he shocked 8,000 astounded All-England spec-tators by the elegant murder of hot favourite Liem Swie King, 15–3, 15–10. No crude bludgeoning here. It was death by a thousand

cuts: nagging length to the base-line; tape-hugging net-shots; effortless strokes allied to an almost languid ease of movement that enabled him to take the shuttle tape-high; deceptive pushes that kept King on the rack until he was cleanly dispatched with a stiletto-pointed smash.

In the 1980–81 Championships, although seeded only 6th he won his way to the final again. Behind him the 'bodies' of Pongoh and Hartono. Taking the first game of the final against Liem Swie King 15–11 with unhurried assurance, he looked set for a double. But when the latter stepped up the pace, Padukone couldn't match it (4–15, 6–15). In modern singles the accent must, like it or not, be on speed and power rather than elegance and deception. Perhaps (backed by Japanese sponsors Akai and Yonex) his transfer from the heat of Bangalore to the cold of Copenhagen had taken its toll.

SVEN PRI (Denmark)
'Over the hill' he might be, but not out of sight and certainly not out of mind.

Sven did not pillage All-England titles as ruthlessly as other Viking raiders have done. His tally? Three All-English Mixed Doubles titles (the first in 1967 under his original name of Anderson) all with the bouncing Ulla Strand; and a solitary Singles title. The latter was his highlight. Twice runner-up to the seemingly invulnerable Hartono, and with the sands of time running out, in 1975 he beat him at last 15–11, 17–14.

Beat him rapturously – tears in eyes he raced off court to embrace his wife. It endeared him to English spectators as much as his refusal to be beaten by humidity and boisterous crowds in a Jakarta Thomas Cup final did to Indonesian ones when other Danes had crumpled under heat and pressure.

Now that his zest is a little less effervescent, he has become something of a 'Nastase without the nastiness'. Showmanship and gamesman-ship bubble out. This, together with delicacy of touch, power of smash and acrobatic returns from off the floor, round his back and between his legs, make him a crowd-puller, a gin-fizz champion!

Sven played a novel retirement game against Flemming Delfs in a Copenhagen shopping arcade, but fortunately he will be seen on court for a year or two yet, testing out rackets under tournament conditions, and as Denmark's chief coach.

STEEN SKOVGAARD (Denmark)

At 6ft 6in you're a bit too big for singles. Twenty-eight year old Steen has therefore wisely used his height and reach to maximum effect in doubles. More especially in mixed doubles. Although he has never won the coveted All-England Mixed title he was World Champion, with Lene Koppen in 1977–80, and has been Danish Champion, with two different partners, for the last six years.

From the very outset, dominating on the front service line with his racket only 2–3ft from the tape, he pressures his opponents. With backhand brushes or orthodox rushes and pushes, he has made himself the most feared receiver in the game. Even Nora Perry will ruefully admit that he is one of the meanest men in the business to serve to.

Not so fast or so acrobatically back as a Tjun Tjun, he nevertheless uses his full height to intercept flicks or forces them almost into the category of high serves. Conversely, with his slow, deliberate and limited swing, his own low serve is no easy target for his opponents.

He has a much sharper smash than his partner, the other 'Great Dane', Flemming Delfs. And he can be equally lethal at the net where, crouched, he holds his racket surprisingly low. Although not a good mover he uses reach and anticipation to good advantage, seldom lifting, frequently snapping up winners. A surprise, flat, round-the-head smash awaits the defender who seeks to by-pass him down the left side-line.

Dropping back in defence but particularly strong off the body, he likes to bore in after his flat return to recapture the net. He can produce a not-too-rare round-the-back defensive shot played with studied nonchalance when demand dictates it.

A student of marketing and commerce, Steen obviously loves things English, else why should he marry pretty Ann Statt (who has represented both England and Denmark) and sweep her off to his home town, Copenhagen? In his spare time he is a keen tennis player who must surely pound down a Roscoe Tanner-style serve.

RAY STEVENS (England)

The iron man of English badminton. Training took him through the pain barrier. A kicking mule wouldn't disown his smash.

Pre-eminently England's No 1 singles player, his consistency and iron determination have kept his volatile young contender, Kevin Jolly, at bay. Even at thirty he hoped to keep the National title, which he took in 1980 for a record fifth time, but has had to give best to Andy Goode. Not built by nature for speed, he gets there by hard work. It is the lack of that extra flash of pace that has robbed him of top honours.

But success and world ranking he has achieved in partnership with Mike Tredgett in men's doubles. He loves the challenge of pitting his stonewall defence against the sharpest attack. And likes nothing better than a bout of all-out – but shrewdly placed – smashing from rear court. ('You must smash tight if you want a kill at the net'.) The whole is spiced, even in a moment of crisis , with irrepressible trick shots and round-the-back or between-the-legs returns of smash which keep the spectators happy.

Two games stand out in 1980. In the Friends' Provident Masters he ran Hartono neck-and-neck for two games, actually taking the first game after a remarkable pull-up from 5–14 to 17–14. But even his new found head of steam could not maintain pressure under the Indonesian's relentless early-take attack which really puts the screws on.

And in the All-England, he and Mike Tredgett made their second finals appearance; only one other English pair, Dave Eddy and Bob Powell, had reached that stage since World War Two. Although losing, they made Tjun Tjun and Wahjudi go all the way.

A serious student of the game ('I'm still learning'), Ray nevertheless spices his game with humour as quick-reflexed as his strokes. One of the first in this country to pioneer the slice-serve, he persevered with it during a rough patch and made history perhaps by using it throughout the National Singles final with complete success.

Thoroughly professional in his approach he now works with Gordon Richards, of Jim Fox

(*Overleaf*) Plate 54. Magnificently muscled Great Dane, Sven Pri, appears to have made an early – too early? – take (*Mervyn Rees*)

and army pentathlon fame, as his trainer and manager. Deeply interested in coaching, he may well become the first of the greats to turn to full-time coaching as a career when his playing days are over. No bad thing for English badminton!

IIE SUMIRAT (Indonesia)

Even in the shadow of his thirties, snub-nosed Iie Sumirat cannot yet be written off. And, as one of badminton's most colourful characters, why should he be?

Fit and a fighter, he has lightning reflexes but not used with the easy style of more 'hit-the-headlines' compatriots Hartono and Swie King. He can still smash, and prod and push his way to victory, even in a gruelling three-setter.

His greatest moment undoubtedly was in 1976 at the Asian Invitation when he beat not one but both of the Chinese legends, Hou Chia Chang and Tang Hsien Hu. Second to that must be his victory in the 1979 Thomas Cup over wily Sven Pri, a victory that set the Indonesian steam-roller on its juggernaut path.

His outspokenness led to his temporary 'exile' by the Indonesian Badminton Association. His ebullience (after the victories described above) led to cartwheels that ended in the net and a series of frenetic 'star jumps' – that, after three torrid sets in high humidity.

TJUN TJUN (Indonesia)

His name sounds like a runaway train – and he certainly plays like one. Perhaps the world's most electrifying player, 10,000 volt Tjun Tjun is a men's doubles specialist.

No fewer than six All-England titles hang at his belt – all in partnership with fellow Indonesian, Wahjudi. They also won the title at the Malmo World Championships in 1977 and doubtless would have retained it before their home crowd in Jakarta in 1980 but for injury that prevented Tjun Tjun playing.

Dark skinned and with a darker fringe cut only just above his eyes, he is a menacing receiver who kills low and flick serves with equal impartiality and relish. The latter he deals with with a jack-in-the-box smash as he leaps backwards. It is one of the sights of the game to see him use the same acrobatic agility to play jump smashes. For a fraction of a second he seems to coil up, then explode upwards two or three feet clear of the floor to smash at the top of his leap.

He is equally aggressive in defence. Not for him a passive resistance. Smashes are driven back with interest as he pushes forward to wrest back the initiative. Then, on the right stroke, he follows in with almost psychic anticipation to cut down the return off the tape.

The same reflexes, quick eye and quicker movement are invaluable when partner Wahjudi is serving. A slightly lifted or flat return is met early and skilfully placed to force another lift. When the receiver is on the rampage, pushing and dabbing into his body, Tjun Tjun defends with the resolution of a man at bay and the cool ease of a fencer – a great and vital skill.

Late 1980 saw his marriage; early 1981 defeat in the Men's Doubles final at the All-England. His hopes of eclipsing that great Danish pair of the 1960s Finn Kobbero and Hammergard Hansen, with a record seven wins (in eight years) was dashed by his compatriots Kartono and Heryanto, World Championship runners-up. And for the first time he seemed to have lost the urge to fight it out to the last point. Had marriage softened his badminton ruthlessness?

MIKE TREDGETT (England)

A great doubles player in his own right – and no slouch at singles if really pressed into action. With pale, dead-pan face he is the perfect foil for ebullient Nora Perry in mixed doubles. He lapsed, sadly and unaccountably, in the 1980 World Championships but three All-England mixed titles must be balm.

He is perfect in badminton terms, too. His left-handedness is a double-edged weapon: not only does it bring forceful lifts to his forehand – a lethal one at that – but also gives him a wide range of sweeping round-the-head strokes. And no matter how far he leans over, he's quickly back on balance and moving.

Speed and an eager ruthlessness permeate his play. He's quick down the sides to take the half-court push early; fast across to challenge the cross-court drive, and fast back too, jumping, to discourage any 'flick' nonsense.

No time for gallantry on court, he relentlessly attacks the lady if she drops back. Few except Wigoeno withstand it.

Tredgett has his own unintelligible brand of

communication with Nora. On occasions, a flicker of pain crosses his face when one of Nora's wilder flights of anticipatory fancy drags him further out of position than he relishes.

In men's doubles, with Ray Stevens, he is world class. A fact underlined in the 1980 All-England when they defeated current world champions Christian and Chandra in the semi-finals and gave long-time holders Wahjudi and Tjun Tjun some very nasty moments in the final. In 1981, with Stevens injured, Mike partnered left-handed Martin Dew to win the F. P. Masters.

A stinging pin-pointed smash, a lightning reflexed short arm defence, flat and fast, and eye-catching leaps to pick off fractionally high shots at the net, are his fortes. Is this agility due perhaps to the fact that he was once a county gymnast?

Mike has an even more enduring partnership with England's 'B' team former, Kath Whiting, the girl with the charming smile. When Mike isn't jetting around the world you'll find them in a delightful old cottage near Ross-on-Wye, with a donkey or two in the paddock.

HELEN TROKE (England)
England's answer to Nettie Nielsen – a winning answer at that. For twice in the 1981 European Junior Championships, both in the team and in individual events, did sixteen-year-old Helen beat sixteen-year-old Nettie.

An intriguing contrast: Helen, pale and quiet, does not immediately catch the eye as does the more flamboyant, rumbustious Dane. Her qualities are less obvious but no less effective.

Her characteristic style and game? A touch drop-shot off early intercepted attacking clears; round-the-head, cross-court drop-shots too, out of the same deceptive mould as those of Karen Bridge and Gillian Gilks; a carefully judged and hit high serve with a homing affinity for the base-line; pertinacity and above all, a defence by-passing smash – one tipped with accuracy rather than speed. Time and again it is hit within inches of the line, to leave a disbelieving opponent stretching unavailingly.

Helen has more than strokes, she has vision. With a wisdom beyond her years she can look to tomorrow rather than today. She sacrificed coveted All-England Under 18 titles that might have been too easily earned to join an Under 23

tour of Sweden and Denmark that would give her tougher opposition and greater experience.

In 1981 too she was one of the youngest-ever players to qualify for the All-England Championships. Malaysia's and Canada's best, Katharine Teh and Jane Youngberg, both fell to her. And a 6–11, 11–4, 8–11 defeat by Japan's talented Yonekura was surest proof of her potential. Proof too that the quiet Hampshire schoolgirl has a temperament that will take her far in world badminton.

WIHARJO VERAWATY (Indonesia)
Striking in name and looks, often referred to simply as Verawaty, she makes her own impact with an almost statuesque build rare among Indonesians. Black hair slicked back from a broad forehead, heavily lidded almond-shaped eyes, high cheek bones: she is obviously of the exotic East. A full-lipped mouth seldom breaks into an easy smile. Impassive on court she was yet tearfully and joyfully emotional in 1979 when, with contrastingly fragile Imelda Wigoeno, she won the All-England Ladies' Doubles and wept unashamedly. She looks like and is a PE student in Jakarta.

In the same year she had used her power and deception to startling effect in the Danish Randers tournament when she beat both Lene Koppen and Gillian Gilks in the Singles with quite a lot in hand. And in 1980 she set the seal on her career when before an adoring home crowd, she showed that Indonesian women as well as men could win world titles – even if it was at the expense of her compatriot, Lie Ivana. She was runner-up in the Ladies' Doubles too.

Verawaty and Wigoeno – the names had a ring, almost a masculine one, and one that made players drawn against them more than a little anxious. Their success, as with all great partnerships, stemmed not merely from individual skills but the subtle blending of complementary ones. Ideally it was the powerful Verawaty who covered the rear-court whilst 5 foot-nothing Wigoeno commanded the net. Their combination never had to be stereotyped for the dancing feet of Wigoeno, and a smash like a wasp sting, could take over effectively at the back, whilst Verawaty, racket held very high, impressively dominated the net even from 18in behind the front service line.

It is at the back though that Verawaty is most

183

effective. Steep drops elicit the weak return of which powerful straight smashes take full advantage, an advantage which she doesn't willingly yield. In defence, she is in the Indonesian mould favouring the backhand which she uses effectively to whip back flat returns. When it comes to drops, she is happy to let the more fleet-footed Wigoeno take the lioness' share.

Both in receiving (upright stance; racket high) and serving she is within a foot of the front service line. She likes too to be almost dangerously close up to Wigoeno when the latter is serving. But anticipation and a surprisingly supple back enable her to deal with even the shrewdest of lifts to the backhand corner.

A tight low serve played with a shortened grip, quickly followed in to a crouched attacking position, often forces an early lift.

In singles, power and reach are again her mainstays. She plays a very strong round-the-head clear to the backhand which she likes to attack and jumps to intercept the attacking clear – ringing the changes on smash or drop return. But allied with strength is a fluent wrist that drags the shuttle down in steep and disguised drops. In the forecourt she gladly takes up the challenge of cut net-shots with an even tighter return.

IMELDA WIGOENO (Indonesia)

Dark and trim, the Jakarta bank clerk is the Eastern Nora Perry. Singles are not for her; ladies' and mixed doubles are.

In the former she makes an excellent foil for the tall Verawaty. In the latter her quicksilver movement and instant reflexes enable her to blend most effectively if unorthodoxly with that will o' the wisp, Christian Hadinata.

Her vintage year was 1979. Not content with winning the All-England Ladies' Doubles she became, with Christian, the first ever Asian pair to break down the European domination of the Mixed event. And in 1980, they went one better by lifting the World title before their own delirious fans.

In mixed, she is a Jekyll and Hyde character. One moment she is at the back smashing with an insistency and a waspish venom quite alien to her real character. The next, light as a feather, she is at the net exchanging touch shot for touch shot, intercepting half-court pushes and returning them with interest or dropping them short with a roll of the wrist. She is very quick too to follow her tape-skimming cross-court net-shots across the width of the court. And in between, dropping back, she'll more than do her bit with a solidity of defence belied by her fragility.

The quintessence of the lady's role in mixed, the serve, bears her own hallmark: a squarish stance close to the front line, then, backhanded, shuttle held down just above racket, a six-inch swing. With reflex-deceiving suddenness, the shuttle skims the tape to the centre or, held flat, is occasionally deftly angled to the side-line, sometimes even driven flat down the centre-line. She follows in quickly to tumble back, tape-high, any net-returns of her serve.

Wigoeno has recently married Rudi Hartono's brother, Ferry.

YOSHIKO YONEKURA (Japan)

Thin-faced and pale, frail and little taller than the net, Yoshiko doesn't look a threat to the world's best. But, packing a crisper than crisp smash, moving neatly, and having more than a fair share of Japanese tenacity, she is just that.

Currently Japan's No 1 singles player, she defeated long time champion Hiroe Yuki in three hard games to gain the title. In 1978, only twenty and on her first visit to the All-England, she reached the Ladies' Doubles final giving best only to 'T 'n T' (Tokuda and Takada). The rating of coach Sheila Tyrrell was 'young, vibrant, strong, enthusiastic and entertaining'.

In 1980, with Tokuda, she put paid to holder Verawaty and Wigoeno in the semi-final. But not even her defence could withstand the cold steel of Perry and Gilks in full cry in the final.

Yoshiko chatters on court with the best of them; she's solemn-eyed but there's a hint of a smile in the wide mouth. She works for Japanese Telephone Services.

Note her ideal aggressive receiving stance, and how close she stands to her partner when the latter is serving. From there she can maintain the attack elicited by her partner's tight serving. Her nimbleness takes care of returns lifted deep.

Plate 55. Hiroe Yuki illustrates that vital Japanese motto: 'Never Say Die!' *(Mervyn Rees)*

She compensates for lack of pounds and inches by putting body and soul into a smash in which her shoulder does its full share.

The same aggression is there in defence. She and her partner bore in to take the shuttle early, flat. Crouched or even slipping, sitting on the floor, she still defends. 'No surrender!' is her watchword.

HIROE YUKI (Japan)

It might be considered ungallant to reveal that Hiroe is now 32, that it is thirteen years since she first won the All-England Singles title, were it not for the fact that on court she shows few signs of the years' advance. A little slower perhaps – but then speed was never the ace up her sleeve.

Her success was founded on honest basics: drop-shots of oriental mystery, of exquisitely cruel brevity; and clears, forehand and backhand, of perfect, grinding length. The two were welded indissolubly by typical determination that no shuttle was going to land on Japanese-held territory, even if she had to run till the boilers burst.

In 1974 and 1975 she was 'Public Enemy No 1' when she defeated England's Gillian Gilks in the All-England Singles. In 1977, she made the trophy her own by beating Lene Koppen. For good measure, partnered by her 1969 victim, Norikao Takagi, she won the Ladies' Doubles in 1971 – Gillian once again the hapless victim.

Hiroe was little seen in 1980–81 as she was, unfortunately, at odds with her National Association.

Index